THIS BOOK IS DEDICATED TO TWO MEN
WHO HAVE GUIDED ME IN THE
JEWISH WAY OF LIFE:

MY MATERNAL GRANDFATHER

הרב הגאון יהושע בוימעל, זצ"ל

RABBI YEHOSHUA BAUMOL

died, September 7, 1948

ד' אלול תש"ח

author of *Emek Halakhah* who, as a creative thinker and
renowned leader, left a tradition of scholarship and humaneness. He was profound enough to be lenient within
the law, and compassionate enough to be understanding of
human weakness.

and

MY PATERNAL GRANDFATHER

ר' יעקב דוד לאם, זצ"ל

YAAKOV DAVID LAMM

died, March 27, 1939

ז' ניסן תרצ"ט

who lived proudly and nobly, and whose patriarchal bearing and saintly humility inspired devotion in all who knew
him. He died in dignity as he lived in dignity. His death,
the first in my experience, remains forever etched in my
memory as the climax of a full and rich life.

The Jewish Way in Death and Mourning

by

MAURICE LAMM

JONATHAN DAVID PUBLISHERS
New York

Address all communications to:

JONATHAN DAVID PUBLISHERS INC.
68-22 Eliot Avenue
Middle Village, N. Y. 11379

1991   1993   1994   1992
12 14 16 18 20 19 17 15 13

ISBN 0-8246-0126-2

Library of Congress Catalogue Card No. 69-11684

PRINTED IN THE UNITED STATES OF AMERICA

THE JEWISH WAY IN DEATH AND MOURNING

Contents

Introduction xi

Preface xvii

1. FROM THE MOMENT OF DEATH TO THE FUNERAL
   SERVICE 1
   Initial Care of the Deceased 3
   Preparation of the Remains: Taharah 6
   Autopsy 8
   Embalming 12
   The Casket 16
   Flowers 18
   Timing the Funeral Service 18
   Between Death and Interment: Aninut 21
   Viewing the Remains 26
   The Night Before the Funeral Service 35

2. THE FUNERAL SERVICE AND THE INTERMENT 36
   Location of the Service 37
   Rending the Garment: Keriah 38
   The Funeral Service 45
   The Eulogy 50
   Escorting the Deceased to the Cemetery 52
   The Interment 55
   Cremation 56
   Mausoleums and Concrete Vaults 57
   Burial of Limbs 58
   The Burial Service 59

CONTENTS—continued

The Burial 64
The Kaddish 65
The Cemetery Plot and Grave 67
Disinterment 70
Reinterment 71
Cemetery Etiquette 74
Memorial Gifts 75

3. MOURNING OBSERVANCES OF SHIVA AND SHELOSHIM   77
The Mourning Pattern 77
The Mourner and the Mourned 79
Which Relatives Are Mourned? 83
Shiva: Its Origins 86
When Does Shiva Begin? 87
The Duration of Shiva and Sheloshim 93
The Sabbath During Shiva and Sheloshim 94
Holidays During the Mourning Period 94
Summary of Holiday Regulations 95
Where Shiva Is Observed 97
Upon Returning from the Cemetery 97
Prayers in the House of Mourning 104
The Mourner and the Minyan 105
Leaving the House During Shiva 109
Sitting Shiva 111
Working and Conducting Business During Shiva . 112
When Is Work Permitted? 116
Wearing Shoes 121
Greetings and Gifts 122
Personal Hygiene and Grooming 125
Laundering and New Garments 130
Marital Relations 133
Study of Torah 134
Comforting the Bereaved 136
Psychological Symptoms of Grief 141
End of Shiva 144
Sheloshim Observances 144

CONTENTS—continued

4. YEAR-LONG MOURNING OBSERVANCE 147
   Counting the Twelve Months 147
   The Kaddish 149
   History of Kaddish 150
   The Function of the Kaddish 153
   The Significance of Kaddish 158
   Kaddish Observances 162
   Mourners Obligated to Say Kaddish 165
   Is the Kaddish Obligation Transferrable? 167
   For Whom Kaddish Is Said 169
   When Kaddish Is Said at Services 171
   Posture of Kaddish Recitation 173
   If Parent Requests Kaddish Be Not Said 174
   When Mourner Cannot Attend Services 174
   Joyous Occasions During Mourning 175
   Social and Business Gatherings 178
   Religious Celebrations 180
   Celebration of the Talmud 182
   Festivities on the Sabbath 183
   The Mourner and Marriage 184

5. POST-MOURNING PRACTICES AND PROCEDURES 188
   The Monument 188
   Grave Visitations and Prayers 192
   The Unveiling 194
   Yizkor 196
   Yahrzeit 201
   Memorial by Proxy 206

6. SPECIAL SITUATIONS 208
   Delayed News 208
   The Kohen 211
   Suicides 215

7. THE WORLD BEYOND THE GRAVE 221
   Life After Death 221
   The Concept of Immortality 224

CONTENTS—continued

Messiah 226
The Resurrection of the Dead 228
Resurrection: A Symbolic Idea 231
Life After Death: A Corollary of Jewish Belief .. 233
The Meaning of Death 235

APPENDIX

The Preparation of the Remains: A Guide for the
    Chevra Kadisha 239
    Infant Deaths 247
Bibliography 249

Glossary 251

Index 259

Introduction

DEATH IS THE CRISIS of life. How a man handles death indicates a great deal about how he approaches life. As there is a *Jewish* way of life, there is a *Jewish* way of death.

As the Jewish way of life implies a distinctive outlook and a unique life-style based on very specific views of God and the place of man in society and the universe, so does the Jewish way of death imply singular attitudes toward God and nature, and toward the problem of good and evil; and it proffers a distinctive way of demonstrating specific *Jewish* qualities of reverence for man and respect for the dead.

For example, the prohibition of both cremation (the unnaturally speedy disposal of the dead), and embalming (the unnatural preservation of the dead), bespeak a philosophy of man and his relationship to God and nature. Repugnance to the mutilation of a body expresses a reverence for man, because he was created in God's image. The ban on necromancy is founded on very precise theological concepts of creature and Creator. Likewise, the commandment to bury the dead without delay draws a very fine, but clear, line between *reverence* for the dead and *worship* of the dead. The profound psychological insights implicit in the highly-structured Jewish mourning observances speak eloquently of Judaism's concern for the psychological integrity of the human personality.

The writing of this book was a chore, perhaps even an exercise in agony. This is not because of the arduous and difficult task of research into the numerous customs and beliefs, which tend to leave one moribund in the constant preoccupation with death. Primarily, it is a result of a sense of futility—the feeling that such a book must fail in its educative task, and that the failure is built into the very fabric of the work. The futility can be expressed in a paradox simply stated: People do not wish to learn about how to deal with death until they are confronted with death, and when they are confronted with death they are not inclined to study how religion approaches it.

People do not desire to study the Jewish way of death because of what Geoffrey Gorer calls "the pornography of death," the distaste of contemplating the problems raised by death in the family, the compulsive shying-away from discussion, the use of every possible euphemism to shield themselves verbally and visually from its sting. We who live in one of the most violent societies in all history, who calculatingly refer to "over-kill," and "body-counts," and "mega-corpse," the measurement of millionfold mutilation of human beings as a consequence of nuclear bombing; we who feed on a daily diet of crime reportage and who view every conceivable method of dying on television; we are frightened sick by the consideration of the eventuality of our own deaths. We are, in fact, deathly afraid of death. In view of this attitude, the study of mourning observances is not likely to be undertaken before it becomes absolutely necessary.

But the crisis will come. If thinking on the subject is to be deferred, if there is to be no education *before* the crisis, what chance is there that we shall know how to handle the crisis when it arrives? And if we are not privy to this information, will those who lived as Jews be able to be buried as Jews? Will we not inevitably succumb to the standards established by commercial funeral directors, rather than by authentic spiritual teachers? Will we not tend blindly to embrace every American practice, whether its origin be in the church or in some transitory fraternal organization? What will be left that is Jewish in our Jewish way of death? And if there is no Jewish way of death, what Jewish way of life could there have been?

The book was, therefore, written for the layman. There are no footnotes. No scholarly disputes are hidden in abbreviated italics. No complicated rabbinic analyses are here disentangled. I have, in short, made no effort to impress the reader with profundity. The scholar, I hope, will detect the traces of my research and recognize the sources in Bible, Talmud, Midrash, Codes and Responsa literature. In this age of unprecedented Jewish ignorance, the major task of the scholar is to popularize the law, rather than to apply himself solely to pure research.

For this reason, too, I have decided on a different method of presentation for this work. Heretofore, popular texts on Jewish law have been written in one of two styles. One has been the exhaustive listing of the details of the law, presented in cookbook fashion, without providing any rationale. This technique left the reader confounded by a maze of halachic by-ways, with no direction, no criteria for discriminating between major and minor laws or between biblical mandate and local usage, and no intellectual underpinning. An illustration of this genre is the English edition of the *Abridged Shulchan Aruch.*

Another style places the emphasis on major observances, leaving all details and nuances to be decided by local rabbis and educators—if they are asked, that is. The reader of this kind of text is left intellectuallly stimulated, but with no guidance as to where to begin the actual practice of the law he now understands.

Both these styles surely have useful functions for specific audiences, but they leave the reader unsatisfied—either intellectually or practically.

In *The Jewish Way in Death and Mourning,* I have

strenuously sought to avoid both extremes. Nevertheless, if
I have failed, the fault lies with me, and surely not with
the subject matter. My work will not be demeaned if it is
to be considered a handbook, nor will I be offended if it is
to be pegged "apologetics." I have tried to trace the religious practices in detail, as well as the rationale that appears to underlie the observances. I have made every effort
to interpret the ancient tradition in a manner relevant to
moderns, and to make palatable to the contemporary Jew
that which on the surface appears to be esoteric.

In this attempt I may have raised more questions than I
have answered, created more problems than I have solved.
I have not attempted to bypass a custom out of fear that it
might be misunderstood, or viewed in an unsympathetic
light by readers with little Jewish background. Whether
the subject be physical resurrection or family relations
during *shiva,* or "paying" for the Kaddish, I have tried to
be forthright—perhaps to a fault.

I have rendered decisions on numerous complex problems—probably to the chagrin of many of my colleagues.
Naturally, it is an absurd and altogether impossible task
to decide on every individual issue, with its abundance of
subtle nuances and complex ramifications. In such cases, I
have referred the reader to local religious authorities who
are specially trained and able to make halachic decisions.
At the very least, the reader will "know how to ask." If this
work provokes only questions it will, to me, have been
supremely worthwhile. We are suffocating, today, from too
many answers to questions we have never learned to ask.

I must express my profound gratitude to those who un-
selfishly assisted me in preparing this volume: To Rabbi
David Silver of Kesher Israel Congregation, Harrisburg,
Pa., who helped me as a respected mentor rather than in his
position as Chairman of the Beth Din of the Rabbinical
Council of America; to Rabbi Norman Lamm, rabbi of The
Jewish Center, New York City, and professor of Jewish

Philosophy at Yeshiva University, who reviewed my work as scholar, not as brother; to Rabbi Sidney Applbaum, rabbi of Congregation Beth Judah, Brooklyn, N. Y., and chairman of the Funeral Standards Committee of the Rabbinical Council of America; to my wife who prodded my pen from planning to publication; and to the members of the Hebrew Institute of University Heights who have been a source of encouragement.

I owe a great personal debt to my publisher, Rabbi Alfred Kolatch, whose unimaginable patience has given me a four-year-long guilt conscience, and whose insight into the mind of the lay reader has caused me more work in rewriting than the original work of research. His friendship through these few years has truly been in the spirit of Jonathan and David.

MAURICE LAMM

Ten Mile River
Narrowsburg, N. Y.
July, 1968

Preface

DURING THE COURSE of a lifetime, virtually no one can avoid an encounter with death. Yet it is an experience for which one is rarely prepared. Psychologists explain why, but they do not condone the evasion. Perhaps this excellent volume by a learned and sensitive colleague, Rabbi Maurice Lamm, will help many to think and act maturely when having to deal with this inevitable circumstance of life.

The book differs radically from earlier attempts with the subject, for Rabbi Lamm has written with feeling and insight about every aspect of the problem. He has collated all the relevant laws and customs of Judaism; he has added interpretation; he has related the behavior and practices of our forbears to modern practices and evaluated their relative merit. He has brought to his theme the legal scholarship of the Orthodox rabbi, the competence of one well-versed in the behavioral sciences, and the humanity and empathy of a warm human being. Indeed, he is to be congratulated on the wide scope, depth, and thoroughness of his presentation which will help all people to cope with the circumstances surrounding death. In addition, Rabbi Lamm's approach will give the Jewish reader a greater appreciation of his ancestral heritage.

The Jewish Way in Death and Mourning fills a definite gap that has long existed in the field of Judaica. Rabbi Lamm's superb contribution provides the English reader with the first readable and comprehensive study in an area of vital importance.

Dr. Emanuel Rackman
Assistant to the President
Yeshiva University

THE JEWISH WAY IN DEATH
AND MOURNING

1 ✧ From the Moment of Death to the Funeral Service

LIFE IS A DAY that lies between two nights—the night of "not yet," before birth, and the night of "no more," after death. That day may be overcast with pain and frustration, or bright with warmth and contentment. But, inevitably, the night of death must arrive.

Death is a night that lies between two days—the day of life on earth and the day of eternal life in the world to come. That night may come suddenly, in the blink of an eye, or it may come gradually, with a slowly receding sun.

As the day of life is an interlude, so is the night of death an interlude. As the day inevitably proceeds to dusk, so does the darkness inevitably proceed to dawn. Each portion— the foetal existence, and life, and death, and eternal life— is separated by a veil which human understanding cannot pierce.

We, the survivors who do not accompany the deceased on their journey into the night, are left alone staring into the veiled, black void. There is a rage of conflicting emotions that seethes within us: bewilderment and paralysis, agony and numbness, guilt and anger, fear and futility and pain— and also emancipation from care and worry. The golden chain of the family link is broken and swings wildly before our eyes. Our whole being is convulsed. Love and warmth and hope have vanished, and in their place remains only

1

despair. The precious soul that touched our life and enhanced its sense of purpose and meaning is no more. Our only consolation is that he once was. There is a past, but the past is no more; and the future is bleak indeed. The broken, swinging chain hypnotizes us and we are frozen.

✓   ✓   ✓

Judaism is a faith that embraces all of life, and death is a part of life. As this faith leads us through moments of joy, so does it guide us through the terrible moments of grief, holding us firm through the complex emotions of mourning, and bidding us turn our gaze from the night of darkness to the daylight of life.

At the moment of death painful questions gnaw at our innards—existential and philosophical problems so stubborn, they will not go away: Why was this person, of all the people that fill our great world, fated to end his days just now? Why did the end come before the logic of life ordained that it come? Death should be, we feel, a sum under the bottom line—a total of all of life's varied experiences. It should add up to a meaningful conclusion, and end naturally. It should not intrude in the midst of the equations of living, starkly disrupting all calculations, confusing all the figures, belying all the prepared solutions. But, too often, the end is abrupt. Life remains an unknown quality— a large, incalculable problem, bedevilled by death.

At the moment of death there is severe disorientation. We are perplexed not only by the large questions of life and death, but by problems of how to feel and how to conduct ourselves properly: How shall we react to the tragedy? What is the proper respect that we should give the dead? How do we achieve a measure of dignity during an interment? Shall we mourn the unfulfilled life of the deceased, torn away before finishing the business of living, or may we feel a loss to ourselves, agonizing over our own personal distress?

And how should we comfort ourselves? Should we ap-

pear before family and friends brave, dignified, courage-
ously unruffled? Or may we give vent to our anguish in a
stream of tears? Shall the usual amenities of a social occasion obtain at the gathering of the family, or should we
concern ourselves with the soul-wound of our own loss and
let the world manage for itself?

Thousands of years of our rich tradition provide us with
direction during these moments of crisis. The accumulated
wisdom of the ages is a source of great consolation.

✔   ✔   ✔

In the pages that follow, you will find clear guidelines
that the Jewish tradition has laid down to lead mourners
through the complex maze of uncertainties and ambiva-
lences that attend the tragic moment. The ache of the heart
will not suddenly disappear. There will be no miraculous
consolation. But Judaism does teach the aching heart how to
express its pain in love and respect, and how to achieve the
eventual consolation which will restore us to humanity and
keep us from vindictiveness and self-pity.

Initial Care of the Deceased

The principle governing the care of the body immediately
following death is the sacredness of man. A human being is
equated with a Torah scroll that was impaired and can no
longer be used at religious services. While the ancient scroll
no longer serves any useful ritual purpose, it is revered for
the exalted function it once filled. Man was created in the
image of God and, although the pulse of life is no more,
the human form must be respected for having once embodied
the spirit of God, and for the character and the personality
it housed. The manner of respect is governed and detailed
by religious tradition rather than by personal sentiment
and whim alone. The following are some of the basic guidelines for the care of the deceased at the time of death:

1. During the last minutes of life no one in the presence

of the deceased may leave, excepting those whose emotions are uncontrollable, or the physically ill. It is a matter of the greatest respect to watch over a person as he passes from this world on to the next.

2. After death has been ascertained, the eyes and the mouth of the deceased must be closed, either by the children or friends or relatives, and a sheet should be drawn over his face.

3. While it has been a custom for many years to rend the clothes and recite the blessing of the "True Judge" at the time of death, it is now customary to do this at the funeral service. At that time all the relatives are assembled, the rabbi supervises the correct manner of rending the clothing, and leads in the correct recital of the blessings. The details of the rending may be found in a separate chapter below.

4. The position of the body should be so oriented that the feet face the doorway. Other than this, the deceased should not be touched or moved, except for his own honor (such as straightening the body if it is found in an awkward position, or moving it if it has been found in environs not considered sufficiently respectful). Some Orthodox Jews retain the custom of placing the body on the floor approximately 20 minutes after death and pouring water on the floor as a sign to friends and neighbors that a death has occurred.

5. A candle should be placed near the head of the deceased. According to some customs many candles should be placed all around the person.

6. A beautiful and moving custom calls upon relatives and friends to ask forgiveness of the deceased, at this time, for any harm or discomfort they might have caused him during his lifetime.

7. The mirrors in the entire house are covered to deemphasize the beauty and the ornamentation of the flesh at a time when, in the same house, another person's body has begun to decay. Mirrors are covered also to avoid personal

vanity during moments of tragedy and to diminish the usual over-concern with one's appearance. Another explanation of this custom is that the image of God, reflected in the mirror, has been diminished by the recent death. This subject is considered in greater detail below.

8. Psalms 23 and 91 are recited. The text and commentary are found below.

9. Personal behavior in the room of the deceased should be consonant with the highest degree of respect for his person. There may be no eating, drinking or smoking in his presence. Outside the room proper, however, these are permitted. No derogatory remarks about the deceased may be voiced, even though, objectively, they may be true. Discussion in the room should concentrate solely on the deceased and his personal qualities, or on the funeral arrangements. There should be no singing or playing of music.

10. The rabbi should be called. He will notify the *Chevra Kadisha* (Burial Society) which will care for the remains. Then the funeral director, who will arrange for the local attending doctor to provide the medical certification of death and for the removal of the body, should be called.

11. From the moment of death until burial, the deceased may not be left alone. Therefore, the family must arrange for a person called a *shomer* (watcher) to be at his side at all times. While it is preferable for the watcher to be a member of the family or a personal friend, this is not always possible. In such cases, a person must be engaged to watch the body and recite from the Book of Psalms. The rabbi or funeral director will be able to make such arrangements for you, but the mourner should ascertain clearly whether the watcher is reliable, for he must remain awake and should recite Psalms all through the night.

12. If death occurs on the Sabbath, care should be taken not to light the candles near the deceased. Only the most minimal arrangements may be made on the Sabbath, and these only out of respect for the dead. The dead may not be

removed on the Sabbath by Jew or gentile. A watcher should be present during the Sabbath.

If death occurs in the hospital, 4 and 5 may not be practicable, but all other customs should be observed in the hospital room and later at the funeral chapel.

The funeral director is paid to serve you and your family, your religious sentiments and your wishes. He is certainly able to accommodate you in the observance of all traditional Jewish customs. There is no valid reason for him not to comply with your wishes. If you experience difficulty in this regard, consult competent rabbinic authority.

Preparation of the Remains: Taharah
טהרה

"As he came, so shall he go," says Ecclesiastes. Just as a newborn child is immediately washed and enters this world clean and pure, so he who departs this world must be cleansed and made pure through the religious ritual called *taharah* (purification).

The *taharah* is performed by the Chevra Kadisha (the Holy Society, i.e. the Burial Society), consisting of Jews who are knowledgeable in the area of traditional duties, and can display proper respect for the deceased. In addition to the physical cleansing and preparation of the body for burial, they also recite the required prayers asking Almighty God for forgiveness for any sins the deceased may have committed, and praying that the All-Merciful may guard him and grant him eternal peace. Membership in the Chevra Kadisha has always been considered a great communal honor bestowed only upon those who are truly pious. Non-Jews, under no circumstances, should perform these sacred tasks of preparing the body, for the ritual of *taharah* is by no means a merely hygienic performance. It is a Jewish religious act.

It is advisable that members of the immediate family absent themselves during the purification, for while their presence would constitute a symbol of respect, it is considered too painful for them to bear. The rabbi can arrange for this purification through the communal Chevra Kadisha or through the funeral director. The *taharah* is the age-old Jewish manner of showing respect for the dead. This is not merely "an old custom," or a "nice tradition," but is an absolute requirement of Jewish law.

It is tragic that fewer and fewer Jews appreciate the magnificence of serving on the Chevra Kadisha, let alone of using its services. In order to clarify the specific procedures of *taharah* that may be helpful to burial societies, there is a special chapter on the subject in the appendix.

Dressing

Jewish tradition recognizes the democracy of death. It therefore demands that all Jews be buried in the same type of garment. Wealthy or poor, all are equal before God, and that which determines their reward is not what they wear, but what they are. Nineteen hundred years ago, Rabbi Gamaliel instituted this practice so that the poor would not be shamed and the wealthy would not vie with each other in displaying the costliness of the burial clothes.

The clothes to be worn should be appropriate for one who is shortly to stand in judgment before God Almighty, Master of the universe and Creator of man. Therefore, they should be simple, handmade, perfectly clean, and white. These shrouds symbolize purity, simplicity, and dignity. Shrouds have no pockets. They, therefore, can carry no material wealth. Not a man's possessions but his soul is of importance. The burial society or funeral director has a ready supply of such shrouds available. If time must elapse before they can be obtained, the funeral should be delayed, as they are considered very important.

Shrouds may be made of muslin, cotton or linen. The

rule of thumb is that one should not go to greater expense than the cost of linen, but a less expensive cloth may be used.

The deceased should then be wrapped in his *tallit*—regardless of whether or not it is expensive, or how new it is. One of the fringes should be cut. One who was not observant, and unaccustomed to wearing a *tallit* may, if so desired, be buried in one purchased specifically for this purpose. The family of the deceased should decide the matter in this case.

Autopsy

Post-mortem examinations often include autopsies. The purpose of this dissection of the corpse is to establish the cause of death and the pathological processes involved. The pathologist strives to acquire reliable information concerning the nature and cause of the disease, and perhaps to investigate the medical procedures used on the patient. The initial autopsy incision opens the entire body in a "Y" shape. It begins below one shoulder, continues under the breasts, and extends up to the corresponding point under the other shoulder. This incision is then joined by another in the midline extending down toward the pubis, to complete the "Y." The scalp incision begins under one ear, extends across the top of the scalp and ends behind the other ear. The organs are removed and studied to the extent of each individual autopsy requirement. It should be noted that the standard autopsy permit form in the Autopsy Manual published by the United Hospital Fund of New York includes, as a matter of course, authorization for "the retention of such parts and tissues as the hospital staff may consider necessary for diagnosis."

Consent from next of kin is required for autopsy. Such consent may be given by the legal custodian of the body who is responsible for the burial, usually the husband or the wife. If there are more than one "next of kin" (and the interpretation of that phrase is elastic) and controversy arises, the hospital may forego autopsy or elect the most amenable relative as "the" next of kin.

In truth, however, it may be fairly surmised that the cause of death is accurately known in most cases, and only rarely is this a medical mystery. From experience with modern medical procedure, it is evident that autopsies are most frequently recommended in order to enable medical students and internes to study and practice by dissection and observation of the corpse. Many articles in medical journals have asserted that recent progress in patho-physiological science has made possible the reliable determination of cause of death without an autopsy. It is now held by many authorities that, with some exceptions, autopsies are no longer considered as vital as they once were.

Nonetheless, it appears that the percentage of autopsies is still considered one of the best indices of the standard of medical practice in hospitals. For this reason the Joint Commission on the Accreditation of Hospitals requires the maintenance of a satisfactory autopsy percentage. The United Hospital Fund standard manual urges obtaining consent in every possible case. "Indeed," says the Autopsy Manual, "when permission is not obtained, the physicians in attendance should be expected to account reasonably for such failure."

Hospital administrative staffs outdo themselves in perfecting techniques of extracting consent. Arguments are offered to counter typical family objections—some of these often untrue, and far below the high ethical practice the public has come to expect of the medical profession. One such argument often advanced is, "There are on record authoritative statements from religious leaders of all faiths indicating that nowhere is there any justification for opposition to autopsies on religious grounds." It is unfortunate that the religious sensibilities of traditional Jews should be so cavalierly dismissed by such misleading statements. Although there are notable exceptions to the rule, there is definite religious objection to autopsy.

Even though the motive of medical study is a worthy one, Jewish tradition forcefully rejects autopsies performed for teaching medical students, because this violates a higher principle: that of mutilating the body of the deceased. Jewish law is governed by several basic principles:

First, man was created in the image of God, and in death his body still retains the unity of that image. One may not do violence to the human form even when the breath of life has expired. Judaism demands respect for the total man, his body as well as his soul. The worthiness of the whole of man may not be compromised even in death.

Second, the dissection of the body, for reasons that are not urgent and directly applicable to specific existing medical cases, is considered a matter of shame and gross dishonor. As he was born, so does the deceased deserve to be laid to rest: tenderly and lovingly, not scientifically and dispassionately, as though he were an impersonal object of some experiment. The holiness of the human being demands that we do not tamper with his person.

Third, we have no permission to use his body without his own express desire that it be used, and even then it is questionable whether the person himself may volunteer to mutilate the image in which he was created. Certainly, where the deceased in his lifetime gave no express permission, even his children have no rights of possession over his body. Thus, we have no moral right, except for the cases to be mentioned, to use the body of the deceased by offering it as an object for study.

Autopsies are indeed valid in certain unusual cases, and these are exceptions to the general prohibition. While the possibilities of religiously-permitted autopsies are listed below, a competent rabbinic authority *must* be consulted in *every* case:

A) Cases which fall under the jurisdiction of governmental authorities. Here the decision must be made by the

Medical Examiner. For convenience and clarity, such hospital cases can be divided into two groups:

GROUP 1. Cases with impelling legal implications *in which an autopsy is usually performed* by the Medical Examiner, and in which permission for autopsy is never requested by the hospital physician.

Examples of such cases are:
a. Death by homicide or suspicion of homicide.
b. Death by suicide or suspicion of suicide.
c. Death due solely to accidental injury.
d. Death resulting from abortion.
e. Death from poisoning or suspected poisoning, including bacterial food poisoning.

GROUP 2. Cases in which the Medical Examiner *may decide that it is not necessary* for him to do an autopsy as part of his post-mortem investigation.

Examples of such cases are:
a. Death occurring during or immediately following diagnostic, therapeutic, surgical, and anesthetic procedures, or following untoward reactions to medication.
b. Death occurring in an unusual or peculiar manner, or when the patient was unattended by a physician, or following coma or convulsive seizure the cause of which is not evident.
c. Death resulting from chronic alcoholism, without manifestation of trauma.
d. Death in which a traumatic injury was only contributory, and in which the trauma did not arise out of negligence, assault, or arson, such as a fracture of the neck resulting from a fall at home and contributing to the death of an elderly person, or accidental burns occurring in the home.

B) Cases of hereditary diseases, where autopsy may serve to safeguard the health of survivors.

C) If another known person is suffering from a similar deadly disease, and an autopsy is considered by competent medical authority as possibly able to yield information vital to his health.

D) In cases where the deceased specifically stipulated that an autopsy be performed there has been much rabbinic disagreement. The circumstances must be investigated on an individual basis, and only an informed, highly competent religious authority may decide.

Even in cases where the rabbis have permitted the post-mortem, they have always insisted that:

Any part of the body that is removed must thereafter be buried with the body, and that it be returned to the Chevra Kadisha for this purpose as soon as possible.

The medical dissection must be performed with utmost respect for the deceased, and not handled lightly by insensitive personnel.

Because these matters are of great religious concern, questions on post-mortem examinations must be answered by a competent rabbi who is aware of both the medical requirements and the demands of the tradition. In addition, some forms of autopsy, such as the removal of fluid or blood only, or the insertion of an electric needle, may be considered permissible in many instances. The decision to perform an autopsy should not be made by the physician, no matter how close he is to the family and how reputable a doctor he may be. The prohibition is of a moral-religious nature, and permission should be obtained from an authority on religious law after consultation with medical authorities.

Embalming

The procedure of embalming was instituted in ancient times to preserve the remains of the deceased. Preservation was desired for many reasons:

1. For sanitation purposes—the assumption being that the fresh remains were a hazard to health;

2. For sentimental reasons—the family feeling that it wanted to prevent deterioration of the physical body as a comforting illusion that the deceased still lived; and

3. For presentability—to avoid visible signs of decay while the deceased was being viewed by the public prior to the funeral service.

It is worthwhile to analyze the three reasons in order to determine their validity today. First, however, it should be clear that *there is no state law* in the United States that *requires* the deceased to be embalmed, except when it is to be carried by public conveyance for long distances.

Is there a *sanitary* purpose for embalming? From all available evidence, the unembalmed body presents no health hazard, even though the deceased may have died from a communicable disease. Dr. Jesse Carr, quoted in *The American Way of Death* by Jessica Mitford, indicates that there is no legitimate sanitation reason for embalming the deceased for a funeral service under normal circumstances.

Do reasons of respect and love warrant embalming to preserve the remains as long as possible? Many relatives feel, naturally, that they wish to hold on to their beloved in his human form as long as possible. If this is the major purpose of the embalming, several points should be taken into consideration:

1. The body will keep, under normal conditions, for 24 hours, unless it has been dissected. If it was kept refrigerated, as is the standard procedure, it will unquestionably keep until after the funeral service.

2. The body must eventually decompose in the grave. Under optimum conditions, even were the embalming fluids to retard the deterioration of the outer form for considerable length of time, reliable reports of reinterments indicate that the remains soon become sickening to behold and totally unnatural, as a consequence of the embalming.

3. Sentiment should attach to the person as he lived his life, as he appeared during the years of good health, not to the corpse as it appears while entombed. The deceased himself undoubtedly would want his loved ones to remember him as he was during the peak of his lifetime. The prohibition of embalming for the purpose of viewing the deceased is considered in a separate chapter later in the book.

In the entire procedure of embalming today there is great confusion. There is not general public knowledge as to the methods of embalming, and certainly very little is known of "restoring," or cosmetology, a term used by the funeral industry for propping, primping, berouging, and dressing the remains to be placed on view. There is little doubt that if the family were aware of the procedures they might be too horrified to request it. A detailed description is available in Jessica Mitford's *The American Way of Death.*

The guiding religious ideal in regard to embalming is that a person upon his demise should be laid to rest naturally. There should be no mutilation of his body, no tampering with his remains, and no handling of the body other than for the religious purification. Disturbance of the inner organs, sometimes required during the embalming procedure, is strictly prohibited as a desecration of the image of God. The deceased can in no wise benefit from this procedure. So important is this principle, that Jewish law prohibits the embalming of a person even where he has specifically willed it.

It is not a sign of respect to make lifelike a person whom God has taken from life. The motive for embalming may be the desire to make of the funeral a last gift or a lasting memorial, but surely mourners must realize that this gift and this memorial are only illusory. The art of the embalmer is the art of complete denial. Embalming seeks to create an illusion, and to the extent that it succeeds, it only hinders the mourner from recovering from his grief. It is, on the contrary, an extreme dishonor to disturb the peace in which a person should be permitted to rest eternally.

It is indeed paradoxical that Western man, nourished on the Christian concept of the sinfulness of the body, which is considered the prison of the soul, should, in death, seek to adorn it and make it beautiful. Surely, the emphasis on the body in the funeral service serves to weaken the spiritual primacy and traditional religious emphasis on the soul.

There are, however, several exceptions to the general prohibition of embalming. These are:

1. When a lengthy delay in the funeral service becomes mandatory.
2. When burial is to take place overseas.
3. When governmental authority demands it.

In these cases, all required because of health regulations, Jewish law permits certain forms of embalming. Rabbinic authority must be consulted to determine the permissibility of embalming and the method to be used. One method frequently used is freezing. This is an excellent modern, clean method of preserving, also recommended by Dr. Jesse Carr, Chief of Pathology at San Francisco General Hospital.

The injection of preservative fluid, without the removal of the organs of the body, frequently has been used. If the blood has been released from the veins it should be collected in a receptacle, which should then be buried with the body. Bloodied clothes, worn by those killed accidentally or by violence, should be buried with the body. The blood is considered part of the human being and even in death they are not to be separated. As time goes on, and our knowledge of chemistry advances, other methods may be developed which Jewish law may consider legitimate.

The foregoing paragraphs are only general guidelines, and do not offer specific dispensation. Specific cases require individual attention and special permission from competent religious authority.

The Casket
ארון

"For dust thou art, and unto dust shalt thou return"
(Genesis 3:19), is the guiding principle in regard to the
selection of caskets. The practice in Israel and in many
parts of Europe has been to bury the deceased on a bed of
intertwined reeds, in no casket at all, thus, literally, fulfilling
the biblical prescription of returning the body to the bosom
of the earth. The casket was used in ancient times either
for purposes of honor, such as for the burial of a priest, or
to avoid a horrible sight, such as when burying a person
who was badly burned or maimed, or to avoid a public
health hazard, as in the case of one who died of a contagious
disease.

In this country, however, the dead are always buried in
caskets. The type of casket purchased should not be determined by cost, and one should not worry excessively about
how visitors will consider it. The following are the basic
criteria:

1. The coffin must be made completely of wood. The
Bible tells us that Adam and Eve hid among the trees in
the garden of Eden when they heard the Divine judgment
for committing the first sin. Said Rabbi Levi: "This was a
sign for their descendants that, when they die and are
prepared to receive their reward, they should be placed in
coffins made of wood."

Another reason for the use of a wood coffin is so that the
body and shroud should not decompose too much sooner
than the coffin. The body, the cloth and the wood have com-
parable rates of deterioration. A metal casket would retard
that process. "Unto dust shalt thou return."

2. Caskets made with metal handles and nails theoretically may be used. This satisfies both previously mentioned reasons for the use of wooden caskets. There is a
long-standing custom, however, one which is subscribed to
by a majority of Jews, which demands that only wooden

pegs be used. In funeral chapels these wooden-pegged caskets are called "Orthodox."

3. Casket interiors. Often, so-called "Orthodox" caskets are purchased with the interior lined, and bedded, and pillowed, preparatory to viewing the deceased—a totally objectionable procedure in truly Orthodox belief and practice. Lined interiors are not considered proper. They, like the embalming, suit-dressing and viewing which usually follow violate the basic principles of the Jewish funeral. The interior adds neither "comfort" nor dignity nor respect. It is only an artificial appendage, unless designed for "viewing," and viewing the body is surely not to be condoned religiously.

4. Type of wood. It really makes no difference what style or quality of wooden casket has been selected. Whether it is mahogany or pine, polished or plain, is unimportant. Many insist on drilling holes at the bottom of the casket to fulfill the "unto dust" requirement. This is quite proper and should be encouraged.

5. Earth from the Holy Land is frequently buried along with the deceased. This is a touching and meaningful custom. Those who wish to observe it should not be discouraged from doing so. The funeral director can easily arrange for it.

6. The casket does not have to be either costly or inexpensive. The Sages did not consider the expense a barometer of honor to the dead. To some it may be preferable to contribute monies to charity in memory of the deceased, rather than purchase lavish caskets. The cost is a personal matter, and should fit the budget of the survivors. The essential requirement is that dignity should prevail.

7. Ostentatious caskets are not in good taste. President Franklin Delano Roosevelt left explicit instructions that "'the casket be of absolute simplicity, dark wood, that the body be not embalmed, or hermetically-sealed, and that the grave be not lined with brick, cement, or stones." Likewise, while the remains of President John F. Kennedy were con-

veyed in a bronze coffin, before explicit arrangements could be made, his widow wisely decided that the President's spirit and life demanded a simple coffin, and he was removed from the bronze coffin and was interred in a wooden casket.

Flowers

In ancient days, the Talmud informs us, fragrant flowers and spices were used at the funeral to offset the odor of the decaying body. Today, this is no longer essential and they should *not* be used at Jewish funerals at all. In our days, they are used primarily at Christian funerals, and are considered to be a non-Jewish ritual custom which should be discouraged. It is much better to honor the deceased by making a contribution to a synagogue or hospital, or to a medical research association for the disease which afflicted the deceased. This method of tribute is more lasting and meaningful. However, if flowers *are* sent to the chapel, and the sender cannot be discouraged, the following procedure is recommended:

1. If the sender does not mind, they should be kept for the house of mourning. Failing this they should be placed at graveside, but not displayed during the service.
2. If the sender is so sensitive and the relationship so delicate that he will be offended, and these recommendations will cause insult or anger, and no alternative presents itself, it is preferable to accept them graciously and display them as intended, but not in an ostentatious manner.

Timing the Funeral Service

The Bible, in its mature wisdom, required burial to take place as soon as possible following death. It established this requirement by both a positive and a negative command. Positively, it stated, "Thou shalt surely bury him the same day." Negatively, it warned, "His body shall not remain all night" (Deuteronomy 21:23). Jewish law, therefore, demands that we bury the deceased within 24 hours following death.

The religious concept underlying this law is that man, made in the image of God, should be accorded the deepest respect. It is considered a matter of great shame and discourtesy to leave the deceased unburied—his soul has returned to God, but his body is left to linger in the land of the living. Even a Priest, on his way to enter the sanctuary on Yom Kippur, was commanded to render this honor of immediate burial even to a strange corpse, although he is normally forbidden to handle the remains. This is the proper honor that Jewish tradition accords those who die.

There is, secondarily, a psychological benefit to be derived from following the tradition. It becomes a matter of almost unbearable mental strain for the family to dwell for a long time in "the valley of the shadow of death." No one deserves to be subjected to the despair and anguish of being continually in the physical company of the deceased, no matter how deep his affection. As it is proper for the deceased to be buried without tarrying, so is it advisable for the family not to have to undergo the emotional pain of an unduly long delay.

Interring the dead may occasionally be delayed, but only for the honor of the dead. Thus, the rabbis allowed a delayed burial in the following cases:

1. When the government requires delay, such as for the legal transportation of the body, or for the completion of forms and papers, or for post-mortem examinations which must be performed prior to burial.

2. If delay is caused by having to wait for the delivery of shrouds or a proper casket.

3. If close relatives have to come from great distances, and it is considered an honor to the deceased for these relatives to be present. There should be, however, no unduly

long period of waiting such as the common misconception
of the permissibility of waiting three days would imply.
Also, the delay should be based not on arbitrary guesswork
as to when "most" people will attend, but on definite knowledge of the time of the arrival of close relatives such as
children or parents.

4. If the eulogizing rabbi is delayed and the presence
of this particular rabbi would be an honor to the deceased.

5. Rather than to hold the funeral late on Friday afternoon, the funeral may be postponed until Sunday (because
the Sabbath intervenes).

6. On major festivals, Jewish law forbids Jews to inter
their dead on the first day of the holiday, but permits non-
Jews to perform the burial on that day. On the second day
of such festivals it permits even Jews to do the burying, but
other than the actual interment, no other violation of the
sanctity of the day is permitted. Because conditions in contemporary society are such that funerals on either day of
the festival invariably result in needless transgressions
of the law, it is preferable to postpone the funeral until
after both days of the holiday.

The best time to hold the funeral service is during the
morning hours, and this for three reasons:

1. It is proper to perform the *mitzvah* of burial with
dispatch; the earlier the better.

2. For practical reasons, most persons will be able to
attend the service, and will then be able to return to their
own affairs.

3. It will leave time for those mourners living far from
the cemetery to begin the mourning period before dark, and
thus count this day as the first day of *shiva*. (This subject
will be treated in greater detail later.)

The timing also depends on the Funeral Home. They
must consider the scheduling of other funerals, and also
must plan the time so as to avoid arriving at the cemetery
during the lunch hour when cemetery employees frequently

are not available. The family should consult the rabbi before a time has been established, so as to determine his availability.

Between Death and Interment

אנינות

Each immediate relative of the deceased is considered an *onen* from the moment he has learned of the death until the end of the interment, regardless of how much time has elapsed in between.

The *onen* is a person in deep distress, a person yanked out of normal life and abruptly catapulted into the midst of inexpressible grief. He is disoriented, his attitudes are disarranged, his emotions out of gear. The shock of death paralyzes his consciousness and blocks out all regular patterns of orderly thinking. "The deceased lies *before* him," as the sages said and, psychologically, he is reliving the moment of death every instant during this period.

In this state of mind, unfortunately, the mourner must make detailed and final arrangements with the funeral director, burial society, cemetery and rabbi. He must also notify friends and family. Yet, inwardly, his primary concern is with his own loss, the great gap created in his personal life and in the life of his family. Often, at this time, he is burdened with guilt for the moments of unhappiness he may have caused the deceased. The suddenness of his grief, the dismay at the news of death, leave him in a state of disbelief. It is simply inconceivable, impossible, that one who was just alive is now dead, cut off and gone.

Practically, then, the *onen* must make immediate and significant decisions based on the reality of death. *Psychologically*, however, he has not yet assimilated it or accepted it. These two elements, plus the need to act with respect and reverence in the presence of the deceased, are the fundamental principles of the laws governing the *onen*.

WHO IS AN ONEN?

An *onen* is one who has lost a close relative for whom he is required to mourn. Those who are obligated to mourn, and to be mourned for, are:

1. father
2. mother
3. brother } —married or unmarried; on the father's
4. sister   }   or mother's side.
5. son
6. daughter
7. spouse

Minor children. A boy under the age of thirteen, and a girl under the age of twelve—are not properly considered *onenim* (pl.), and they are not bound by the laws of mourning that take place after interment. They are required only to rend their clothes, as will be discussed later.

Suicides. In the case of true suicides, as determined by Jewish law, the laws of *onen* or mourning do not apply. The obligation for arrangements and care of the deceased, according to Jewish law, falls technically upon the whole community, and not solely upon the relatives. The relatives, thus, have neither the obligation to participate in the arrangements nor to pay special courtesies to the suicide. A suicide—for reasons other than insanity—is considered to have destroyed the image of God and to have deprived his family of his presence. By treating the suicide in this manner Judaism plainly expresses its abhorrence of such actions, and this has served as a deterrent. (However, the costs of suicide burial, in our day, are borne by the family.) The subject of suicides is treated in greater detail in a separate chapter below.

A relative is an *onen* only if:

1. He busies himself with some aspect of the funeral arrangements.

2. Even if he does not so concern himself, that he be in a position to do so should it become necessary. He is *not* considered an *onen* if there is absolutely no possibility of his participation in the arrangements.

Thus, he is not an *onen* if:

1. The deceased is not in the possession of his relatives, as when the government has not released the body to the family, or if he was drowned, or if he is missing in combat and cannot be found, although there may be certain knowledge of his death.

2. He could not physically be present at the funeral preparations because he is under military obligation, or is confined in a hospital or prison, or is overseas, or is in a city too distant from the funeral. If, however, there is the possibility that he might have arrived in time for the funeral service, he is considered an *onen*, providing no other immediate relatives were present during arrangements.

The *onen* is required to abide by the following rules:

1. He may not eat in the presence of the body.

2. He may not eat meat or drink wine or liquor any place.

3. He may eat no festive meal or attend a party.

4. He must deny himself the luxuries of self-adornment, of bathing for pleasure, shaving, taking a haircut, and indulging in conjugal relations.

5. He may not conduct normal business during this time.

6. He may not study Torah, as this is considered a source of enjoyment.

7. All observances practiced by the mourner during *shiva* devolve also upon the *onen*, except that he is permitted to wear shoes and to leave the house in order to expedite the burial arrangements.

8. Because of the need to make and conclude the funeral arrangements, the *onen* is released from the obligations of

prayer, and many other specific positive observances, such as reciting the *motzi* over bread or the grace after meals. He, therefore, cannot be included in a *minyan.* While he is exempt from performing the positive commandments, he remains part of society and must obey all the negative commands. Thus, for example, while he need not recite a blessing over the washing of hands before breaking bread, he must take care to wash and cleanse himself properly. One is a positive commandment, the other a negative rule of religiously sanctioned hygiene. The *onen* should *not* perform commandments from which he is exempted. This would indicate a lack of concern for the deceased, and the Rabbis insisted that there is no virtue in this action.

9. On the Sabbath most laws that apply to the *onen* are cancelled. He is permitted meat and wine and is obligated to perform all the mandatory Sabbath observances. However, he must not participate in matters of private enjoyment, such as conjugal relations and the delight that is reaped from the study of the Torah. The *onen* should attend religious services. Preferably he should not serve as reader or cantor. He should not recite the Kaddish if other mourners are present, unless he has Yahrzeit or is in the midst of the year of mourning for one of his parents.

10. If the burial must take place on the second day of the holiday (even though, as mentioned above, burials should be strongly discouraged at this time) *aninut* (the state of being an *onen*) goes into effect immediately, even though it be a holiday. In such a case, the *onen* does not recite the Kaddish, or eat meat or wine.

11. On Succot the *onen* is not obligated to sit in the *succah.* If he desires to do so, he should not recite the blessing for that *mitzvah.* On the first night of Succot, however, seeing that burial cannot take place on the first day, he should recite the Kiddush and perform other observances connected with the holiday.

12. On the first night of Passover, the *onen* should observe all the *mitzvot* of the Seder night. On *Sefirah*

days, between Passover and Shavuot, the *onen* should refrain from reciting the counting of the days with the blessing, until immediately after burial. After the funeral, he may count the days *and* recite the blessing.

13. On Purim, the *onen* must listen to the reading of the *Megillah*, and is permitted to eat meat and wine in fulfillment of the religiously prescribed festive meal of the day.

14. On Hanukkah, the *onen* should have the candles lit for him, but the blessings recited by someone else. If no one else is present, he should kindle the candles himself without reciting the blessings.

15. *Tefillin:* The laying of the *tefillin* may not be performed on the day of death and on the day of burial. This is not because of the general exemption from positive obligations during the time of *aninut,* but rather because *tefillin* is considered an object of beautification and ornamentation, and this is inconsistent with the inner bitterness experienced by the mourner so soon after the loss of his loved one.

The following are some clarifications and ramifications of this law of *tefillin:*

1. Even if burial occurs on the day following death, or two days thereafter, *tefillin* are not donned during this entire period. One resumes the practice on the day after burial. Thus, also, if for some reason burial took place at night, the entire following day is considered unsuitable for wearing the *tefillin.*

2. If three or four days elapse between death and burial, then:

   a. If the mourner is personally involved in making arrangements for the funeral or interment, he does not don *tefillin* on any of these days, including the full day of burial.

   b. If the mourner is not involved in these matters, he then follows the laws of *aninut:* he does not don *tefillin* on the day of death, but resumes wearing them immediately thereafter. On the day of interment he is prohibited from doing so before the time of burial, but upon returning from the funeral should promptly don them.

3. If he received news of the death after interment already took place, but this was within thirty days of the time of burial, he may not wear the *tefillin* on the day the news arrived. If the news came at night, he refrains from wearing *tefillin* on the following day.

4. If the interment occurred during a holiday, or during the intermediary days (*chol ha'moed*) of Succot or Passover (when the mourning period begins later), there is no prohibition against the wearing of the *tefillin* (for those who normally put on *tefillin* during *chol ha'moed*).

5. Likewise, a groom who has suffered the death of a relative during the week immediately following the wedding, and whose mourning period begins later, should wear the *tefillin* during this week.

Viewing the Remains—A New American Custom*

It has become a common practice at American funerals, among all religious faiths, to display the body of the deceased as part of the funeral ritual or service. This custom is of recent American origin, having no roots in ancient culture or contemporary European usage, with the exception of the "lying-in-state" of kings and emperors.

The lifeless body is removed from the hospital or home and taken to the funeral establishment. There it is embalmed and "restored" by manipulating it, injecting it with chemicals, covering it with cosmetics, dressing it neatly, and supporting it with mechanical devices. It is then displayed

---

* This chapter was written with the kind assistance of a noted psychiatrist, Dr. Naftali Eskreis. It was published as-a separate article in the April, 1966 issue of the *Journal of Religion and Health*.

in a "reposing room," or in the chapel, before the religious service begins. Clergymen usually insist that the casket be closed during the service itself.

The viewing of the corpse is one of the fundamentals of the economy of the funeral industry. Before the body is offered for presentation to relatives and friends, it must be perfumed, restored to a look of perfect health, dressed in expensive garments, and placed in a respectable, "comfortable-looking" casket. These requirements of viewing usually constitute the bulk of the funeral costs.

I

The new, American, quasi-religious ceremony is justified to the public by two high-sounding phrases. One is that viewing the corpse is "paying your last respects." This form of farewell to the deceased is made to seem the minimal courtesy a man can pay his beloved; it has become the natural and logical thing for mourners to do. The second is that it is a necessary aspect of "grief therapy," helping the bereaved to remember a sweet, content, smiling face rather than the vacant, pain-ridden, drawn look of a cadaver.

To the layman, both these arguments seem quite plausible, requiring no further investigation—certainly not at the time of death. The practice of viewing the remains has, therefore, become standard, and a "traditional" part of the American funeral.

Viewing the corpse is objectionable, both theologically and psychologically. It shows no respect for the deceased, and provides questionable therapy for the bereaved. On the contrary, we believe that while viewing may seem desirable superficially, deeper consideration will show it to be devoid of real meaning, and, in fact, detrimental in terms of both religion and mental health. Religiously, it expresses disregard for the rights of the dead and a perversion of the religious significance of life and death. Psychologically, it may serve to short-circuit the slow therapy of nature's grief process that begins from the moment of the awareness of death.

Traditional Judaism regards burial procedures, for the most part, as *yekara d'schichva*, devoted to the respect, honor, and endearment of the deceased. Mourning laws are primarily *yekara de'hayye*, therapy for the living, devoted to the mitigating of intense grief, the slow disentanglement from the web of guilt, anger, fear, hatred, and rebellion that enshrouds the mind of the mourner after his relative has been taken from life.

The sages wisely noted that one cannot and should not comfort the mourners while their dead lie before them. Comfort and relief come later, after funeral and burial arrangements have been completed and the dead have been interred. Until that time, the deceased remains the center of concern. His honor and his integrity are of primary importance.

II

Whether, in fact, respect for the deceased is primary, or the comfort of the mourners is the principal goal, it is difficult to justify this new practice of viewing the remains as a standard feature of the funeral service.

First, if that sublime concept in Genesis that "God created man in His own image" is right—and all of our major religions are based on it—then the whole procedure for preparing the body and restoring it, which is prerequisite for viewing, is offensive and abominable. If man is fashioned after his Creator, how can we allow the stippling and the nailing, the molding and the smearing, literally the "man-handling" of that which was created in the image of God?

It is a horrifying experience to witness the restoring process for those who died after sustained illness, or intense suffering, or as a result of accident, or, for that matter, for all except those who died in the bloom of health. Can this handling of the deceased be considered a tribute to God's creation and to man's living in the image of God?

Isaiah's description of the righteous dead (Is. 57:2) : "May peace come, may they rest in their resting place," is all but absurd with the development of the restoring process. There is no rest for those who should rest in peace (not even, we may add, if the ceremony takes place in what is called a "reposing room"). The image that is born, fondled, loved, respected and honored, the dignity that inheres in man as a creation in the image of God, is now desecrated. A person's last right should be the right of utter privacy, the privilege of remaining untampered with after death. It is amazing that this process of disturbing the rest of the deceased is called, "paying our last respects."

Secondly, Judaism postulates that the dignity of man derives from two basic sources. One, mentioned above, is that man is the creation of an all-good God. This endows him with the spark of divinity, and it is the divine image in man that grants him innate value. The other derives not from man's creatureliness, but from his personal social development as a human being living among other human beings. What is important here is man as he exercises the freedom of his will, the person as he develops his own *anschaung,* how he handles the existential crises that beset him, what he does with the qualities that were inborn in him, his unique individuality. The sum total of his personal experiences and his reactions to them grant him "value" in addition to that innate dignity he derives from being a creation of God.

The Talmud records a dispute between Rabbi Akiva and Ben Azzai as to the most significant phrase in the Bible. They disagree as to which of the two foregoing qualities endows man with greater value. Rabbi Akiva declares that it is man's righteous exercise of the freedom of his will, the love of neighbor, the social values that are primary. Ben Azzai dwells on the creation of man in God's image as the major source of his dignity.

If we reject manipulating and masking the cadaver in preparation for viewing as a violation of the image of God, we must also reject holding up for display the physical remains of the human being who achieved dignity from the sum of his life experiences, his loves and interests, the *élan vital* that was the hallmark of this man.

In Jewish literature and law, the human being is compared with the scroll of the Torah. The death of a man, for example, is equivalent to the burning of a Torah, and, in both cases, the onlooker is required to rend his garments. As the Torah, used for holy purposes, retains its holiness even when it becomes religiously disqualified, so man, having lived for noble purpose, retains dignity even in death. The remains possess the holiness that characterizes the Torah itself. Thus, too, one may not dishonor a corpse, as one may not desecrate the holy Scroll. In Traditional Judaism, the dishonoring of the dead includes not only untoward and derogatory remarks, or joking and jesting, but even eating, drinking and smoking—even studying the Bible in the presence of the deceased—any indulgence in the pleasures and needs of the living in the company of the helpless and nonparticipating corpse. One may not deal with the dead as though he were living, as if he were merely sleeping. For those who thus ridicule the dead, the sages apply the phrase from Proverbs 17:5: "Whoso mocketh the poor, blasphemeth his Maker."

When we place on display the remains of the person we loved, we may, in fact, bring ourselves some temporary comfort, but this, surely, does not constitute respect for the dead. What we are doing, essentially, is holding up a lifeless, bloodless, mindless mass of flesh and bones. The "color" of the deceased lay in his wit, character and personality—or lack of these qualities—not in the embalmer's rouge and lipstick. What should be remembered is the indelible impression upon us of a full-blooded, living person, not the expression on his lips as fashioned by mechanical devices.

What we view is the ghost of a man, not the man. It is

sheer mockery to parade before this ghost to say, "Goodbye," or to take one last look by which to remember him. This is not the person, but a death mask, even if prettied up artificially. When we display our dead, we exhibit not their loves and fears and hopes, their characters and their concerns, but their physical shapes in their most prostrate condition. Strangely enough, we readily understand sick people who, wracked with pain and emaciated from suffering, do not wish to be seen in their deteriorated condition. Yet, while we appreciate the vanity of the living only too well, we are insensitive to the ghastliness of holding up the helpless ghost, painted and propped, in morbid exhibitionism.

Jewish mystics refer to the look of the deceased as *mar'eh letusha*, "a hammered image." Indeed, the viewer emerges, after the ordeal of the funeral, with a new and sordid dimension added to his memories and feelings. This is not the person he knew in life, nor is it the cadaver gripped by death; it is a make-believe, a figure out of a wax museum, a being neither dead nor alive.

Thirdly, both Judaism and psychotherapy express in their own idioms the view that a masking of reality will not enable the human being to cope with reality. The truth is that the end has come. The deceased shall no longer walk the earth and share happy occasions with his relatives. To extend into the time of death the countenance of cheerful life is to disguise the end, to introduce by subterfuge the possibility of continued, though passive, existence and to risk causing severe damage to the mental state of the bereaved.

Judaism explicitly postulates that the funeral must be a finale. The service, the prayers and the rituals do not attempt to hide death, much less to deny it. They confirm it and acknowledge it unhesitatingly. It is only the acceptance of the *reality* of death that enables man to overcome the *trauma* of death.

During the cleansing and purification of the deceased in

preparation for burial, a very ancient prayer—more than a thousand years old—is recited. The prayer is, as it were, a presentation of the dead before God, asking for His mercy and for forgiveness for the dead. The prayer at graveside is likewise a justification of the God of truth: the Lord who has given and the Lord who has taken. There is no mask of death in the Jewish ritual. The deceased is buried in the earth itself, dust to dust, and the grave is filled in the presence of the relatives and friends. Indeed, it is the closest of friends and the greatest of scholars who are invited to be the first to fill in the grave. The thump of the clod of earth upon the wood of the casket sounds the sure finale to a precious life.

It is a perversion of the true religious import of the funeral to disguise the reality of death. The display of the dead in the most lifelike appearance, the semblance of life through the use of cosmetics, the clothing in gowns or tuxedos, the propping of the head and use of pillows, the facsimile of a happy person asleep, is contrary to the spirit that religion seeks to engender. Man does not, as the happy phrase would have it, merely "go to sleep with his forefathers." Man dies and decays, and his physical existence is no more. His good works live on after him, but his body returns to the earth as it was. His personality, his goodness go on to a greater dimension of existence; the chemical elements decompose and return to their original state.

III

From the standpoint of psychotherapy, the idea of viewing the corpse as standard funeral procedure because of the therapeutic value inherent in the practice has not been proved clinically and, in fact, appears to contradict the very basic thrust of its method. "Grief therapy" works, it is claimed, to soften the shock of death. It alleviates that sudden cut-off and, momentarily, returns those lost to us. But, if therapy is conceived as a form of self-enlightenment and self-understanding, what valid function can viewing perform? Shall we believe that man requires a neurotic distortion of truth in order to protect himself from the trauma of truth? It seems far more sensible to rely on the faith that man can summon the strength with which to confront the raw, if sometimes bitter, truth without the aid of fabricated distortions. Viewing is as much "grief therapy" as painting a jail with bright colors is "thief therapy."

It may also be that not only is viewing not therapeutic, but is, in fact, injurious to the viewer. The first stage of mourning is characterized by anger, despair, and the denial of death. Fixation on any one of these reactions represents, from the psychological point of view, a pathological response. It is entirely conceivable that viewing may lead to a fixation on the denial of death. The refusal to give up the object of love is perpetuated by the illusion of life that the embalmers strive so mightily to create. The religious ritual of the funeral compels one to acknowledge the finality of the physical loss, and thus enables the "working through" of the grief process. To fix one's mind on what should be an ephemeral reaction is possibly to short-circuit the entire effectiveness of the grief process.

To speculate further, is it not possible that viewing may meet the bizarre needs of certain individuals and precipitate vicarious deviations from the usual grief reactions? Indeed, it is possible that in a predisposed person it may give onset to excessive fantasies or delusions. It does not mean, of course, that the result must be pathological, but it may certainly create a variant response to mourning.

There is, unfortunately, little statistical data available on the entire subject, but speculation compels one to regard this self-styled "grief therapy" with the gravest suspicion.

IV

In addition to the foregoing, it is interesting to note that this new ceremony of viewing the remains is but a reflection of our general value system. By making a display of the flesh minus the mind, we are, in fact, demonstrating our lifelong emphasis on appearance over value, on externals and possessions over the inner life and growth of the sensitive and sentient human being. As such, viewing is an extension into death of the kind of attitudes that tax life: to use Buber's terms, the attrition of the "thou" in favor of the "it." When we take a human being to whom we once related as a subject, as an equal, as a "thou," and manipulate him as one would a piece of merchandise, we reduce him to an object, a mere "it." The tendency of those attending funerals is to note that "he looks good" rather than "he was good," and conversations tend to dwell on the person as a man of means, rather than a man of ends. But the person himself, in his own intimation of immortality, hopes and expects not that the shape of his nose and jaw, or the tilt of his chin, will be remembered, but that his deeds, his teachings, his attitudes, his strivings, his good intentions and efforts, and the accomplishments of his children will somehow bring him the immortality he craves.

We cannot agree that man's soul is so impoverished that he cannot remember the living image of his departed; that he is so neurotic that he cannot be permitted to confront the ultimate truth; that he is so self-indulgent that he will willingly disturb the departed for the sake of his own peace of mind; that he is so afraid of fact that he must create for himself a fiction.

From both viewpoints, that of Traditional Judaism and that of psychotherapy, there is no valid reason for this new, American, quasi-religious ceremony. On the contrary, man, created in the image of God, participating in the dignity of human life, deserves to rest in peace. And the mourner deserves, at this traumatic moment of intense grief, to be allowed to work through, naturally and at his own pace, an acknowledgment and an acceptance of his loss.

The Night Before the Funeral Service

The deceased may not be left alone before burial. As noted previously, the watching over of the deceased may be performed by a relative or by any other person, preferably an observant Jew who will recite portions from the Book of Psalms. This can be arranged by the funeral director or the rabbi.

The "wake" is definitely alien to Jewish custom, and its spirit does violence to Jewish sensitivity and tradition. The custom of visiting the funeral parlor on the night before interment to comfort the mourners and to view the remains is clearly a Christian religious practice, and not merely an American folkway. In Judaism, which requires no additional ceremonies to buttress its own authentic millennial customs, respect to the dead is not paid by viewing their remains, for it is, as we have said, rather offensive. And it is futile to attempt to comfort the mourners when their dead lie before them in the chapel. The place for offering condolences is at home, during the seven special days of mourning called *shiva.*

In addition, the wake is often reduced to the level of a social gathering. The conversation is often inane, and the evening has the barest facade of dignity. The family itself must suffer prolonged hours of trivial chatter in the face of terrible grief.

The wake, therefore, should be discouraged at Jewish funerals, under any and all circumstances.

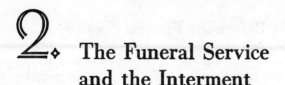

2.♦ The Funeral Service and the Interment

THE JEWISH FUNERAL service is a starkly simple, but emotionally meaningful, farewell to the deceased. The service does not attempt to comfort the mourners. The Sages wisely noted that it is sheer mockery to comfort the bereaved while their beloved lies dead before their eyes. Moreover, it is psychologically futile to effect a reconciliation between the mourner and his fate at this time.

The service is directed, rather, at honoring the departed. The tribute to him takes the form of the recitation of a eulogy; chanting of several Psalms and the Memorial Prayer; following the casket and accompanying the deceased to his final resting place; speaking only well of him; and many other small ways in which each individual pays his own heartfelt respect.

In order to render the proper homage to the deceased, tradition serves as a wise and able instructor. The cumulative wisdom of the Jewish people's experience with grief for over 3,000 years is distilled in the laws and customs pertaining to this area of life. The following pages offer the most important details of these traditions, and some of the wise principles underlying them.

Location of the Service

From the days of the Second Temple until modern times, funeral services have taken place in either the home of the deceased or at the cemetery. The Talmud indicates that the service of farewell took place in one of these two places, most often in the home.

The use of the synagogue for such occasions was rare. When the service was held at the local synagogue or religious school it was only so that the entire community might pay honor to an exceptional person. In modern times, the funeral chapel is almost always used. The chapel provides a dignified setting, is able to accommodate many people, and is, therefore, to be encouraged in most instances.

There are occasions, however, when one or another of these four choices—home, synagogue, chapel or cemetery— is preferable, depending upon the family's decision. It should be noted that the holding of funeral services within the precincts of the synagogue sanctuary is very rare. It is done only for those who, like Rabbi Judah the Prince, are scrupulously observant, great Torah scholars, and noted leaders in communal activities. Respect may be rendered those who are deserving, although they may fall somewhat short of this ideal person, by taking the hearse to the cemetery via the synagogue, and pausing in front of the synagogue. The rear door of the hearse is opened, the cantor chants the memorial prayer in honor of the deceased, and then the cortege continues to the cemetery.

If there is no Jewish chapel available, then the community should set aside some room in the local synagogue for such occasions. The vestry or auditorium is the most appropriate place to hold such services. If this facility is not available, then the home should be used. If this too is impossible, the cemetery should be the place for the eulogy and prayers. In inclement weather, when there is no other place for the funeral, a hospital auditorium or a non-sectarian chapel, *with all religious symbols removed,* may be used.

Rending the Garment: Keriah

קריעה

The most striking Jewish expression of grief is the rending of garments by the mourner prior to the funeral service.

The Bible records many instances of rending the clothes after the news of death. When Jacob saw Joseph's coat of many colors drenched with what he thought to be his son's blood, he rent his garments. Likewise, David tore his clothes when he heard of the death of King Saul, and Job, who knew grief so well, stood up and rent his mantle.

The rending is an opportunity for psychological relief. It allows the mourner to give vent to his pent-up anguish by means of a controlled, religiously sanctioned act of destruction. Maimonides, according to the interpretation of B. H. Epstein (*Torah Temimah* on Lev. 10:6), notes with sharp insight that this tear satisfies the emotional need of the moment, or else it would not be permitted as it is a clear violation of the biblical command not to cause waste. For this reason, we may assume, the tear for parents must be made with bare hands.

Geoffrey Gorer, in his book *Death, Grief and Mourning*, notes that "although our culture gives no symbolic expression to anger, a considerable number of others have done so." This is seen in such rituals as the "destruction of the dead person's property or possessions or, slightly more indirectly, by the various mutilations which mourners have to inflict upon themselves as a sign of the pain which the dead have caused them. According to some psychoanalysts, this anger is a component of all mourning, and one of the main functions of the mourning *process* is to *work through* and dissipate this anger in a symbolic and, to a great extent, unconscious fashion."

Keriah may serve also as a substitute for the ancient pagan custom of tearing the flesh and the hair which symbolizes the loss of one's own flesh and blood in sympathy for the deceased and which is not permitted in Jewish law (Deuteronomy 14:1-2).

The halachic requirement to "expose the heart" (that is, that the tear for deceased parents must be over the heart), indicates that the tear in the apparel represents a torn heart. The prophet Joel (2:13) chastises the Jew to rend the heart itself, not only the garment over the heart, indicating that the external tear is a symbol of the broken heart within.

Another, and relatively unknown, reason is advanced in the Jerusalem Talmud (*Moed Katan* 3:5) : The "exposing of the heart" is performed because the mourner has lost the ability to fulfill the biblical command to honor father and mother. We suffer deeply when we can no longer give love to our beloved. Of course, respect for parents can, and should, be expressed after their death, but, according to many authorities, it is a rabbinic, rather than a biblical enactment. *Keriah*, thus, also symbolizes the rending of the parent-child relationship, and confronts the mourner with the stabbing finality of this separation, expressed on his own clothes and on his own person for all to see.

Who Must Rend the Clothing?

1. Seven relatives are obligated to perform this command: son, daughter; father, mother; brother, sister; and spouse.

2. They must be adults, above the age of thirteen. Minors, who are in fact capable of understanding the situation, and appreciating the loss, should have other relatives or friends make the tear for them. For pre-Bar Mitzvah youngsters who are too immature to understand the gravity of the situation, one should nonetheless make a slight symbolic cut in the garment. This unites them with the family at the terrible time of tears and tragedy.

3. Divorced mates may cut their clothing, but they are not *obligated* to do so. They also may, of course, bemoan the

death with the others and accompany the deceased to the cemetery.

4. Sons-in-law or daughters-in-law, if this is their sincere desire, may rend their garments out of respect for their spouse's tragedy. This should be done only with the assurance that their own living parents will not object.

5. Bride and groom should not perform the clothes-tearing ritual during the first seven days following the wedding. This time is one of inviolate joy even in the face of grief.

6. Mentally ill patients, who cannot appreciate the gravity of their loss, or may not see the death in its proper perspective, should not tear the clothing. If it is the patient's parent who has died, rending should be performed after sanity has returned. In the case of the death of other relatives, once it has been delayed it is not to be done at all.

7. The physically handicapped, or those too weak to make the tear themselves during the *shiva*, should not have their garments cut subsequently, even though they recover. They felt the pain and anguish at the time of the occurrence of death, and the later rending is purposeless, as the rending must take place during the time of most intense grief.

When Should the Rending Take Place?

The garment should be torn at either one of three times:

1. At the moment of hearing of the death, wherever the mourner may be at that time.

2. At the home or the chapel, immediately prior to the service.

3. At the cemetery, prior to the interment.

Today, it is usually done at the funeral chapel; this is the preferable procedure. At this time, the rabbi is present and can supervise the rending in accordance with the traditional laws. Also, this is the time that the entire family is gathered together, and the relatives can stand by one another united through this emotionally charged expression of common bereavement.

The following are the laws of rending for special circumstances:

1. On Sabbaths and holidays the mourners should certainly be encouraged to delay the *keriah* until the service at the chapel. If, however, they desire to do so as soon as is possible, they must wait at least until nightfall.

2. During *chol ha'moed*, the days between the first and last days of Passover and Succot, the *keriah* may be performed. Some rabbis may prefer to wait until after the holidays, especially if there are no sons or daughters, and it is, therefore, proper to allow the rabbi to make that decision.

3. If news of the death of one of the seven relatives, noted above, reached the mourners after interment, but *within* 30 days thereafter, they must rend the garment upon hearing the news. If the news reached them more than 30 days after the death then:

a. For parents there is no time limit. The garment must be rent no matter how late.

b. For other relatives there is no obligation to rend after 30 days.

If the mourners forgot to rend at the proper time, then:

1. *For parents*—they should rend as soon as they recall their omission. This may be done even if the time elapsed is very long.

2. *For other relatives*—if it was recalled during *shiva* (the first seven days of mourning), the tear should be made then. Afterwards, it should not be made.

However, the blessing that usually accompanies the *keriah* should be recited only within the first *three* days after death, but not later. The reason for this is that the blessing may be recited only in the midst of intense grief, and this stage of grief is considered by the law to last until the fourth day, after which time it slowly diminishes.

Which Clothing Should Be Rent?

The clothing to be rent is customarily the outer clothing usually worn at room temperature. This precludes the cutting of the overcoat and underclothes.

1. For men, the vest should be cut, if it is usually worn by the mourner. If it is not usually worn, the suit, jacket or sweater should be rent.

Some Orthodox rabbis have permitted, and declared valid for the performance of *keriah*, the rending of a tie which is always worn. The reason for this is that it satisfies the conditions required for *keriah:* It is close to the neck, so that it is recognizable as not merely another tear, and it is a garment that is almost always worn. It is, technically, an article of clothing in that its size is the width of three fingers square, which is considered permissible with regard to carrying it on the Sabbath. (Were it not an article of clothing it would not be permitted to be worn on the Sabbath.)

2. For ladies, the dress, or blouse, or sweater should be cut. Clothing may be changed for this rending. It is not necessary or desirable that new clothes be worn. The mourner may change into used clothing for this occasion.

Should a Pinned Ribbon Be Used?

The rending of the clothes expresses the deepest feelings of sorrow and anguish. It is the symbol of a broken heart and a genuine mark of separation from one who was dearly beloved, with whom one had a blood relationship, or ties of matrimony.

The grief we express at such moments taps the deepest wells of our humanity, and the manner in which we manifest it should be equally authentic. The anguish is exquisite and, one might even say, sacred, and the way in which we express it should be no less sacred. It is appropriate that this form of release of sorrow be sanctioned by faith and by centuries of ancient custom, going back often to biblical times.

How shallow, how disappointing, how pitiably trivial, therefore, to symbolize these authentic sentiments not by an act of historic and religious significance, but by the little black ribbon or button—invented by enterprising American undertakers! Tradition calls upon us to tear *our* garments, to put the mark of the broken heart on our *own* clothing—and not to vent our feelings on a meaningless and impersonal strip of cloth pinned on us by a stranger.

Keriah is too personally meaningful to substitute for it a petty gimmick, the expression of penury, rather than grief, thereby desecrating our own most genuine human experiences.

Nevertheless, if for some reason the ribbon has been used at the funeral service, the mourner should make a tear in the proper clothing upon his return home.

Where Should the Cut Be Made?

For parents: The tear should be made on the left side— over the heart—and should be plainly visible.

It should be torn vertically, beginning near the neck and cut down approximately three inches. The initial cut may be made with a knife (by anyone close by), but then should be torn by hand by the mourner himself.

The tear should not be made along a seam, as it must appear to be a purposeful scar in the clothing, and not merely an accidental unthreading.

For other relatives: The tear is made on the right side, and need not show. Thus, the cut may be inside the lapel of a jacket, or the lining of a sweater or dress. Also, it may be done by others, not necessarily by the hand of the mourner himself.

The woman mourner must retain her modesty and, consequently, the tear in the garment should be made by herself in a relatively inconspicuous part of the clothing so as not to expose herself immodestly.

How Long Should the Rent Garments Be Worn?
For parents: The rent should be clearly visible during *shiva*. If a change of clothes is required during that time, the changed clothes, too, should be cut. After *shiva* the rent clothes need not be worn. A daughter, for reasons of dignity and modesty, may baste the clothing that was torn as soon after the funeral as she wishes. The son may baste his clothing only after thirty days. But neither son nor daughter may ever permanently sew these clothes. The wound left by the passing of parents may be healed, but the scar never completely disappears.

If a major holiday occurs during *shiva*, the clothes may be basted before sundown. The torn garments are not worn on the Sabbath during *shiva*.

For other relatives: Mourners for relatives other than father or mother are required to perform the rending of the clothes, but need not make the rend visible. Thus, if they change their clothing during the *shiva*, they need not rend the new set of clothes. The clothes may be basted after the *shiva*, and sewn completely after the thirty-day period of mourning. If a major holiday occurs during *shiva*, the mourner may sew the clothes before sundown. "There is a time to rend the garment, and a time to mend it," says Ecclesiastes (3:7).

Posture During Keriah

The law requires that the rending of the garments be performed while standing. The posture of accepting grief in Jewish life is always erect, symbolizing both strength in the face of crisis, and respect for the deceased.

The Funeral Service
לויה

The funeral service is a brief and simple service designed primarily as *yekara d'schichba*—for the honor and dignity of the deceased. The worthy values he lived by, the good deeds he performed, and the noble aspects of his character are eulogized. The function of the eulogy, however, is not to comfort the bereaved, although by highlighting the good and the beautiful in the life of the departed it affords an implicit consolation for the mourners.

There is also great psychological benefit from the funeral service itself although this, too, is not its primary purpose. It enables many friends and relatives to participate in the situation of bereavement and, thus, relieve the terrible loneliness of the mourners. In addition, since it not only praises the deceased, but also confronts all who attend with the terrible fact of their own mortality, it impels them to "consider their days," to take stock and live their lives creatively.

The service consists of a selection from the Psalms appropriate to the life of the deceased, a panegyric of his finer qualities which his survivors should seek to implant in their own lives, and a Memorial Prayer asking that God shelter his soul "on the wings of His Divine presence."

The most commonly used Psalm at the funeral service is Psalm 23.

Psalm 23

מִזְמוֹר לְדָוִד: יְיָ רֹעִי, לֹא אֶחְסָר. בִּנְאוֹת דֶּשֶׁא יַרְבִּיצֵנִי,
עַל מֵי מְנֻחוֹת יְנַהֲלֵנִי. נַפְשִׁי יְשׁוֹבֵב, יַנְחֵנִי בְמַעְגְּלֵי צֶדֶק לְמַעַן
שְׁמוֹ. גַּם כִּי אֵלֵךְ בְּגֵיא צַלְמָוֶת לֹא אִירָא רָע, כִּי אַתָּה עִמָּדִי,
שִׁבְטְךָ וּמִשְׁעַנְתֶּךָ, הֵמָּה יְנַחֲמֻנִי. תַּעֲרֹךְ לְפָנַי שֻׁלְחָן נֶגֶד צֹרְרָי.
דִּשַּׁנְתָּ בַשֶּׁמֶן רֹאשִׁי, כּוֹסִי רְוָיָה. אַךְ טוֹב וָחֶסֶד יִרְדְּפוּנִי כָּל
יְמֵי חַיָּי; וְשַׁבְתִּי בְּבֵית יְיָ לְאֹרֶךְ יָמִים.

The Lord is my Shepherd; I shall not want.
He has me lie down in green pastures,
He leads me beside the still waters.
He revives my soul;
He guides me on paths of righteousness for His glory.
Though I walk through the valley of the shadow of
      death,
I fear no harm,
For you are with me.
Your rod and your staff do comfort me.
You set a table in sight of my enemies;
You anoint my head with rich oil; my cup overflows.
Surely goodness and mercy shall follow me all the days
      of my life,
And I shall abide in the house of the Lord for ever.

Commentary

This Psalm expresses the most intimate, personal relationship of man with his beloved God. Troubles may abound, agony may strike the soul, but there is this one comforting thought—"the Lord is my Shepherd." As a shepherd seeks to guide and care for his flock, as he seeks fertile pastures in which his sheep may graze, as he always stays close to his flock and helps them grow and develop; as he lovingly embraces and raises up the sheep who have been injured; so does God, the Divine Shepherd, watch over His flock. We, the members of the flock, may sometimes, in our despair, doubt the justice of the Shepherd, we may not understand His ways, but we are confident that He is concerned with our welfare.

"He has me lie down in green pastures: He leads me beside the still waters." And so, even if sometimes, as is inevitable, "I walk through the valley of the shadow of death, I fear no harm, for You are with me: Your rod and Your staff do comfort me." For I know that the rod of the Shepherd seeks to guide me, however strange that path may seem to be, however puzzled I may be by the evil that has befallen me. My faith in the Divine Shepherd gives me the confidence to proclaim, "Only goodness and mercy shall follow me all the days of my life, and I shall abide in the house of the Lord forever."

What Is Man?

A second selection recited at most funeral services is "What Is Man," consisting of verses from various Psalms.

יְיָ: מָה אָדָם וַתֵּדָעֵהוּ, בֶּן־אֱנוֹשׁ וַתְּחַשְּׁבֵהוּ.

אָדָם לַהֶבֶל דָּמָה, יָמָיו כְּצֵל עוֹבֵר.

בַּבֹּקֶר יָצִיץ וְחָלָף, לָעֶרֶב יְמוֹלֵל וְיָבֵשׁ.

לִמְנוֹת יָמֵינוּ כֵּן הוֹדַע, וְנָבִא לְבַב חָכְמָה.

שְׁמָר־תָּם וּרְאֵה יָשָׁר, כִּי אַחֲרִית לְאִישׁ שָׁלוֹם.

אַךְ אֱלֹהִים יִפְדֶּה נַפְשִׁי מִיַּד שְׁאוֹל, כִּי יִקָּחֵנִי סֶלָה.

כָּלָה שְׁאֵרִי וּלְבָבִי, צוּר לְבָבִי וְחֶלְקִי אֱלֹהִים לְעוֹלָם.

וְיָשֹׁב הֶעָפָר עַל הָאָרֶץ כְּשֶׁהָיָה, וְהָרוּחַ תָּשׁוּב אֶל הָאֱלֹהִים אֲשֶׁר נְתָנָהּ.

"O Lord, what is man that You regard him, or the son of man that You take account of him? Man is like a breath, his days are like a passing shadow. You sweep men away. They are like a dream; like grass which is renewed in the morning. In the morning it flourishes and grows, but in the evening it fades and withers. The years of our life are threescore and ten, or even by reason of special strength fourscore; yet their pride is but toil and trouble. They are soon gone, and we fly away. So teach us to treasure our days that we may get a wise heart. Observe the good man, and behold the upright, for there is immortality for the man of peace. Surely God will ransom my soul from the grave; He will gladly accept me. The Lord redeems the souls of His servants; none of those who take refuge in Him will be condemned. The dust returns to the earth as it was, but the spirit returns to God who gave it."

Commentary

What is expressed here is despair over the brevity of man's life. It asks: "What can be the significance of a life that withers so quickly?" But faith informs us that, nonetheless, there is a God who guides us. Observe the good man! God will care for the upright in heart. He shall ascend the mountain of the Lord.

Other Psalms or selections from the Book of Proverbs are chosen by the rabbi for appropriate occasions and for different personal qualities of the deceased. Frequently, "A Woman Of Valor" is read for a kind and gracious lady. Other selections are chosen for a person who died at a young age.

The Memorial Prayer

The Memorial Prayer is a beautiful one having been chanted in the same way for many years.

For a Male

אֵל מָלֵא רַחֲמִים, שׁוֹכֵן בַּמְּרוֹמִים, הַמְצֵא מְנוּחָה נְכוֹנָה
תַּחַת כַּנְפֵי הַשְּׁכִינָה, בְּמַעֲלוֹת קְדוֹשִׁים וּטְהוֹרִים כְּזֹהַר הָרָקִיעַ
מַזְהִירִים, אֶת נִשְׁמַת_____שֶׁהָלַךְ לְעוֹלָמוֹ. בַּעֲבוּר שֶׁנָּדְרוּ
צְדָקָה בְּעַד הַזְכָּרַת נִשְׁמָתוֹ, בְּגַן עֵדֶן תְּהֵא מְנוּחָתוֹ. לָכֵן בַּעַל
הָרַחֲמִים יַסְתִּירֵהוּ בְּסֵתֶר כְּנָפָיו לְעוֹלָמִים, וְיִצְרוֹר בִּצְרוֹר
הַחַיִּים אֶת נִשְׁמָתוֹ. יְיָ הוּא נַחֲלָתוֹ וְיָנוּחַ עַל מִשְׁכָּבוֹ בְּשָׁלוֹם,
וְנֹאמַר אָמֵן.

"O God, full of compassion, Thou who dwellest on high! Grant perfect rest beneath the sheltering wings of Thy presence, among the holy and pure who shine as the brightness on the heavens, unto the soul of . . . .
. . . . who has gone unto eternity, and in

whose memory charity is offered. May his repose be in
paradise. May the Lord of Mercy bring him under the
cover of His wings forever, and may his soul be bound
up in the bond of eternal life. May the Lord be his
possession, and may he rest in peace. Amen."

For a Female

אֵל מָלֵא רַחֲמִים, שׁוֹכֵן בַּמְּרוֹמִים, הַמְצֵא מְנוּחָה נְכוֹנָה
תַּחַת כַּנְפֵי הַשְּׁכִינָה, בְּמַעֲלוֹת קְדוֹשִׁים וּטְהוֹרִים כְּזֹהַר הָרָקִיעַ
מַזְהִירִים, אֶת נִשְׁמַת—שֶׁהָלְכָה לְעוֹלָמָהּ. בַּעֲבוּר שֶׁנָּדְרוּ
צְדָקָה בְּעַד הַזְכָּרַת נִשְׁמָתָהּ, בְּגַן עֵדֶן תְּהֵא מְנוּחָתָהּ. לָכֵן בַּעַל
הָרַחֲמִים יַסְתִּירֶהָ בְּסֵתֶר כְּנָפָיו לְעוֹלָמִים, וְיִצְרוֹר בִּצְרוֹר
הַחַיִּים אֶת נִשְׁמָתָהּ. יְיָ הוּא נַחֲלָתָהּ, וְתָנוּחַ עַל מִשְׁכָּבָהּ בְּשָׁלוֹם,
וְנֹאמַר אָמֵן.

"O God, full of compassion, Thou who dwellest on high
Grant perfect rest beneath the sheltering wings of Thy
presence, among the holy and pure who shine as the
brightness on the heavens, unto the soul of . . . .
. . . . who has gone unto eternity, and in
whose memory charity is offered. May her response be
in paradise. May the Lord of Mercy bring her under
the cover of His wings forever, and may her soul be
bound up in the bond of eternal life. May the Lord be
her possession, and may she rest in peace. Amen."

The prayer is self-explanatory. Unlike the Kaddish, this
is a prayer in behalf of the dead. While it is not *technically*
to be considered a "lament," nonetheless custom dictates
that it should not be chanted when *Tachanun* is not recited
in the synagogue. For this prayer you will have to know
the Hebrew name of the deceased and the deceased's father.
If these names are not available, the English names will
have to be used.

The Eulogy
הספד

The eulogy is a significant focus of the funeral service. One of the most important obligations of mourners and heirs is to provide for this eulogy. Abraham, the first patriarch of the Jewish people, eulogized his wife Sarah, and that has been the custom of Jews to this day.

Purpose of the Eulogy

Following the lesson of Abraham, the purpose of the eulogy is twofold. First, is *hesped*—the praising of the deceased for his worthy qualities. Second, is *bechi*—expressing the grief and the sense of loss experienced by the mourners and the entire Jewish community.

Very wisely, the Jewish tradition requires the eulogizing of the deceased to be *kara'ui*, balanced and appropriate. It may not grossly exaggerate, or invent, qualities that the deceased did not in fact possess. Such praise is a mockery and an effrontery to the departed, rather than a tribute to his personal virtues. In addition, the mourners should remember that although the deceased may have been undistinguished in many ways, and lacking certain moral qualities, there is always a substratum of goodness and decency in all men which can be detected if properly sought. Sometimes, the mourners are too close to their departed and see only mediocrity and perhaps meanness. But, sometimes, a more objective view reveals virtues unknown or latent: honesty or frankness or humaneness or respect or tolerance, or simply the ability to raise decent children in a violent and unstable world.

Where Is the Eulogy Delivered?

The eulogy is spoken, almost always, at the chapel, or at the home or, occasionally, at the cemetery prior to burial. For outstanding scholars or community leaders, it may be delivered during *shiva* or on the thirtieth day after the funeral.

Eulogies generally are not delivered if the funeral occurs on major festivals, such as Passover, Shavuot and Succot, or on other holidays such as Hannukah, Purim, Rosh Chodesh (the first day of the Hebrew month), on afternoons immediately preceding these holidays, or on Friday afternoons, or on days immediately following the three major festivals. The reason for this is that although the funeral is an occasion of grief for the family of the deceased, the joyous spirit of the holiday, which devolves on the entire community, overrides the obligation and desire for lamentation by individuals. However, while *bechi*, the bewailing, contradicts the spirit of the holiday, *hesped*, spoken in the correct manner, often does not; hence it is, on occasion, permitted to speak a very short eulogy emphasizing only the praise of the deceased, and encouraging the relatives to incorporate these qualities into their own lives.

Eulogies should not be made if this was the specific request of the deceased. Because the eulogy is *yekara d'schichba*, for the honor of the dead rather than for the survivors, an individual may elect to forego the honor. However, the mourners should not take this decision upon themselves if they merely conjecture that this is what the deceased would have wanted. Most people deserve a eulogy and should not be deprived of it because of speculation, although the conjecture may have been made in good faith.

Preparing for the Eulogy

Frequently rabbis must deliver eulogies for people they have never met. Under conditions peculiar to the modern American Jewish community, this is almost inevitable. In order to make a dignified and honest presentation, the rabbi will have to know certain basic facts of the life of the deceased. Be prepared to tell him all of the departed's good qualities, and do it enthusiastically. Every man has a unique image. Do not hesitate to put your heart into the description.

Also, the rabbi will want to know the relationship of the deceased with the family, how he earned his livelihood, what was his educational background, the extent of his observance of Judaism, and his identification with the Jewish people. If there has been a divorce or a particular hatred or difficulty or frustration in his life, advise the rabbi of these facts. This discussion with the rabbi should be held by one close to the deceased, but who is not so emotionally exercised that he cannot impart the necessary information.

Rituals of a Fraternal Order

A secular ceremony is out of place during a religious service. However, a non-sectarian burial program of a fraternal order which is designed solely to honor the deceased and is accomplished only by kind words from friends, may be used. The family should ascertain that there are no christological elements in the service, such as the "Lord's Prayer." Even though this prayer contains no specific mention of Christianity its source is the Christian Bible, and it is out of place at a Jewish funeral. Care should be taken that there be no physical contact with the body, and that this ceremony take place before, not after, the religious service. It should be brief and unostentatious. This ceremony should take place only if it was the sincere and express desire of the deceased.

The recessional, performed by wheeling the casket from the chapel to the hearse, should be attended to by members of the Jewish faith.

Escorting the Deceased to the Cemetery

The profound significance of this aspect of the funeral is generally not appreciated. The sages considered the preparing and escorting of the deceased to his final resting place an extremely important symbol of respect. They refer to it as *gemillat chesed shel emet*, an act of genuine, selfless kindness. They insisted, as they did in few other instances, that a man should interrupt even the study of Torah to assist in removing the deceased from the home and conveying him to the cemetery. The sages of the Talmud declared that one who sees a funeral procession and does not accompany the dead—at least briefly—deserves to be banished from the community.

Preparing the Body and Escorting It

1. When no other Jews are available to care for the deceased, the dead person is considered technically a *met mitzvah*, an "abandoned" corpse, which places the obligation for burial upon the first Jew who finds it. Even the High Priest in ancient times who was not otherwise permitted to handle a strange corpse, was under full obligation to bury the deserted dead. Thus, when no other Jews are available, one must sacrifice even very important work, or the study of Torah and the performance of other religious duties, and certainly other pleasurable activities, to help prepare the body for burial, and also to accompany the deceased to the grave and bury it. There is no difference as to whether or not one is related to, or acquainted with, the departed.

2. When other Jews are available for preparing the body, but one is not sure as to whether there will be a *minyan* for the average deceased, or a respectable representation for the scholar and community leader, there is no requirement to cease working or studying during the period of preparation. However, there *is* an obligation to escort the departed to the cemetery even if one must sacrifice time from work.

3. When Jews are available both to prepare and accompany the body, and if one is not doing required and important work or study, one should escort the deceased to the cemetery at least symbolically by walking in the direction of the hearse some six or eight feet to indicate respect for the deceased and sympathy for the mourners. It does

not matter whether or not one knew the departed. There is
an obligation of respect for all Jews.

4. When Jews are available for preparing and escorting
the body, and one is involved in urgent business or studying
Torah, it is sufficient to stand in respect as the procession
passes.

5. When pressed for time, the priorities for attendance,
in order of their importance are:

   a. Attend the service and then, briefly, follow the
hearse.

   b. Be present at the cemetery during actual burial.

   c. Visit during the *shiva* mourning period.

Visitation in a chapel before the service is not a Jewish
custom, as indicated previously, and should not be practised.

6. For a child under 30 days of age attendants for the
funeral procession are not required. A minimum of three
people in attendance at the cemetery is sufficient.

May a Divorced Mate Attend Funeral Services?

There is no Jewish legal requirement that a divorced
person attend a former mate's funeral service, but this is
certainly not prohibited. For one contemplating divorce,
obligations for mourning depend on whether there was
agreement to proceed with the divorce. If only one mate
contemplated divorce, and no legal action had been taken,
there is an obligation to mourn. If both agreed to the
divorce, although no action was taken, there is no positive
requirement to mourn according to Jewish law.

Should Bride and Groom Attend Funeral Services?

A bride and groom, during the first seven days after the
wedding, are not required to attend any funerals at all, even
for parents, if they are honeymooning away from home. If,
within the seven days, they returned to their work, however,
they must attend the funerals of the seven close relatives.
They may attend funerals of other acquaintances.

Should Mourners Attend Funeral Services?

Mourners, within the first three days after the interment, should not attend funerals except if it is for one of the seven closest relatives: father, mother, brother, sister, son, daughter and mate, or for one who has no Jewish attendants escorting him. They should not, however, escort the dead to the cemetery.

After the third day and until the end of *shiva*, the mourner may attend the funeral for other members of the family (not the seven relatives). He should accompany the hearse for six or eight feet and then return home, but not go to the cemetery.

Accompanying the Non-Jewish Deceased

One may accompany the gentile dead to the cemetery. If his absence would be noted, and it might be considered disrespectful, one should also attend the ceremony at the interment. While one should not, by any means, be discourteous in these matters, one may not participate in the Mass or other religious service held at the chapel. No intelligent gentile would quarrel, or even question, a friend's religious scruples. We are living in an age of understanding and tolerance, and people of diverse creeds need not sacrifice their religious conscience for fear of being misunderstood.

The Interment
קבורה

Jewish law is unequivocal in establishing absolutely, and uncompromisingly, that the dead must be buried in the earth. Man's body returns to the earth as it was. The soul rises to God, but the physical shelter, the chemical elements that clothed the soul, sink into the vast reservoir of nature. God's words to Adam are, "For dust thou are and unto dust shalt thou return." Later, the Bible crystallizes God's words into positive law, *ki kavor tikberenu*, "Thou shalt surely bury him" (Deuteronomy 21:23).

In our society there exist contradictory tendencies that reflect man's confusion in treating the dead. Shall he hasten the dispatch of the deceased, or preserve the body and delay the inevitable decay? Some choose to embalm the deceased, deposit them in metal cases, encase the caskets in concrete vaults, or store them in mausoleums. They strive to preserve the remains, although they know quite well that eventually the forces of decomposition will triumph. Others wish to avoid even the normal, steady decay of nature, and choose to cremate the remains and reduce the deceased to ash— without pomp or ceremony. The ash is either stored in an urn and shelved, or left in the basement of the chapel, or strewn over the ocean by plane, or buried in a small box.

The Torah absolutely and unqualifiedly insists on the natural decomposition of the remains. The wood of the casket, the cloth of the shrouds, the unembalmed body decompose in nature's own steady way. No artificiality, no slowing or hurrying of this process is permitted. The world goes on in its own pace. Those who die must follow the law of nature and the world.

Cremation

Cremation is never permitted. The deceased must be interred, bodily, in the earth. It is forbidden—in every and any circumstance—to reduce the dead to ash in a crematorium. It is an offensive act, for it does violence to the spirit and letter of Jewish law, which never, in the long past, sanctioned the ancient pagan practice of burning on the pyre. The Jewish abhorrence of cremation has already been noted by Tacitus, the ancient historian, who remarked (upon what appeared to be a distinguishing characteristic) that Jews buried, rather than burned their dead.

1. Even if the deceased willed cremation, his wishes must be ignored in order to observe the will of our Father

in Heaven. Biblical law takes precedence over the instructions of the deceased.

2. Cremated ashes may not be buried in a Jewish cemetery. There is no burial of ashes, and no communal responsibility to care, in any way, for the burned remains. The only exception is when the government decrees that the ashes be buried in the ground, and there is no other burial plot available to the family. For such unusual cases a portion of the Jewish cemetery must be marked off and set aside.

3. Jewish law requires no mourning for the cremated. *Shiva* is not observed and Kaddish is not recited for them. Those who are cremated are considered by tradition to have abandoned, unalterably, all of Jewish law and, therefore, to have surrendered their rights to posthumous honor.

Mausoleums and Concrete Vaults

The specific biblical mandate of interment refers to burial in the earth. This means that:

1. A mausoleum is permissible only if the deceased is buried *in the earth itself*, and the mausoleum is built around the plot of earth. This was frequently done for scholars, communal leaders, those who have contributed heavily to charity, and people of renown.

2. However, to have the deceased buried above the ground, not surrounded by earth within the mausoleum, is unquestionably prohibited. The Bible repeats its injunction: *kavor tikberenu*, "bury thou shalt surely bury," to emphasize that it is not a legal burial if the casket is left above the earth.

3. If the deceased willed burial in a mausoleum, one should not follow the will in such a case, even though in most instances his will is iron-clad and obligatory upon the mourners.

4. In certain parts of the country the earth is unstable and shifting, and government authorities require caskets to be enclosed in concrete vaults. In such cases, vaults are ac-

ceptable. In other instances, where the motive is solely to preserve the remains, it is preferable not to use the vault. Clearly, the concrete vault is not in the spirit of the tradition, and should be avoided where possible. However, theoretically it is permitted.

Burial of Limbs

The blood and limbs of an individual are considered by Jewish law to be part of the human being. As such, they require burial. If the deceased was found with severed limbs, or with blood-stained clothes, both the limbs and the clothes must be buried with him.

If limbs were amputated during one's lifetime, they require burial in the person's future gravesite. If he does not own a plot as yet, or if he is squeamish in this regard, it should be buried in a separate plot, preferably near the graves of members of his family. The limbs are cleansed and placed in the earth. No observance of mourning is necessary.

Donation of Limbs to Hospitals

Jewish law generally discourages contribution of one's limbs to hospitals. If one has absolutely stipulated that a limb be donated for medical research, the question of following his will depends on many details, and requires rabbinic research. It is best, therefore, to consult an expert on Jewish law. At any rate, even if it were permitted, the limb would require burial when it is no longer in use by the medical institution.

The donations of eyes to an eye bank is a subject of rabbinic discussion. Important authorities have considered it entirely permissible. Other transplantations, such as heart and kidney, etc., are too complex an issue of medical ethics and *halacha* for discussion in these pages.

The Burial Service

An attitude of somberness, regret and hesitation should prevail during the procession when the casket is carried from the hearse to the grave and then deposited in the grave. It should also be viewed as a sacred occasion which requires one's personal participation in the final honoring of the deceased. Both of these aspects, the personal duty to give honor, and the hesitation to perform that which is necessary, govern the program and style of the processional.

Pallbearers

Pallbearers from among the family or friends should carry the casket and deposit it in the grave. This custom dates back to the Bible when Jacob's children carried him to his last resting place. In ancient times the body was carried on the shoulders. Regardless of whether carried on shoulders or by hand, or wheeled on a special cemetery device, this should be considered a signal honor and a symbol of personal tribute for those who participate.

There are several customs as to who shall be selected as pallbearers, any one of which is acceptable to Jewish law. One is that the primary carriers should be the children and brothers of the deceased. Others say that friends or other relatives should do this, but not the immediate family, However, it would seem more advisable for others to carry the casket, rather than the immediate family, for fear of their being overcome with grief. If there is no such fear, children or brothers may participate, if they so desire. In any case, if there are no others, the immediate family must perform this task.

Those who handle the casket must be of the Jewish faith. It is a violation of Jewish law to consign the deceased to anonymous gravediggers, especially when their faith is not known and their personal behavior and moral standards are not known to the family. Handling the casket is not merely a physical activity which requires brawn; it is a personal one which demands love and respect.

Personal enemies may help carry the casket, and their efforts should not be considered hypocrisy, but a form of regret. Surely the family should be consulted, but they should be encouraged to use sympathetic judgment and compassionate concern.

In light of the requirement of pallbearers, it is necessary to tell the funeral director or the driver of the family car *not* to follow their customary practice of holding the family limousines far behind the hearse so that the casket may be removed and carried to the grave by cemetery gravediggers. Some cemetery officials encourage this because of the possible insurance hazard in case of accident while family members are carrying the casket. Proper cemetery insurance coverage, however, takes into consideration the traditions of the Jewish people on a Jewish cemetery.

The Processional

Because the spirit of the processional is governed not only by the desirability of personal participation and accompaniment of the deceased, but also by hesitation and unwillingness to remove the presence of the dead, the procession pauses briefly several times before it reaches the gravesite, except on festive days when the spirit of communal joy modifies the expression of grief at funerals.

There are several customs regarding the number of pauses made in order to indicate our unwillingness to end the service, and when and for whom they should *not* be made. One custom establishes seven stops, another three stops, and another maintains that the procession should stop every six or eight feet. Seven pauses are customary in most communities.

The Midrash cites a strange, but insightful, reason for halting seven times. Death confronts men with the need to re-assess their own existence and ponder the "big" questions of life: What is the use of all our strivings? Does life have a deeper meaning? Does man, after all, come to naught? These are the great issues that disturb Ecclesiastes as he seeks to understand the true meaning of life. "Vanity of vanities," said Ecclesiastes, "vanity of vanities, all is vanity" (1:2). Vanity, in this context, signifies the vapor (*hevel*) that appears when one exhales on a cold day. It has no substance, and disappears into "thin air."

Is life only vapor? The sages noted that "vanity" in the oft-quoted verse, is said three times in the singular, and twice in the plural, which adds up to seven times. Each of these "vanities" is symbolized by a pause, as one carries the casket to the grave. With each stop, the fact of ultimate death teaches us to avoid the life of vanity, to be creative and kind, to repent of evil, to walk in the path of goodness.

All those in the funeral party should follow the casket, not walk before it. Usually, only the rabbi precedes the procession to indicate where and when to pause.

During the procession, the very beautiful and moving Psalm 91 is recited. This Psalm has been ascribed by Bible commentators to Moses, or a poet under his influence. It is said to have been recited at the building of the Tabernacle in the desert. Others ascribe it to a dialogue held between David and Solomon, or recited by them, at the dedication of Jerusalem and the Temple. It is referred to as the "Song of the Spirit," guarding man against the evil that surrounds him. It is an expression of confidence that God will watch over His people, and that nothing will again befall them because they trust in the Lord.

> For He will give His angels charge over thee,
> To keep thee in all thy ways.

It concludes with a prayer for the living:

> With long life will I satisfy him,
> And make him to behold My salvation.

Recitation at Graveside

The *tzidduk ha'din,* or justification of the divine decree, is a magnificent and moving prayer recited immediately before, or immediately after, the body is interred (depending on local Jewish usage) when the reality of the grave confronts the mourners.

TZIDDUK HA'DIN

צדוק הדין

The Rock, his work is perfect, for all His ways are judgment: A God of faithfulness and without iniquity, just and right is He.

The Rock, perfect in every work, who can say unto Him, "What workest thou?" He ruleth below and above; He ordereth death and restoreth to life: He bringeth down to the grave, and bringeth up again.

The Rock, perfect in every deed, who can say unto Him, "What doest thou?" O Thou who speakest and doest, of Thy grace deal kindly with us, and for the sake of him who was bound like a lamb, O hearken and do.

Just in all Thy ways art thou, O perfect Rock, slow to anger and full of compassion. Spare and have pity upon parents and children, for Thine, Lord, is forgiveness and compassion.

Just art Thou, O Lord, in ordering death and restoring to life, in whose hand is the charge of all spirits; far be it from Thee to blot out our remembrance. O let Thine eyes mercifully regard us; for Thine, Lord, is compassion and fogiveness.

If a man live a year or a thousand years, what profiteth it him? He shall be as though he had not been. Blessed be the true Judge, who ordereth death and restoreth to life.

Blessed be He, for His judgment is true, and His eye discerneth all things, and He awardeth unto man his reckoning and his sentence, and all must render acknowledgment unto him.

We know, O Lord, that Thy judgment is righteous: Thou art justified when Thou speakest, and pure when Thou judgest, and it is not for us to murmur at Thy method of judging. Just are Thou, O Lord, and righteous are Thy judgments.

O true and righteous Judge! Blessed be the true Judge, all whose judgments are righteous and true.

The soul of every living thing is in Thy hand; Thy might is full of righteousness. Have mercy upon the remnant of the flock of Thy hand, and say unto the destroying angel, "Stay thy hand!"

Thou art great in counsel and mighty in deed; Thine eyes are open upon all the ways of the children of men, to give unto every one according to his ways, and according to the fruit of his doings. To declare that the Lord is upright; He is my Rock, and there is no unrighteousness in Him.

The Lord gave, and the Lord hath taken away; blessed be the name of the Lord. And He, being merciful, forgiveth iniquity and destroyeth not. Yea, many a time He turneth His anger away, and doth not stir up all His wrath.

The prayer has three major themes:

1. God ordained this dreadful end, and His decree is justified. God gives to each his due, in accordance with reasons He alone knows. Although we may not understand His ways, we know that there can be no imperfection in Almighty God.

2. We pray that God be merciful to the survivors. Although He has taken the life of this dear one, may He, in His great mercy, spare the lives of the remainder of His flock and stay the hand of death. Even at this most personal moment of grief, the Jew must concern himself with unselfish thoughts and pray for all of humanity.

3. God's decree must be accepted. To the very end we must remember that as God in His kindness was beneficent to give us this dear one and bring him into life, He is the same just God when He beckons that soul to return to him. "The Lord has given and the Lord has taken." We thank the Lord for the years that were given to us. "Blessed be the name of the Lord."

This prayer is not recited for children under 30 days of age. It is also not recited if the burial occurs at night, or if the funeral is held on one of the major festivals such as Passover, Shavuot or Succot, or on other holidays such as Hannukah, Purim, Rosh Chodesh, or on all afternoons preceding the holidays and the Sabbath, or on the days immediately following the three major festivals, as it would conflict with the spirit of joy that should obtain at these times.

The Burial

The sacred principle of the Jewish burial law which establishes that the deceased be buried in the earth, requires lowering the casket to the bottom of the grave. Leaving the casket at ground level during the service, in the company of the entourage, and then, without completing the interment, to turn one's back on the unburied casket and return home, is a distinct affront to the dead.

The minimum dimensions of the grave must provide, at least, that the opening should be as wide and as long as the casket, and at least ten *tefachim,* or forty inches deep.

The use of a mechanical device to lower the casket into the grave is *not* contrary to Jewish law. It is, however, a slow process, and surely not as quick as lowering by hand. Its use, therefore, is a matter of family preference. A Jewish friend or relative should release the lever to begin the operation of the mechanism.

The grave must be filled at this time. At the very minimum, the casket must be fully covered with earth to take on the form of a grave. After that, the laborers may assist in filling the grave if the others cannot perform this deed.

Some follow the practice of covering the open grave with a green, plastic, grass mat, but do not fill it with earth. This is *not* the traditional Jewish way. Indeed, it is a signal honor and duty to help in shoveling the earth to cover the casket. This duty is usually reserved for the learned in attendance, for the community leaders who are present, and also for the closest relatives and dearest friends. It is the personal "good-bye" of beloved neighbors. That this duty is a heartbreaking one is all too evident. But this spells the finality of death, and it must be faced and accepted as such.

Psychologically, the heart-rending thud of earth on the casket is enormously beneficial. In proclaiming finality, it helps the mourner overcome the illusion that his relative still lives; it answers his disbelief that death has indeed claimed its victim; it quiets his lingering doubts that this may be only a bad dream. The earth-filling process dispels such illusions and starts the mourner on the way to recovery and reconciliation. To attempt to spare him this unpleasantness merely retards the psychological healing process.

Is there a specific method of filling? The earth originally dug out should be replaced. Custom has it that the shovel should not pass from hand to hand, but each person should replace it in the earth. This is a silent, symbolic gesture expressing the prayer that the tragedy of death be not "contagious," and that the remainder of family and friends may live long and peaceful lives. The law does not stipulate how many shovelfuls should be used. Some customarily use the back of the shovel to indicate a difference from its use for other purposes.

The Kaddish

The *Burial* Kaddish is different from the other forms of Kaddish recited in the synagogue. (The *Mourner's* Kaddish is considered in detail in a later chapter of this book.) It takes the form of a prayer, and not a formal doxology. It is, therefore, not circumscribed by all of the regulations regarding the Kaddish of the synagogue service. This is why it may be recited directly following burial, whereas the synagogue Kaddish is recited only after a portion from the Psalms or Torah is read.

The Burial Kaddish is a prayer affirming that God, in His good time, will create the world anew, and that the deceased will be raised up to everlasting life. With the advent of the new world, the Temple will be reestablished, and the true worship of the one God will replace the idols of the masses. It bespeaks the hope that there is a future for the deceased, and it gives new faith to the mourners, even as its recitation at the moment of interment evokes new tears.

The Burial Kaddish is recited after the grave is filled with earth. In cases of emergency, such as excessive grief at the time of great tragedy, or if the hour is late and the Sabbath or a holy day is approaching, it is permissible to say the Kaddish after the casket is fully covered with a layer of earth. In such case it is not necessary to wait for the grave to be completely filled.

The Burial Kaddish is omitted on festivals and during "joyous celebrations" (which is defined later) when *tacha-nun* is not recited in the synagogue. At such times, Psalm 16 is recited and the traditional Mourner's Kaddish is said. The special Burial Kaddish is replaced by the Mourner's Kaddish if no mourners are present. Kaddish is not recited at all when the grave cannot be filled in the presence of a *minyan*.

Recessional from the Gravesite

The purpose of the recessional is to redirect our sympathies and concerns from the deceased to the mourners. It marks the transition from *aninut* to *avelut*, the new state of mourning which now commences. The theme changes from honoring of the dead to comforting the survivors. To act out this transition, those present form parallel lines, facing one another. The mourners solemnly pass through as they come away from the site of their bereavement. As the mourners walk by, those present recite words of comfort: *Ha'makom yenachem et'chem b'toch she'ar avelei tziyon vi'Yerushalayim*, "May the Lord comfort you among the other mourners of Zion and Jerusalem." If no mourners are present, the parallel lines are dispensed with, as words of comfort are obviously out of place. A beautiful Israeli custom has the mourners place a stone on the covered grave and ask forgiveness for any injustice they may have committed against the deceased.

Washing of the Hands

After the funeral, those in attendance wash their hands. This is symbolic of the ancient custom of purification, performed after contact with the dead. It emphasizes the Jew's constant concern with life, its value and dignity, rather than over-zealous attention to, and worship of, the dead. The washing is done upon returning from the cemetery, before entering the home, or, if this is not feasible, at the cemetery office itself. It is performed with a cup of water poured alternately on both hands. As with the shovel, at the filling of the grave, the cup is not passed from hand to hand.

The Cemetery Plot and Grave

The Gravesite: Purchasing a Plot

It is an ancient Jewish custom to purchase a gravesite during one's lifetime and to own it outright prior to burial. The Bible states explicitly that Abraham *bought* a grave for Sarah. Likewise, Joseph was buried in the family plot that his father Jacob had *acquired* in the city of Shechem.

The purchase may be made through a burial society of a fraternal or religious organization, or directly from the cemetery owners. It must be located among other Jewish graves, or on grounds bought by a Jewish organization for use as a Jewish cemetery. This has been the custom through the centuries. On first settling in a new country the community purchased land for a synagogue, a school, and also a cemetery.

The following are criteria for determining whether a particular cemetery is a proper burial place for Jews:

1. The purchase contract should stipulate that the area of the plot is designed exclusively for Jews.

2. Burial rights must be permanent. The cemetery corporation should not be permitted to exercise any authority with regard to the removal of the remains from any grave.

3. All facilities for Jew and non-Jew must be absolutely separate—with separate entrance gates, and with each section fenced completely.

The Family Plot: Basic Grave Formation

1. The basic grave formation in most cemeteries is arranged according to families. There has been a custom in later centuries, observed by many memorial societies, of burying men and women in separate sections. Neither custom is obligatory. One should make inquiry regarding this procedure before one joins the society, in order to avoid problems during the moment of crisis when it is too late to make any change.

In many cemeteries it is standard procedure—and a religiously proper custom—not to bury a woman next to any man other than her husband. This is of concern especially when contemplating erection of a double monument. Therefore, the graves alternate—husband, wife, wife, husband, husband, wife, etc.

2. If man and wife were separated in marriage, they

may nevertheless be buried alongside one another. If one of the partners, however, stipulated that he be buried separately, the request must be followed.

3. One who has been unmarried should be buried alongside his or her parents.

4. *Married children.* It is customary, though not mandatory, that the wife be buried with the husband's family. When no graves are available, they should be buried elsewhere in the same cemetery. If they live far from the parental grave, or if there are other personal advantages to selecting another cemetery, they may establish their own family plot.

5. If, by being buried in a family plot, the departed will be buried alongside a lifelong enemy, he should be buried elsewhere in the family plot. If this enemy died more than a year before, this is not necessary, and should be left to the discretion of the relatives and friends.

6. *Second marriages.* If a preference for burial location was expressly made, it must be honored. If this preference was not made expressly, but was implied, in that he clearly and undoubtedly lived better with one mate than the other, then he should be buried with the more beloved mate.

If no preference is known, then:

a. If there are children from the marriage of only one of the mates, whichever it be, he is to be buried at that mate's family plot or at the discretion of those children.

b. If there are children from both mates, or no children from either mate, some customs suggest burial with the first mate.

7. *Intermarriages.* If the Jewish partner remained Jewish he is entitled to burial in a Jewish cemetery.

The unconverted gentile partner may not be buried in the Jewish cemetery. Even if that person has been circumcized, but for purposes other than conversion, he is considered non-Jewish, and may not be buried on the cemetery.

Children of a Jewish mother may be buried on the Jewish cemetery even if they have not been circumcised.

Children of a gentile mother, who themselves have not been converted, may not be buried in the cemetery even if they had been circumcised, but without intent to convert, and even if they were educated in a Jewish school.

Genuine converts are buried as full Jews, in the plot of the Jewish mate, or in a newly-established family plot. This situation is not considered an intermarriage.

8. *Suicides.* Traditionally, those who commit the stark offense against God and man by taking their own lives wilfully, and in full sanity, are buried separately near the cemetery gate, or at least six feet from other Jewish dead. The chapter below discusses the subject of suicides fully.

9. The observant and ethical Jew should not be buried alongside confirmed sinners. Wherever possible, this principle should be adhered to, and other arrangements should be made.

10. *Burial in Israel.* The burial of Jewish deceased in the Holy Land, especially those who ardently loved the land, were religiously observant, or contributed to the support of Israel, is considered an act of pious devotion, even though visitations to the grave may be rare or not at all possible.

The Bible records that Joseph made the special request to be buried, not in the land where he reigned as vice-regent, but in the land of his forefathers, the Holy Land. Burial in Israel is considered by the rabbis equal to being buried directly under the altar of the Temple. Reinterment is permissible for such purposes (see section on reinterment). For making the proper arrangements the mourners should consult the rabbi, or funeral director or a rabbinic organization.

11. Burial land bought in a cemetery, even though it was officially designated for a specific person, may be sold.

Disinterment

The removal and opening of the casket after the burial had once been completed is prohibited in Jewish law. The abhorrent sight of the decomposing flesh is considered to be a disgrace to the deceased. It is revolting and depressing to the living to see the end of man as a mere rotting skeleton. The law, basing itself on the twofold reason that disinterment is an indignity to the deceased and a disturbance of his peace, is very strong in its condemnation of those who needlessly open graves after burial. Disinterment may never be undertaken without first consulting an authority in Jewish law. Most cemeteries or societies require written approval of a rabbi.

The following are cases that might warrant such consultation:

1. If it is believed that valuables have fallen into the earth that was used to fill in the grave.

2. If a very large sum of money was placed on the casket, or if the deceased was wearing very expensive jewelry that was somehow not removed before burial, and the survivors are indigent, or creditors will have to take great losses because of lack of funds.

3. If the remains were not prepared according to religious law, disinterment may be possible if this was realized shortly after burial.

4. If the body was not identified accurately before burial, thus preventing the wife's remarriage for fear that her husband yet lives.

If any of these circumstances have occurred after the casket has been placed in the grave but before the grave has been filled, it is permissible to open it without further consultation.

Reinterment

The deceased may not be moved from one grave to another even if the second gravesite is a more respectable one. By holding up the lifeless corpse, once the glory of creation, and now in its ugly, decomposed state, one is manifesting disrespect to the image of God. Reinterment is, thus, frowned upon by the rabbis of the Talmud. The medieval sages add that after death man stands in judgment before God, and reinterment disturbs that state of judgment. Also, it is added, the removal of the remains to another site is a "mocking of the dead," and a slight to others who have passed on and are now reposing in the same cemetery.

Reinterment may be permitted, after consultation with a rabbi, in the following instances:

1. The removal of the remains from an individual plot to a family plot where other immediate members of the family are already buried. This may be done even if the deceased did not know of this plot.

2. If the deceased was not buried in his own gravesite, as for example:
   a. He was mistakenly placed in someone else's grave.
   b. He was placed in a stolen grave.
   c. Part of the grave is on public land.
   d. He was placed in a grave with the owner's permission, but it was never fully paid for.

3. If he is interred in a non-Jewish cemetery, even though he owned the plot himself.

4. If the present gravesite is not guarded against destruction by vandals.

5. If it may be destroyed by water or other natural phenomena.

6. If the government appropriates the property for highways or other communal needs.

7. If the deceased is to be reinterred in Israel.

8. If the grave was considered temporary, and expressly so stipulated when the deceased was originally interred.

9. If it was discovered that the deceased expressly desired to be buried elsewhere, even though there was no stipulation that he be moved after burial.

10. War dead buried in national cemeteries may be reinterred in Jewish cemeteries at home.

The above-listed exemptions are merely guidelines. A decision regarding reinterment was considered to be of such a serious nature that it was not made even by a duly-ordained rabbi without first consulting other rabbis. There are many specific questions to be considered, such as the time that has elapsed since death, the state of the remains, the state of the casket. These, and a multitude of other details require competent, rabbinic authority to decide.

The vacated grave, following reinterment, may be given to the indigent dead, although the value of the monument after the engraving has been obliterated is questionable, if it has any value at all by presentday standards. It may not be sold, nor any material benefit derived from it.

Ritual of Reinterment

The exhumed remains, no matter what the state of decomposition, must be guarded and respected as on the day of death.

There are prescribed mourning laws for the day of reinterment. The following must be observed:

1. Mourners must rend their garments. See above for the details of this law.

2. Full mourning, as during *shiva,* is observed for the one day on which reinterment takes place, from morning only until nightfall, even if reinterment was not completed by nightfall. No further mourning need be observed after this time. Relatives who know of the reinterment and the date on which it is to occur must observe these mourning laws on that one day. If they are made aware of the reinterment after that date they are not required to observe any of the mourning laws.

3. A child should not personally participate in the reinterment of his parents.

4. All foods, including meat and wine, may be eaten.

5. There should be no words of grief; only praise for the deceased.

6. The interment should not take place on the intermediate days of Passover or Succot.

7. It should be begun in the morning or early afternoon. If it commences too close to nightfall there will be no time for the mourning observances.

8. Three hand-breadths of earth from the area immediately adjacent to the body must be reinterred with the body if it was originally buried without an enclosing casket.

Cemetery Etiquette

The subject of proper conduct at the cemetery is generally neglected. The consequence of this neglect is, frequently, gross impropriety and a super-abundance of superstition. There are two basic principles which can serve as a guide to correct Jewish etiquette on a cemetery. These are:

Kalut Rosh

The holiness of the cemetery is equivalent to the holiness of the sanctuary. Our actions within its confines must be consonant with the high degree of this holiness. Also, because the graves in the cemetery are places from which we may derive no benefit at all, we are restricted from lounging in the area. *Kalut rosh* is a spirit of levity and undignified behavior. Under the category of the prohibition of *kalut rosh*, the following points must be observed, and should be followed not only at the gravesite, but within the boundaries of the entire cemetery.

1. Eating and drinking may not take place on the cemetery. This holds true for unveilings as well! The frequent, but unfortunate, frivolity that marks such occasions should certainly be discouraged. It is a violation of every code of honor.

2. Dress should be proper to the occasion and the place. One should not dress to impress relatives who attend. When one visits the cemetery or the grave of a deceased, it is certainly not the time for scant or frivolous-looking dress, athletic attire, or work clothes.

3. One may not step over or sit on the gravestone which directly *covers* a grave. One may, however, sit on seats near the graves or on roadside railings and gates.

4. Flowers which, perchance, have blossomed on the grave itself may not be picked for use at home. Naturally, trimming the grave is permissible and commendable.

Lo'eg Larash

As noted previously, indulging in pleasurable activities, even religious observances, that the deceased or any of the other occupants of the graves once enjoyed participating in, but now cannot, represents a slighting of the dead. Thus:

1. One should not study Torah, or recite the Psalms, or conduct formal, daily services within approximately six feet of a grave.

2. One should not carry *tefillin* or a Torah with him into the cemetery.

Memorial Gifts

Those who wish to honor the dead, or their survivors, may do so in a genuinely religious spirit. They may bring a token of their esteem with them during *shiva* or send it through the mails.

It is not in keeping with the traditional spirit for this memorial gift to be flowers or fruits. It is more significant and more useful to contribute a sacred article for synagogue or school use. This might include Bibles, prayerbooks, scholarly works, Torahs and Torah ornaments, etc. These will usually be acknowledged by the synagogue or school immediately so that the mourners will be notified of the gift during *shiva*.

Donations to charities at the time of the funeral is an ancient Jewish custom. The custom has three roots in our tradition:

1. The biblical verse, "Charity saves one from death," is meant to be taken not only literally, but in the spiritual sense, that one who is evil is not considered to be truly alive. Charity saves from "spiritual death." The association of charity and death here is a direct one.

2. Charity symbolizes the unity of all Israel. Contributions of time and effort and substance for the good of the community is an expression of unity. At the funeral it symbolizes the anguish felt in common by all Jews for the family of the deceased.

3. The mystical tradition, embodied in the *Chapters of Rabbi Eliezer*, says that because of charity will the dead be resurrected in the world to come.

It is in the spirit of dignity, and in keeping with Jewish tradition, to make such contributions as memorials to the dead, rather than to bring outright gifts to the mourners. Naturally, if the deceased felt close to a specific charity, such as a medical research program, it might be wise to contribute to that fund. The memorial gift may be selected by the giver or left to the discretion of the mourners.

3. ✦ Mourning Observances of Shiva and Sheloshim

The Mourning Pattern

JUDAISM, WITH ITS long history of dealing with the soul of man, its intimate knowledge of man's achievements and foibles, his grandeur and his weakness, has wisely devised graduated periods during which the mourner may express his grief, and release with calculated regularity the built-up tensions caused by bereavement. The Jewish religion provides a beautifully structured approach to mourning.

The insight of the Bible, together with the accumulated religious experience of centuries, has taught the Jew how best to manage the grief situation. It was only with the rise of modern psychology, with its scientific tools and controlled experimentation, that the value of this grief structure has been recognized.

Joshua Loth Liebman, in his book *Peace of Mind*, maintains: "The discoveries of psychiatry—of how essential it is to express, rather than to repress grief, to talk about one's loss with friends and companions, to move step by step from inactivity to activity again—remind us that the ancient teachers of Judaism often had intuitive wisdom about human nature and its needs which our more sophisticated and liberal age has forgotten. Traditional Judaism, as a matter of fact, had the wisdom to devise almost all of the procedures for health-minded grief which the contemporary psychologist counsels, although Judaism naturally did not possess the tools for scientific experiment and systematic study." The Jewish tradition has thus provided for a gradual release from grief, and has ordained five successive periods of mourning, each with its own laws governing the expression of grief and the process of return to the normal affairs of society. It fits so closely the normal cycle of bereavement that some have maintained that the laws of mourning are descriptive rather than prescriptive.

Five Stages of Mourning

The first period is that between death and burial (*aninut*), during which time despair is most intense. At this time, not only the social amenities, but even major positive religious requirements, were cancelled in recognition of the mourner's troubled mind.

The second stage consists of the first three days following burial, days devoted to weeping and lamentation. During this time, the mourner does not even respond to greetings, and remains in his home (except under certain special circumstances). It is a time when even visiting the mourner is usually somewhat discouraged, for it is too early to comfort the mourners when the wound is so fresh.

Third, is the period of *shiva*, the seven days following burial. (This longer period includes the first three days.) During this time the mourner emerges from the stage of intense grief to a new state of mind in which he is prepared to talk about his loss and to accept comfort from friends and neighbors. The world now enlarges for the mourner. While he remains within the house, expressing his grief through the observances of *avelut*—the wearing of the rent garment, the sitting on the low stool, the wearing of slippers, the refraining from shaving and grooming, the recital of the Kaddish—his acquaintances come to his home to express sympathy in his distress. The inner freezing that came with the death of his relative now begins to thaw. The isolation from the world of people and the retreat inward now relaxes somewhat, and normalcy begins to return.

Fourth is the stage of *sheloshim*, the 30 days following burial (which includes the *shiva*). The mourner is encouraged to leave the house after *shiva* and to slowly rejoin society, always recognizing that enough time has not yet elapsed to assume full, normal social relations. The rent clothing may customarily still be worn for deceased parents, and haircutting for male mourners is still generally prohibited.

The fifth and last stage is the 12-month period (which includes the *sheloshim*) during which things return to normal, and business once again becomes routine, but the inner feelings of the mourner are still wounded by the rupture of his relationship with a parent. The pursuit of entertainment and amusement is curtailed. At the close of this last stage, the 12-month period, the bereaved is not expected to continue his mourning, except for brief moments when *yizkor* or *yahrzeit* is observed. In fact, our tradition rebukes a man for mourning more than this prescribed period.

In this magnificently conceived, graduated process of mourning an ancient faith raises up the mourner from the abyss of despair to the undulating hills and valleys of normal daily life.

The Mourner and the Mourned

Who is a mourner? Jewish law formally considers the bereaved to be those who have lost any one of the seven close relatives listed in Leviticus (21:1-3) : *father, mother, wife (or husband), son, daughter,* (married or unmarried), *brother,* and *sister* (or *half-brother* and *half-sister*). The Bible originally enumerated these relationships with regard to the ritual impurity of the *kohen* or priest. The priest who ordinarily was to have no contact with the dead, was, how-

ever, permitted to defile himself in order to bury these relatives. The oral tradition considered that these relationships
apply to the laws of mourning as well. (The concept of
priestly defilement is discussed in a special chapter below.)

1. *Adopted relatives.* There is no requirement to mourn
for adoptive parents, adopted brothers and sisters, or
adopted children. But while there is no legal obligation to
mourn, there should be "sympathetic mourning," namely
abstention from public rejoicing and similar activities˙ in
order to demonstrate a full measure of sorrow.

2. Minors have no obligation to observe the laws of
mourning. Thus, a boy under the age of thirteen and a girl
under the age of 12, need not "sit" *shiva* or follow the other
observances. However, their clothes should be rent for them,
and they should be encouraged to restrict, somewhat, their
daily activities. This procedure should be followed especially
in the case of more mature children, although they are still
minors.

Bride and Groom

1. During the first seven full days following the wedding, bride and groom are not at all obligated to observe
the laws of mourning, even for a parent, but they do attend
the funeral service. However, immediately following these
seven days of formal rejoicing they must begin the observance of *shiva* and *sheloshim.* Now, the law distinguishes
between a case where the death occurred *before* the beginning of the seven days of rejoicing, and one where the death
occurred in the midst of this week. In the former case, the
bride or groom begin the complete period of *shiva* and
sheloshim immediately after the week of rejoicing is over.
In the latter case, he or she rejoins the rest of the family
which is observing *shiva* and finishes the *shiva* observance
together with them. A widow and widower have a formal
period of rejoicing of three days, rather than of seven, after
marriage.

2. If a holiday, which normally nullifies the entire mourning period of *shiva*, occurs during the week of rejoicing which is co-extensive with *shiva*, the bride and groom must, nonetheless, fulfill the *shiva* after the holiday. Thus, if the wedding occurred on Saturday night and the death of a parent occurred on Sunday, the holiday which falls during that week nullifies the *shiva* period only for those who have observed the mourning period. But the bride and groom, because they were not obligated, and did not mourn formally, must observe the complete *shiva* after the conclusion of the holiday.

3. Bride and groom do not rend the clothing until after the week of rejoicing. They do, however, recite the blessing, *dayan ha'emet* ("the true judge") with the other mourners at the funeral service, as this is an expression of immediate and spontaneous grief, and cannot be meaningfully delayed.

4. During their honeymoon week they are, technically, not considered mourners. By law, they are not required to be visited and consoled in the manner of others observing *shiva*.

5. Bride and groom need not accompany a deceased parent to the cemetery, but, by all means, should follow the hearse from the home or funeral parlor for several blocks, so as to give honor to the parent.

6. The groom is obligated to don the *tefillin* even on the day after death, which is not obligatory upon other mourners, for he is considered to be in a state of rejoicing rather than mourning.

7. In the event of the death of a parent of the bride or groom *prior* to the marriage ceremony, or even after the ceremony, but prior to the *consummation* of the marriage, qualified authority should be consulted.

All these foregoing cases concern bride and groom during their formal seven-day honeymoon period, when they have set aside these days exclusively for each other. If, however, they have returned to work or school prior to the death, but during this week of rejoicing, they are obligated to mourn in the usual manner.

Divorced Mate

A divorced mate need not observe any of the mourning laws, and need not attend the funeral. If one of the mates *contemplated* divorce, but took no legal action, he is obligated to mourn. If both agreed in principle to the divorce, and definitely determined to proceed with it, although no legal action was officially started, there is no requirement to mourn.

Converts to Judaism

There is no obligation upon a person who had converted to Judaism to mourn his non-Jewish parents in the prescribed Jewish manner. While it is expected that the convert will show utmost respect for his natural parents, he is, nonetheless, considered detached from them religiously. The grief that the convert expresses, although technically not required by Jewish law, should possess a markedly Jewish character. Therefore:

1. The convert may say Kaddish if he so desires. It is preferable, however, since the deceased was not a Jew, for him to recite a Psalm instead, or to study a portion of Torah in honor of the deceased, as is customary on *yahrzeits*. In that way, a distinction is made between mourning a Jew and a non-Jew. The decision to do either rests with the bereaved.

2. Likewise, the *shiva* procedures should, preferably, not be observed as in full mourning for a Jewish parent. Full observance may indicate to friends, not intimately acquainted with the family, that the parent was Jewish. This may give rise to difficulties. For example, it may encourage the marriage of the convert to an unsuspecting *kohen*, a union which is not permitted.

The converted Jew should not feel that his *emotions* of

grief must be restrained because of the religious difference. It is only the *religious observance* which is at issue. Indeed, those mourners who are converts should be shown special kindness during this period.

Which Relatives Are Mourned?

A life duration of more than 30 days establishes the human being as a viable person. If a child dies before that time he is considered not to have lived at all, and no mourning practices are observed, even though the child may have been normal, but was killed accidentally. (See: Page 220.)

Any human being who has lived beyond this minimum span must be mourned. There are, however, several exceptions:

Apostates

A defector from the faith, who denounces Judaism openly, and adopts another religion without compulsion, is not to be permitted burial in a Jewish cemetery and is not to be mourned at all. For all intents and purposes, his defection is accepted as *de facto* severance from the faith-community and he is, therefore, not honored by the faithful. Permitting burial or any other religious observance for an apostate would leave the door open for others to follow, and would encourage the defection of others. The realization that all privileges and honors of the Jewish people will not be accorded the apostate may serve as a deterrent to those considering such action.

Arrogant Sinners

Those who publicly, purposefully and arrogantly, disown the ways of Israel, her faith and practices, her laws and traditions, but do *not* formally defect from Judaism by embracing another faith, are granted the rights of *taharah* (purification) and the wearing of shrouds. They are also interred, albeit in an obscure part of the Jewish cemetery. However, there is no mourning, such as the rending of the clothing, *aninut*, or *shiva*. The Jewish community must be forgiving up to a certain point; beyond that it must safeguard its own existence. By such treatment of the deceased sinner does it hope to prevent others from following his example.

Non-Intentional Sinners

Those who violate the laws and traditions of Israel out of social necessity, or as a result of ignorance of the details of the law, are not considered in the category of arrogant sinners. These people must receive the full measure of dignity afforded all Jewish dead. They must be mourned in the manner prescribed for all other deceased.

Cremated Dead

Those who choose not to be buried in the ancient Jewish manner have shown a final defiance of the tradition of the faithful, and are not to be mourned. Their ashen remains are not to be buried in a Jewish cemetery. See chapter on cremation above.

Executed Criminals

Those who are executed by the government for reasons that, under Jewish law, would have brought upon them a sentence of capital punishment (such as murderers), are not to be mourned. If the crime would not have warranted capital punishment under Jewish law, the criminal must be mourned and full burial rights are accorded him. This is an unusual problem, and the details of each individual case would require rabbinic interpretation.

Suicides

One who was an obviously intentional suicide is not eulogized or mourned, but certain laws are observed. There are, however, numerous qualifications as to who is legally termed an intentional suicide. See special chapter on Suicides below.

Offspring of Intermarriage

The child of a Jewish mother is considered to be Jewish even if the father was a gentile. Hence, such a person is to be mourned as any full Jew and he, in turn, is obligated to mourn other relatives. Understandably, he is required to mourn his gentile father only if the father converted before conception of the child.

If the mother is not Jewish, then:

1. If the child was formally converted, he is mourned as a Jew.

2. If the gentile mother converted before the birth of the child, even though after conception, the child is considered Jewish. He is mourned, and is obligated to mourn, under the same laws as other Jews.

Children Born Out of Wedlock

If the mother is Jewish, the child is considered Jewish in regard to all laws of mourning, as stated above.

Instructions Not to Be Mourned

In the case of an explicit request by the deceased not to be mourned by the observance of *shiva*, it is questionable whether the will of the deceased should be observed. Much depends on the reason for the request. If the purpose was to alleviate the burdens of the survivors, to enable them to go to work, or to spare the family the trouble of observance, then we may dismiss the request and insist upon honoring the deceased. If, however, the motivation for the will was the intentional violation of the tradition, we must judge whether or not it was issued out of ignorance of Jewish values and their true significance. It would appear that if the reason for the will were based on ignorance, we should certainly observe the laws of mourning. If it was a wilfull denial of Jewish values, however, Jewish tradition would dictate following his will, and not honoring him by the observance of *shiva*.

Shiva: Its Origins
שבעה

That a time be set aside for the expression of grief is indicated in the Bible and is mentioned, recurrently, in its early historical narratives. The High Priest, Aaron, is stunned by the sudden death of his two sons at the apex of their careers. When Moses asks why the sacrificial offering was not eaten on the day of their deaths, Aaron replies: "There have befallen me such things as these, and had I eaten the offering, would it have been pleasing in the eyes of the Lord?" (Lev. 10:20). Aaron's explanation is that the time of mourning is not an occasion for feasting before the Lord; it is, specifically, for the expression of grief.

So too, Amos refers to a special time for mourning. He prophesies the disastrous consequences of injustice and immorality, and declares: "And I will turn your feasts into mourning, and all your songs into lamentations; and I will bring sackcloth upon all loins, and baldness upon every head; and I will make it as the mourning for an only son; and the end thereof as a bitter day" (Amos 8:10). The day of grieving is *yom mar*, "a bitter day."

The sages noted that it was the practice in ancient times, even prior to the revelation at Mt. Sinai, to mourn intensely, not only for one day, but for one week—*shiva*. Thus, Joseph was an *avel* for seven days following the passing of his father, the patriarch Jacob.

After the revelation, Moses established the seven days of mourning by special decree declaring, as formal doctrine, that which had been practiced only as custom. He enacted, the sages asserted, the seven days of mourning as he enacted the biblical seven days of rejoicing of major holidays. The connection between the two opposites is hinted at in the verse from Amos, quoted above: "And I will turn your feasts into mourning." Just as feasts were observed for seven days, so mourning was to last for one week.

Thus, from the earliest moments of recorded Jewish history, the Jewish people have observed *shiva* for deceased relatives as "days of bitterness." The occasional disregard of *shiva* in some quarters of the Jewish community, or the casual decision, without rabbinic authorization, to observe an arbitrary number of days of mourning to suit one's own needs, or to coincide with a weekend, amount, in fact, to a noxious disregard of generations of sacred observance.

When Does Shiva Begin

Avelut, the process of mourning, begins immediately after the deceased is interred and the casket is completely covered with earth. The mourners walk between the parallel lines of friends and relatives and are formally comforted by them. They then proceed directly to the home where *shiva* is to be observed. There, the observances commence as soon as the mourners demonstrate formal acceptance of mourning by removing their shoes and sitting on a low bench or stool.

Mourners who do not accompany the deceased to the cemetery begin their *avelut* at the approximate time of burial or, at the very latest, when the other mourners have returned from the cemetery. There are exceptional circumstances in regard to the beginning of *shiva*.

Burial at Twilight

When burial occurs late in the day, provided it takes place before nightfall (i.e., even during the approximately

eighteen minutes between sunset and dark: the legal duration of *bein hashemashot,* or twilight), mourning should
begin at the cemetery, a short distance from the grave itself. The mourners remove their shoes and then seat themselves on a stone or railing. Thus, while it may already be
nighttime when they arrive at the home where *shiva* will
be observed, the law considers that mourning was formally
begun during daylight at the cemetery. That day is, therefore, counted as the first of the seven days of *shiva.* The
mourners, however, should be informed that mourning
technically began at the cemetery. (This is possible only if
the mourner has not yet prayed the evening *maariv* service.
If he has already prayed the service, *shiva* begins the next
day.)

Thus, too, if one is notified of the burial of a relative at
twilight, and he finds himself on the road, or in another
public place, he should make formal mental note of the fact
that his mourning has begun, and he is then permitted to
count that day as the first of *shiva,* even though he was not
able to remove his shoes and sit on the low bench—the
formal recognition of *shiva.*

Burial Close to Sabbath or Holidays

1. If the mourners have made mental acknowledgement
of *avelut* before the beginning of Sabbath services, or in the
case of a woman before the kindling of Sabbath candles,
even though they have observed the mourning for only a
brief time, mourning is considered technically to have com-
menced on the day before the Sabbath or holiday. The
Sabbath would, thus, be considered the second day. If the
second day falls on a major holiday, which cancels the *shiva*
altogether, there are to be no further observances of mourning as customarily practiced on the first seven days.

2. If notification of the burial came after the Sabbath
had begun (after *kabbalat shabbat*), but before the evening
service (*maariv*) (and for a woman mourner after candle-

lighting, but before nightfall), the day of burial is counted as the first day of mourning. Even if only a gesture of formal observance was performed prior to the nightfall of the Sabbath, we may count Friday as the beginning of mourning. Prior to a major holiday, there also must be some actual observance of mourning, no matter how short its duration, in order for the holiday to cancel the rest of *shiva*.

3. If knowledge of the burial came after *maariv*, or after dark, even though the burial occurred during daylight, the first day of mourning begins as of that night, and not as of the previous day.

Burial on Sabbaths and Holidays

1. If burial occurred on the Sabbath (in case of some emergency—the burial being performed by non-Jews, or by Jews by decree of the government), mourning technically begins on the Sabbath, although there are no outward observances.

2. If burial took place on a holiday, whether on the first or last days, or the intermediate days of *chol ha'moed*, mourning begins on the night following the holiday.

3. If the burial took place on the first day of a two-day holiday, such as Shavuot, and the second day falls on the Sabbath, counting of *shiva* begins on the Sabbath, although the formal practice of mourning is not observed outwardly at that time.

4. If the first day of Rosh Hashanah was the time of burial, counting begins on the second day of the holiday.

Out-of-Town Burials

Those who accompany the casket to the cemetery begin the *avelut* immediately after burial, rather than after the extended period of time required to return to one's home. Those who remain at home should begin mourning when the body is removed from their presence.

Temporary Burial

1. If the intention is to remove the body to a permanent plot at some time during the first seven days, mourning is delayed until the permanent burial.

2. If reinterment is not scheduled until after seven days, mourning begins immediately. If circumstances change, and the body is then transferred during the *shiva* period, the counting of *shiva* begins anew with the permanent burial.

3. If there was no intention of removal at all, and unforeseen circumstances compel reinterment during *shiva*, mourning need not begin anew.

Labor Strike

In the case of a labor strike, or government injunction, or other major obstacles that prevent immediate burial in one's own plot, the following procedure should be observed:

1. The family should provide its own laborers or family and friends if the union will permit this.

2. It is preferable, especially if it is expected that settlement will come only after an extended time, to effect immediate, temporary burial in a non-struck cemetery, and later to remove the remains to one's own plot.

3. If this is not feasible, or if settlement is imminent, the body will be stored by the cemetery and the mourners must proceed with all *initial* mourning practices. They should rend their clothes and recite the blessing, recite the Kaddish and end the period of *aninut*, but not observe the *shiva* and all observances associated with it. They should insist on being called to the interment when it does take place and only then should they begin *shiva*.

4. If delaying *shiva* is impractical, or for some reason cannot be effected, *avelut* and *shiva* begin as soon as the casket is received by the cemetery authorities.

5. In all such cases a rabbi should be consulted.

Notification of Out-of-Town Relatives

One who learned by telephone or telegram of the death of a relative, but lives too great a distance to attend the funeral, should begin *avelut* at the approximate time of burial. Delayed news of death and burial is treated in a special chapter below.

Minors Who Come of Age During Shiva

Boys who reach the age of 13 years and one day, and girls of 12 years and one day are obligated to observe all of the laws of the Torah as adults. If minors come of age during the mourning period for parents, they need not start the entire period from the beginning, but are required to observe only the remainder of the mourning period. However, youngsters immediately prior to Bar Mitzvah should be taught to observe the mourning laws, but without the full strictness of the adult observance. If the child attains his majority after the conclusion of the *shiva*, he need not observe any of the laws of the seven or the 30 day period.

We fear excessively, in this "Age of the Child," the effects of such experiences upon our youngsters. Psychologists, in counselling normally-behaved children, generally consider it preferable for the child to face the unpleasant fact rather than to have it masked and to repress it.

Those Who Neglected to Mourn

Those who did not observe any of the mourning laws at all, out of forgetfulness, or ignorance, or spite, or for some other reason, must begin the *shiva* observance upon the realization of this neglect, so long as it is still within 30 days from the time of burial. If the mourner observes some part of the mourning, even for only a short time, he is considered to have erred in not performing all of the laws, or to have demonstrated a lack of respect in his non-observance. But the *shiva* is considered fulfilled and he is not required to begin the entire process of mourning anew.

If, because of mental illness, or some physical illness, one was not apprised of the death, he should begin mourning when his doctors consider him capable of doing so, provided the thirtieth day after burial has not passed. If the sick person was aware of the death, and was stable enough, mentally, to accept the fact of mourning, he is considered to have fulfilled the *shiva* requirement, although he may have been completely unable to perform the actual observances. In such a case he need not begin mourning at a later time.

Missing Persons Assumed Dead

1. If the remains of the deceased are expected to be found, such as of a person who was drowned in a lake or other land-locked water, or if one was killed by an animal in a known locale, or if he was murdered, and it is anticipated that the body will be found, mourning should begin when the body is discovered, or when, after exhaustive search, all hope of finding the body is abandoned. So long as there is reasonable expectation that the body will be found, mourning need not be observed.

2. If there is no expectation of finding the body, such as of one who was drowned in an ocean, or judged to have been killed in an unknown location; or if an exhaustive search has yielded no results, and there are no witnesses to the death, then:

a. If a wife survives, there should be no demonstrative mourning for fear that others may consider her eligible for remarriage, when, in fact, this eligibility is uncertain in the eyes of the law, since there were no witnesses to the death of her husband. If there is one witness, or one who heard of the death from a witness, rabbinic guidance should be sought.

b. If no wife survives, or the deceased is a bachelor, or divorcee, mourning is begun when the judgment of death is made. However, this is quite an unusual occurrence, and the determination of death is a difficult and complicated rabbinic decision. The reader must appreciate that this is a complex issue for which there is no general rule, and he must, therefore, seek expert advice.

The Duration of Shiva and Sheloshim

The Shiva Period

The seven days of mourning begin immediately after interment. They end on the morning of the seventh day after burial, immediately following the *shacharit* (morning) service. Those present extend condolences, and the mourner rises from his week of mourning. If no public *shacharit* service is held in the mourner's home *shiva* ends after the mourner has recited his private prayers, provided that it is after sunrise.

In computing the seven days, Jewish tradition follows the principle of considering a fraction of a day as a complete day. Thus, the day of burial is considered as the first day, even though interment may have been concluded only a few moments before nightfall. Thus, too, the seventh day is considered a full day even though mourning was observed for only a short time after sunrise. Two fractional days of mourning are counted as two whole days of *shiva*.

To illustrate, if interment occurred on Wednesday, afternoon, Wednesday is the first day, Thursday the second, Friday the third, Saturday the fourth, Sunday the fifth, Monday the sixth, and Tuesday morning is the seventh and final day. A simplified method is to consider the *shiva* as concluding one week from the morning *before* the day of burial.

The Sheloshim Period

The following principles are used in computing the thirty-day period:

1. Counting starts from date of burial, not the date of death.

2. Partial days are to be considered full days (the same as with *shiva*).

3. *Sheloshim* ends after morning services on the thirtieth day after burial.

The Sabbath During Shiva and Sheloshim

The Sabbath day does not terminate *shiva* as does a major holiday, for while *public* mourning observances are suspended, *private* mourning practices are observed. It is, therefore, counted as part of the seven days. Because *public* mourning observances *are* suspended and the bereaved are permitted to put on shoes and leave the house for services, it is necessary to establish the exact duration of the Sabbath respite. Also, the torn garments are not worn on the Sabbath during *shiva*.

The bereaved should not arise from *shiva* (on Friday) until as close to the Sabbath as possible, allowing themselves the time necessary for Sabbath preparations, such as cooking or dressing. This should not take more than approximately one hour and a quarter. In an emergency, approximately two and one half hours is allowed for such preparations. Contrary to popular opinion, *avelut* does *not* cease at noon on Friday.

The bereaved should return to their mourning on Saturday night, immediately after the evening services.

Holidays During the Mourning Period

1. The spirit of joy that is mandatory on major holidays is not consistent with the sorrow of bereavement. In Jewish law, therefore, the holiday completely cancels the *shiva*. Thus, if mourning was begun even one hour before dark, the onset of the festival nullifies the remainder of the *shiva*, and we consider one hour of *shiva* observance as the equi-

valent of seven full days. If, however, death occurred *during* the holiday, or even before the holiday, but without the knowledge of the mourner, *shiva* and *sheloshim* begin after the holiday is concluded.

2. Also, if *shiva* had been completed even as late as on the morning before the holiday, the remainder of the *sheloshim* is cancelled, and all its observances suspended. Thus, a man may shave and take a haircut immediately prior to the holiday, in honor of the festival, the *sheloshim* having been fulfilled. (See: Page 128, paragraph 3.)

3. If the holiday occurred in the midst of *shiva*, not only is *shiva* considered completed, but the days of the holiday are counted toward the *sheloshim*, and the counting of 30 days need not be delayed until after the holiday.

Summary of Holiday Regulations

The following is a summary of the somewhat complicated holiday regulations:
If mourning began before

Passover

1. The partial mourning before the holiday equals seven days.
2. Eight days of holiday, added to the seven, make a sum of 15 days.
3. Required for the *sheloshim:* 15 additional days.

Shavuot

1. Mourning period prior to holiday equals seven days.
2. The first day of Shavuot is considered the equivalent of another seven days, giving the sum of 14 days.
3. The second day of the holiday marks the 15th day.
4. Required for *sheloshim:* 15 additional days.

Succot

1. Mourning period prior to holiday equals seven days.

2. Seven days of holiday, added to the seven, makes a sum of 14 days.

3. The holiday of Shemini Atzeret, which falls on the eighth day of Succot, acts as Shavuot in regard to *sheloshim,* and is regarded as another seven-day period. This makes 21 days.

4. The day of Simchat Torah marks the 22nd day.

5. Required for *sheloshim:* eight additional days.

Rosh Hashanah and Yom Kippur

Although there is no commandment to "rejoice" (technically) on these holidays, they are considered the same as the other festivals in all three respects, namely, a) They cancel the remainder of the *shiva,* if mourning was accepted prior to the holiday; b) They delay the beginning of mourning if interment for some reason occurred during them; c) They cancel the remainder of the *sheloshim* if the *shiva* was completed before the onset of the holiday. Thus,

1. *Rosh Hashanah*
   a. Mourning prior to Rosh Hashanah equals seven days.
   b. Yom Kippur completes the *sheloshim.*

2. *Yom Kippur*
   a. Mourning before the holy day equals seven days.
   b. Succot completes the sheloshim.

If burial took place, for any reason, during the festival itself, or on *chol ha'moed* of Succot or Passover, then:

1. *Shiva* observance begins at the completion of the holiday (in the case of Succot—after Simchat Torah).

2. The last day of the festival (Passover, Shavuot, Succot, and Rosh Hashanah) is counted as the first day of *shiva.*

3. The days of the holidays are, nevertheless, counted as part of the *sheloshim.* (Hence the unusual circumstance of having the *sheloshim* begin *before* the *shiva.*)

4. The day of Shemini Atzeret is counted as only a single day.

Where Shiva Is Observed

1. Ideally, *shiva* should be observed by all relatives in the house of the deceased. Where a man has lived, there does his spirit continue to dwell. It is, after all, in that place that one is surrounded with the tangible remains of a person's lifework, and it is only right that evidence of his life should be evident during *shiva*. In addition, it is of distinct value to have the family united as it was in days gone by.

2. It is permitted to travel even great distances after the funeral in order to observe *shiva* in the house of the deceased. However, in such cases, the acceptance of mourning should be demonstrated formally at the cemetery, in the cemetery office or on the grounds, by sitting on a low stool and removing the shoes for a short while.

3. Circumstances, however, are not always ideal. Thus, if there is a need to sleep in one's own home, the mourner may commute, but should do so after dark when the streets are quiet. He should then return to the house of the *shiva* early in the morning, before people generally arise.

4. Thus, too, if a person desires to sit *shiva* within his own home, in the company of his mate and children, he may do so. He may also travel distances from the cemetery to his home. However, if he is to travel, he should first accept mourning at the cemetery, as noted above.

Upon Returning from the Cemetery

Prior to departure for the funeral service, arrangements should be made for three observances that are obligatory upon returning home: 1. Washing of hands before entering the apartment; 2. Meal of condolence; 3. Proper arrangements in the house for the *shiva* observance.

The Washing of Hands

It is an ancient custom of the Jewish people to cleanse themselves after being in close proximity to the deceased. This is done, symbolically, by washing the hands before entering the apartment. A container of water should be prepared for this purpose at the entrance.

The custom of hand washing is traced to many different origins. One is that it is a symbolic cleansing from the impurity associated with death. This impurity which is in the spiritual-legal category, and has no relation to physical or hygienic cleanliness, underscores Judaism's constant emphasis on life and the value of living. Another reason often given is that it stems from the practice ordained by the Bible when a person was found dead and the cause of his death was unknown. The elders of the city washed their hands and proclaimed, in behalf of the residents of the city, that none of the citizens have directly or indirectly caused this person's death. A third reason some commentaries offer is that the washing is testimony that these individuals participated in the interment service and did not shrink from performing the burial honors due the dead.

Whatever its origin, the custom of washing the hands is universally observed among Jews. The cup of water is not transferred directly from one person to another. This is a symbolic expression of hope that the tragedy should not continue from person to person, but should end where it, unfortunately, began.

The Meal of Condolence   סעודת הבראה

The meal of condolence, the first full meal that the mourners eat upon returning from the interment, is traditionally provided by the neighbors of the bereaved. So important was this basic courtesy considered that some religious thinkers maintain that it was biblically ordained. Indeed, the sages of the Jerusalem Talmud admonished neighbors who caused the bereaved to eat of his own prepared meal. They even pronounced a curse upon them for displaying such callousness and indifference to the plight of their fellow men.

This beautiful custom, which may appear strange to some American Jews, possesses profound psychological insights. One astute medieval rabbi, obviously of the pre-Freudian era, observed that the mourner harbors a strong death wish at the moment he returns home to the familiar surroundings now bereft of warmth and life. His wish is to join his beloved. In this frame of mind he would tend to deprive himself of food in order to achieve a symbolic death. Indeed, a comment frequently heard is, "Who can eat when my husband lies dead in the cold, friendless earth?"

Another aspect of the meal of condolence is that it is the second formal expression of consolation. The first, as mentioned above, is the parallel rows of friends through which the bereaved walk as they depart from the gravesite. That is a silent tribute, with only a Hebrew formula of condolence, but it is eloquent testimony that we share the pangs of our neighbor's anguish. This second stage of condolence takes us one step closer to the mourner in his state of misery; we move from the role of spectator to participant, from sentiment to service. We bring the mourner the sustenance of life, figuratively and literally, the "bread" of his existence. That is why this meal of condolence is mandatory upon the neighbors, and not the mourners.

This expression of consolation should be, as is the first one, a silent one. The meal should not be an occasion for socializing or for idle chatter. This is discouraged during the period of mourning and, in any case, is in very poor taste.

The third formal occasion of consolation, the *shiva* visitation, is the time that is ripe for the beginning of the mourner's verbalization of his feeling of loss. Here, too, the rabbis urge the visitors to sit in silence until the bereaved himself desires to speak. Even then, the rabbis advise visitors to speak only on the subject of the death in the family. This theme will be treated below.

The Menu of the Meal of Condolence

1. Minimally, it should include bread or rolls—the staff of life. It should also include hardboiled eggs, symbolic of the cyclical or continuous nature of life. Some explain that the egg is the only food that hardens the longer it is cooked, and man must learn to steel himself when death occurs. The meal of condolence may also include cooked vegetables or lentils, and a beverage such as coffee or tea. Some custom has it that wine should also be served. It is obvious that this occasion of drinking should not induce lightheartedness or a surfeit of conviviality.

2. The meal of condolence must be the very first meal eaten on the day of interment. This commandment refers only to the first meal and *not* to the second meal of the day nor, if the mourners choose to fast, to the meal taken after dark or the next day. Of course, if neighbors were unwittingly delayed, or ignorant of the custom, the meal should be accepted most graciously.

If interment took place at night, the time for the first meal is considered to be all night or any time during the next day.

3. Who must prepare the meal?

Ideally, as was noted, the neighbors should do so. If they do not, the relatives or the son or daughter of the mourner may perform this *mitzvah*. If that is not possible, the mourners may prepare it for one another.

If no one is available to perform this commandment, the mourner should prepare his own meal. No mourner is expected to fast.

If the meal of condolence is not ready when the mourners have returned from the funeral, they may partake of light refreshments of their own, such as coffee and cake, providing they do not eat bread or cooked food or sit down to a table as at a formal meal.

4. When is the meal of condolence *not* served?

The meal of condolence is not served at a time when there is no formal, public observance of mourning, such as on Sabbath or the major festivals (Passover, Shavuot and Succot), or on the late afternoons preceding these days. However, the meal *should* be served on days of Rosh Chodesh, Hanukkah, Purim, and *chol ha'moed*.

The meal is also not served for those mourning the loss of infants who have not survived thirty days, and after the death of intentional suicides. (See chapter below on Suicides.) Also, if news of the death of a close relative came more than thirty days later the meal is not served.

5. If a second death occurs during *shiva*, another meal of condolence must be served.

Candles in the House of Mourning

The house of mourning must be prepared with candles for the return of the mourners from the cemetery. Candles, in memory of the deceased, should be kindled and kept burning for the entire seven-day period of *shiva*. They are kindled upon returning from the cemetery. (The *shiva* candles are usually provided by the funeral director.)

To the Jew, the candle signifies a special event, some notable occasion in life. There is candlelight on Sabbath, on major holidays, customarily at the *b'rit*, the *pidyon ha'ben*, under the wedding canopy, and often at occasions of *simcha shel mitzvah*—meals celebrating the successful conclusion of a commandment.

During *shiva*, candlelight is the symbol of the human being. The wick and the flame symbolize body and soul, and the bond between them. The flame is the soul that strives ever upward, and brings light into darkness. Jewish mysticism has suggested profound and insightful analogies of the flame and the soul of the deceased in its comments on the *shiva* candle, *yahrzeit* lamp and *yizkor* candle.

1. Because of this deep significance of the flame, the

shiva candle, ideally, should not be an electric fixture, but one of wick and flame, either of olive oil or paraffin. If these are unavailable, an electric light should be used. Also, if there is any danger of fire, the electric light, of course, should be used.

2. *Where* the candle should be kindled is a matter of opinion in the sources. It is most proper that it be lit in the home of the deceased, where he lived and died. This should obtain regardless of where the death occurred. If it is not feasible to observe the *shiva* at the residence of the deceased, it should be kindled wherever the mourners are sitting *shiva*.

3. The candle should be kindled immediately upon returning from the cemetery, or upon hearing of the death within the seven days. The candle is left burning for the duration of the *shiva,* even throughout the Sabbath at which time demonstrative mourning is not observed. Also, on *chol ha'moed* of Succot and Passover the candle is lit immediately, even though *shiva* begins after the holiday is over. In such a case, the candles should remain burning through the holiday and until the end of the *shiva*. It is preferable on those days, however, to place the candles in a room other than the dining room so as to make the symbol of grief less prominent on the holiday which is a joyous occasion for the entire Jewish people.

4. One candle is sufficient for the household. There should be one lit also wherever the mourners observe the *shiva*.

Covering Mirrors in House of Shiva

It has been a time-honored tradition to cover the mirrors in the *shiva* home from the moment of death to the end of *shiva*. While the custom is of uncertain origin, its practice is appropriate to the pattern of *avelut*.

A variety of reasons have been advanced for the custom of covering the mirrors:

1. Judaism has always taught that man was created in the image of God and that he derives, from that resemblance, his dignity and his value. It has supplemented this concept with the idea that the death of one of God's creatures diminishes the very image of the Creator Himself. Man's demise represents a disruption of the relationship between the living man and the living God. The dignity of man is the reflection of his Creator and, therefore, the image of the Creator Himself shrinks with the death of His creatures. At the time of the destruction of the image of God, represented by man, the mirror—which serves to reflect man's "image"—ought not be used.

2. When death strikes, the mourner should contemplate the relationship between God and man, Creator and creature. When, instead, the bereaved dwells vainly on self-adoration (through the use of his mirror) and continues to be concerned with his own image and his own creatureliness, he thereby brings to almost comic proportions the austere moment of tragedy.

3. It should be recognized that the mirror occupies an unusual place in the household. It is the object which, more than any other, serves to enhance the attractiveness of man and wife for each other. The silvered glass reflects the external appeal of each of the mates.

Judaism has taken great care to promote a relationship of kindness, concern, courtesy, and even physical desire between a man and his wife. Nevertheless, with the death of a child or parent or sibling, this intimate relationship must be suspended. One commentator thus states that the ancient custom observed during *shiva*, of *kfi'at hamitah*, the overturning of the bed or couch, served as a means of discouraging marital relations. When the cloud of death settles on a household, the mirror—happy symbol of secure and intimate family living—must be covered, and the mourner must concentrate on the painful loss.

4. It is obvious that the individual, if he were isolated from society, would have little need of the precious reflecting

glass. The mirror is the means of achieving social acceptance by enhancing the appearance. The spirit of Jewish mourning, however, is the spirit of loneliness, the mourner dwelling silently, and in solitude, on his personal loss. Social etiquette and appearance become terribly insignificant. The covering of the mirror symbolizes the sense of withdrawal in *avelut*.

5. The fifth reason is a very practical one: Worship services are customarily held in the home of the bereaved, as will be noted below. Jewish law clearly states that one may not worship an image or stand directly in front of one, whether it be a picture, or a reflected image in a mirror. Thus, mirrors must be covered in this temporary House of Worship.

Additional House of Mourning Preparations

Several other matters regarding the house of mourning should be noted. These will be recorded here and discussed in further detail in the appropriate chapters below.

1. Arrange with the funeral director for *shiva* benches or stools for all the mourners, even for those who are too ill to sit on them constantly throughout the *shiva*. The mourners will also require slippers that are not made of leather.

2. Ask the rabbi or sexton or lay official of the synagogue for a sufficient number of men to constitute a *minyan*, and for prayerbooks for all present, men and women, and skullcaps for the men.

3. Also arrange for chairs for those who will visit during *shiva*.

Prayers in the House of Mourning
תפילות

It is a sacred obligation to hold daily services during *shiva* in the house of the deceased, whether the death occurred there or elsewhere. This is done in order to honor the dead and to show respect for the bereaved.

It is important to hold public services in the presence of a *minyan* so that the mourners observing *shiva* may recite the Kaddish, which requires the attendance of ten adult males. We, thereby, demonstrate respect for the bereaved, as well as honor for the deceased.

Significantly, however, it is considered by many to be *more* important to hold services in the house of the deceased if he left no mourners, and when Kaddish need not be recited, and *shiva* is not observed. The Talmud (Shabbat 152b) records that Rabbi Judah the Prince gathered a *minyan* to accompany him on a condolence visit to the house of one who died in the neighborhood and left no mourners. After *shiva*, Rabbi Judah saw the deceased in a dream and learned from him that he was comforted and set at ease because of the presence of the *minyan*.

Therefore, if there are two deaths that have occurred in a community that can provide but one *minyan*, and one of the deceased left mourners, whereas the other did not, the service should be held in the house of the deceased who is *not* mourned.

The Mourner and the Minyan

1. If the mourners can borrow a Torah Scroll, they should do so, but must provide for it a clean and honorable place in the home. It will be read at each service on Mondays, Thursdays and Saturdays (mornings or afternoons, when the mourners prefer to pray at home).

2. Services need not be held in the home if the deceased was a child of less than one year of age. In places where such services are held, however, they are held solely in honor of the bereaved, so that they may remain at home during *shiva*.

3. The male mourner himself is counted as part of the *minyan*.

4. The mourner may lead the service himself. Although some local customs discourage this, the weight of scholarly opinion urges the mourner to do this.

5. If no *minyan* can be gathered, should the bereaved leave the house of *shiva* to attend services with the congregation, or should they pray at home? While there has been rabbinic controversy regarding this matter, much depends on the commitment of the mourner in observing the *shiva*. If leaving the home for services will tempt him to engage in other activities while he is out-of-doors, it is better that he not attend public services. If, however, he will not abuse this leniency, the mourner should not be deprived of the privilege of reciting the Kaddish and praying with a *minyan*. However, he should first make every effort to secure a *minyan* at home for both morning and evening services. If this is not possible, the *minyan* should be secured at least for either the morning or evening service only, and he can then attend the synagogue for the other service. Failing this, he should keep in mind the requirements of *shiva*, and should go to the nearest synagogue for services, both morning and evening. At the synagogue, he should not sit in his regular seat so as to indicate some change in his personal status during mourning.

CHANGES IN THE ORDER OF THE SERVICE

Following are several changes in the order of service that pertain to the entire *minyan* when it is held in the house of the mourner.

Daily Services

Tachanun is not said; *el erech apayim, lamenatzeiach,* and *va'ani zot briti* are not said. *Tikkabel,* in the full *Kaddish* recitation, is not said, according to some usage. Many local customs do require its recitation.

Friday Evening Services

Hodu before the *minchah* service should not be recited by the mourner. The Sabbath eve service should begin with *mizmor shir le'yom ha-shabbat*, omitting *lechu neranenah* and the introductory Psalms. *Birchat me'en sheva* is not recited. *Shalom aleichem* should not be recited at the table, but *zemirot* may be sung.

Sabbath Morning Services

The mourner may not recite an *aliyah* (the call to recite the blessing over the Torah). During weekdays, he must refuse the honor even after having been called publicly. On the Sabbath he must avoid receiving the honor even though he be a Kohen or a Levi, but if there is no other person available, or he is mistakenly called, he should accept the honor. His refusal of an *aliyah* on the Sabbath would be considered public mourning which is forbidden. The mourner may be called, however, to raise or tie the Torah, or to remove and replace it in the Holy Ark, even on weekdays.

If the mourner was dangerously ill and has recovered, he may recite the blessing of gratitude, the *birchat ha-gomel*, before the entire *minyan*, but without receiving an *aliyah*. *Av harachamim* is recited at this home service.

Sabbath Minchah Services

Tzidkat'cha is recited, although it is the equivalent of *tachanun* which is omitted on the weekday, and *va'ani tefilati* is omitted.

Conclusion of the Sabbath

Vi'yehi noam is not recited, according to some customs; *ve'yiten* should be recited; *havdalah* should begin from the blessings themselves, omitting the introduction, *hineh*, if the mourner recites it himself.

Holidays

On holidays, if the mourner is a Kohen, he should not participate in the Priestly Blessing, but should leave the *minyan* prior to its recital.

Hallel

The *hallel* is not chanted in the house of mourning because it speaks of joy, which is not consonant with mourning, and because it includes the phrase, "The dead shall not praise Thee," which is considered a mockery of the deceased when it is recited during the *shiva* in the house of mourning. A consensus of rabbinic opinion observes the following guidelines with reference to the recitation of *hallel* in the house of mourning:

1. On *Rosh Chodesh:* If the service is held in the house of the deceased, *hallel* should not be recited at the service proper, but the individuals may recite it in their own homes. If it is held in the house of the mourner which is *not* the house of the deceased, the mourner should absent himself while the remainder of the *minyan* recites the *hallel*.

2. On *Hanukkah* and other holidays: All the members of the *minyan must* recite *hallel* individually after the service, if they have not already done so. Likewise, if *hallel* is to be said on a holiday which is coincident with the last day of *shiva* (when at the conclusion of services the *shiva* terminates), *hallel* should not be recited at the service proper, but everyone must recite it later, individually.

Avinu malkenu, during the Ten Days of Repentance, should be recited.

Psalm 49 is recited after every morning and evening service in the house of mourning. Some traditions urge this recitation also after the *minchah* service. On days on which *tachanun* is not recited, Psalm 17 is sometimes substituted. On Sabbath, *chol ha'moed,* and Purim this Psalm, too, is omitted.

Leaving the House During Shiva

The most characteristic tradition of Jewish mourning is the mourner's withdrawal to the sanctuary of his home following the death of a close relative. He does not mix socially, participate in joyous events or take pleasure trips during this time.

This tradition of staying at home is based, generally, on two reasons. First, is a practical reason: If he is prohibited from doing business or experiencing pleasure, home is the most logical place to be. Second, it has positive, curative value: Mourning is an in-depth experience in loneliness. The ties that bind one soul to another have been severed and there is a gnawing sense of solitude. To remain incommunicado is to express grief over the disruption of communication with someone we loved. At certain times every person has a right, even an obligation to be alone. This is such a time. The mourner, therefore, remains at home during the entire period of the *shiva*. It then becomes the moral duty of the Jewish community to come to the door of the bereaved and to comfort him with words of praise for the deceased, and thereby to draw him out of his loneliness and into the social structure once again.

Following are some details of the law of staying at home during *shiva:*

1. If there is a compelling need for the mourner himself to leave the home for the purpose of fulfilling a *mitzvah* that he personally is obligated to perform, such as the circumcision of his son, or the purchase of *tefillin,* where others cannot help him, he may leave the home for this purpose.

2. The mourner may not leave the house to participate in a *mitzvah* that can be accomplished without his presence, such as attendance at a Bar Mitzvah, circumcision of the son of a relative or a friend, attending a wedding ceremony, or paying a condolence call upon other bereaved.

3. If in the house of *shiva* there is no available place for the mourners to sleep, or if they are needed at their own home (especially if one of the mourners is a mother of young children), or if the bereaved wish to change the place of mourning so that personal friends and neighbors may have the opportunity to visit, they are permitted to leave the house of *shiva*. They must do this, however, in the manner described below.

4. If during the *shiva* there occurs the death of another of the seven close relatives for whom he is religiously required to mourn, he may leave the house to follow the funeral procession, inconspicuously. If he is *needed* in order to make funeral arrangements or to act as a pall-bearer, etc., he is permitted to attend the funeral even during the first day of *shiva*. If he is *not needed* for these duties, he may not attend another funeral until the third day of *shiva* (that is, the second morning after interment). At the funeral he may follow the procession for a short distance, always remaining at the periphery of the cortege.

5. If there is no *minyan* that is able to come to the home and if, in accordance with the qualifications stipulated above, he chooses to attend services, he should worship at the closest synagogue. He should proceed alone, or in the company of other mourners. If he is travelling by car, he is considered to be alone. The distance one is required to travel is of no consequence. It should be noted that the mourner may not use this occasion to do *anything*, except attend services.

6. The need to leave the home for business or professional purposes, or for special emergencies, will be considered in a special chapter below, on "work" during *shiva*.

7. A *mohel* may leave the house to perform a circumcision, for this must be performed only on the eighth day after birth. If there is no other *mohel* available, he may perform it even on the first day of his *shiva*. If there is another *mohel* available, and only his services are desired, he may perform

the circumcision, provided it is to take place after the third day of the *shiva* period.

8. A Kohen, required for a *pidyon ha'ben* (the ceremonial redemption of the first-born son, which must be performed only on the thirtieth day after birth), follows the same regulations as for the *mohel*.

9. The mourner may be asked to serve as *sandek* at a *b'rit* after the third day, but it is considered an impropriety to make such a request of him. A person in mourning surely will have ambivalent feelings about accepting this honor.

10. The mourner should attend congregational services on Tisha B'av and Purim. If a *minyan* and Torah Scrolls are not easily available, he should also worship with a congregation on the Sabbath.

11. When leaving the house of *shiva* every effort should be made not to do so until the third day—that is (as explained above), the second morning after interment. He should make every effort to leave only after dark. If this proves impractical he may leave during daylight hours, but should proceed as inconspicuously as possible. He should not wear leather shoes, even out of doors, as will be noted below. If this is impossible, he should place some earth or sand in his shoes, as a constant reminder that he is in mourning. In all complicated situations, of course, a rabbi should be consulted.

Sitting Shiva

It is an ancient Jewish tradition that mourners, during *shiva,* do not sit upon chairs of normal height. Until modern times it was the custom to be seated on the earth itself, a procedure which demonstrated the departure from normalcy during the early stages of bereavement. Thus, expression was given to the sense of loneliness and depression one felt after one's relative was interred in the very earth on which he sat. The Bible tells us that when Job suffered a succession of disasters he was comforted by friends who sat with him "to the earth." It is, almost in a literal sense, a physical adjustment to one's emotional state, a lowering of the body to the level of one's feelings, a symbolic enactment of remorse and desolation.

The mourner today sits "to the earth," in the biblical phrase, by sitting *closer* to the earth on a wooden stool or hassock or footstool, on a mat or on several pillows. The material the mourner chooses to sit on is, at present, unimportant. It is not the stool that is important. Primarily, the tradition stipulates, he must sit on a level lower than that of normal seating height, and whether the seat is or is not comfortable is irrelevant. If he desires, he may put a cushion on the stool. Sleeping on a bed of normal height is permitted.

Following are details of the tradition of sitting *shiva*.

1. One need not "sit" at all during *shiva*. He may stand or walk or lie down. The tradition is concerned only that when the mourner does sit down, he should sit on a stool of lower height rather than usual.

2. Elderly people, the physically weak, and pregnant women may sit on normal seats. However, they should make an effort, whenever practicable, to sit on a low stool when people come for short visits to comfort the bereaved. This demonstrative bereavement is the most important aspect of the tradition of "sitting," and it should not be taken lightly.

3. The mourner need not rise from his seat in respect for any visitor, no matter how important he is, whether he be a renowned scholar, or an eminent public personality, or a government official.

4. If the mourner wishes to sit on a porch or terrace, he may do so, provided he sits on the low stool.

Working and Conducting Business

One of the most fundamental laws of Jewish mourning (over three thousand years old, and later recorded by the prophet Ezekiel), is the prohibition of working and doing business during *shiva*.

Judaism, unlike many ancient (and some modern) cultures, endows labor with dignity, and considers commerce a proper activity of man. However, never must "work" so dominate a man that he becomes a mere cog in society's wheel. The dimensions of man's personality must include his labor or business or career, but must transcend them as well. He must be able to experience life's great moments as an authentic human being, and not restrict his horizon to that of a laborer or professional. Hence, Judaism demands that at moments of great joy or great grief—both of which require concentration and undisturbed meditation—we refrain from our daily pursuits.

Thus, the prophet Ezekiel records the words of the Lord: "And I will transform your festivals to mourning." And the sages taught, "as on festivals labor is prohibited, so in days of mourning." The work prohibition during mourning is not similar to that of the Sabbath, but to that of *chol ha'moed*, the intermediary days in the midst of the festivals of Passover and Succot. Of course, the tradition accurately and wisely noted the different motivations for the work prohibition on festivals and during mourning, and these differences are reflected in the laws of *avelut*.

Following are the basic laws of the work prohibition during *shiva*. We must realize that because of the many possible situations and the variety of personal and business obligations, the decision of a rabbi may be required in some instances. There are a number of contingencies in this law, and only a competent, learned authority can weigh the human need and the religious requirement in order to make a valid decision.

Generally, the law states that one may not do any manner of skilled or unskilled labor, or manage any business enterprise, or direct any investment of monies, by himself or through agents, for all of the days of *shiva*. Included in this prohibition are all those who are *dependents* of the mourner and his immediate domestic help, whether they are Jewish or gentile. A child of a mourner, who is not himself mourning, even if he is past the age of Bar Mitzvah, may work during *shiva*, but only if the profits go to the child, not to the parent. Those who are economically *independent* of the father are not affected by the *shiva* restrictions.

1. If the mourner is an employee—either a manager, executive, craftsman, or laborer—he may employ another person to work in his behalf. The employer is not expected to suffer because of the bereavement of an employee. Likewise, a mourner, if he is a tenant farmer, may designate a replacement so that the percentage of the owner's profit should not be lost thereby. Under ordinary circumstances, however, those who are self-employed may not similarly engage replacements to function in their behalf.

2. If the mourner is an employer, the employees should be allowed to work during their owner's observance of *shiva*. They are considered to be working for their own profit, even though the mourner profits thereby as well.

Similarly, one who is a tenant farmer in the fields of a mourner, either on a percentage or rental basis, or for a stipulated share of produce, may continue working, as he is doing so for his own benefit, even though profit accrues to the mourner as well.

3. If the mourner has contracted work to others before the death occurred, the workers may continue to do their labor. However, this work may not be performed on the premises of the mourner. But the mourner may not contract for new work during *shiva*. This principle holds only for portable items. Contract work on stationary items, such as building construction, may not be done at all by anyone during *shiva*, under ordinary circumstances.

4. A day worker, one who gets paid by the hour, rather than by the piece, may, under ordinary circumstances not work for the mourner during *shiva*.

5. If the mourner has agreed to do contract work for

others, he may arrange to have it completed through others, but not on his own premises.

The mourner may accept contract work during *shiva* for the period after *shiva*, but should not enter into written agreements or contractual arrangements at this time.

6. Items which the mourner rented to others before *shiva* may be used by them without restriction. He may not renew the rental during the *shiva*, unless it is on a continuous renewal basis, and the matter cannot wait until after *shiva*.

7. Retail stores must be closed during *shiva*, under all ordinary circumstances. This rule applies to stores individually owned or owned in partnership. The details of this law are complex:

a. The partner of the mourner, in this case, will, unfortunately, be adversely affected. He may do work for the business in private, but not in the place of business, and not publicly. If the mourner is the major partner, and the business is called after his name, even private work done for it by the other partner is not permitted. If the mourner is a silent partner, the opinion of many scholars is that the other partner may continue normal operations.

b. If the partnership owns more than one store, and each partner manages one, only the store managed by the mourner must be closed.

c. If one of the partners himself dies, the partnership is considered terminated, and the business may operate normally, unless it was explicitly stipulated, previously, that the children will inherit the deceased's portion of the business. If it was *not* explicitly so stated, the store need not be closed at all (except in honor of the deceased, if so desired by the surviving partner).

d. If they are partners merely in the rental of store space, but individually own separate businesses, the partner need not close his part of the store. In fact, in such a case, if the family is in need, the mourner may have others work in his portion of the store, since it is already open, and not specifically open for the mourner.

8. Housework, such as cooking and cleaning, may be performed during *shiva*, but only such work as is necessary for that specific household. This applies not only to the woman doing chores for the members of the family, but also if the residence is located in a commercial establishment, such as hotel or restaurant for customers who eat or sleep there. While this is technically not considered labor, it should be avoided in ideal circumstances. Likewise, mourners who work as servants, bakers, or waiters, (live-in help) may, in critical circumstances where the labor is absolutely required, perform their appointed tasks. However, they should not do so until after the third day, and they should not leave the premises of their employment until the conclusion of *shiva*.

9. A physician may attend to those of his patients who need his personal service during the *shiva*, even if other physicians are available. Of course, the doctor should use his discretion as to whether or not it is important enough to make the house call. If there is any doubt in his mind, the physician should definitely attend to his patient.

10. If the mourner was engaged in his business and, for some reason, did not learn of the death, there is no obligation to inform him of the tragedy. So long as he himself is not aware of the death, the members of his family are not forbidden to work. He and his family may continue business activity until he is made aware of the death. If he is away from home and is notified by his family by letter or telegram, they should estimate the time of his receiving it, at which moment he becomes a mourner and his place of business must be closed by them.

When Is Work Permitted?

There are cases which, by their very nature, must be considered as exceptions to the normal rules of mourning because of the severe hardship that may be entailed.

These exceptions fall into three categories:

The Poor

No one is expected to suffer unduly as a consequence of observing the traditions of Jewish mourning, and relief from the stringencies of the law was thus provided. By the same token, the poor were not simply lumped into an exclusive class, giving them complete exemption from *all* the laws of mourning. Such economic burdens that develop from strict observance of the laws were relieved in accordance with the clear provisions of the tradition. But the remainder of the mourning obligations not pertinent to the exigency, remained in force.

The following laws apply to the indigent mourners. Poverty is defined, in terms of the laws of mourning, as those unable to earn their daily bread unless they work each day.

1. The indigent mourner, even if he must borrow money or accept charity, must observe the first three days of mourning: the day of interment, the following day, and until a short time after sunrise on the third day. He may not work during this time.

2. After the third day he may work, but should do so privately and inconspicuously, if possible. His wife, if she is the mourner, may work in the home. He may work after the third day even if charity or loans are offered him, but he refuses to accept this assistance, because it represents a compromise of his dignity.

3. If there is no possibility of his receiving charitable assistance, he may work even on the very first day, but he should strive to perform this work inconspicuously.

Severe Loss

Not only poverty, but also incurring a severe business loss is grounds for exemption from the prohibition of work during *shiva*. Understandably, each person will tend to evaluate the extent of his loss subjectively. The deeply grieved may look lightly upon the possibility of losing employment. Those who are grieving mildly may consider a half week's wages a major setback. The judgment in such a situation should, therefore, be measured by a religious authority.

The following matters will be taken into consideration:

1. Will the mourner lose trade to competitors if the store is closed?

2. Does the *shiva* fall during one's busy season?

3. Are the goods, that will remain unsold because of the observance, perishables? Is it possible they may be rendered non-merchandisable or lose value after the *shiva?*

4. Will the purchase price of materials that may not be acquired during *shiva*, rise if the purchase is delayed?

5. Is there a possibility of losing a job if the mourner does not work for the entire week?

6. Will employees have to be paid while they sit idle while the employer is mourning? Will rented items, such as delivery trucks, have to be paid for, although they will not be used?

7. Will the cessation of business activity cause an irretrievable loss of capital investment?

8. Will there be a major loss of profit if business is not conducted? The rabbi will decide differently, for example, if one is an investor in his spare time for additional income, and the loss is mild, or if he derives his major income from investments and, thus, faces a serious financial crisis.

9. Will another person suffer loss as a result of the mourner's observance?

10. Are the administrative aspects of the business, such as billing, etc., so important that if they are delayed payment may not be received?

11. Finally, and most important, will an extensive financial loss result in any way, because of the full observance of mourning?

In cases where the hardship is adjudged to be severe, the mourner should abide by the following scale of preferences:

1. The mourner should attempt to have others do the work in his stead.
2. He should attempt to delay the work until after the third day.
3. He should strive to accomplish his work inconspicuously.
4. It at all possible, it should be done at night, and *shiva* should be observed during the day.

Only under exceptional circumstances may the work be done by the mourner himself, or before the third day, or in public. This is true for the employee, the self-employed, the storekeeper, or his partner.

Public Need

Personal mourning should also not intrude on the conduct of public affairs. Thus, the Talmud guards against the cessation of public Torah studies when the teacher is required to observe *shiva* at home. It insists that another person teach in his stead, and if that is not possible, it requires the mourner to perform his normal duties. Public need, thus, received priority, and any disruption of this need was considered an exceptional contingency. In the category of public need are included the following:

1. The *sexton* of the synagogue, if he is personally needed to arrange the sanctuary and prepare for the Sabbath, or care for the burial of the dead in the Burial Society, and there is no other person who can function in his stead, may perform this work during *shiva*.
2. The teacher of religious studies, if there is no available substitute, should not dismiss classes during *shiva*, but should continue teaching himself. If this can be done in his

home, it is preferable. This does not apply to the teacher of secular subjects.

3. The *shochet*, or ritual slaughterer, of a small community which depends on him for daily meat, may perform his duties after the third day so that the community need not go without meat on the Sabbath. If there is no other *shochet* he may go back to work even during the first three days. (This is usually of little concern in our day of pre-packaged frozen kosher meats.)

4. The rabbi, in his professional capacity, may decide points of religious law during *shiva*, if there is no other available rabbi who can decide these matters. If there is a wedding ceremony at which there will be no music played, and he is the only qualified person available, he may perform the ceremony in as inconspicuous and quiet a fashion as possible.

5. A scribe may write a Jewish bill of divorce, if there is a possibility that one of the couple may otherwise renege on the agreement, or that the proceedings may be disrupted because of his absence.

6. The *mohel* for the circumcision, and the Kohen for the ceremony of *pidyon ha'ben*, should likewise perform their respective duties if there is no substitute, as noted above.

7. Public officials, who are personallly indispensable at the time of *shiva*, may perform their duties if they can find no adequate replacement. Similarly, military personnel, policemen and firemen, during times of emergency, when their participation is necessary for the public good, may perform their duties during *shiva*.

It cannot be reiterated often enough that the decision to curtail the practice of *shiva* may not be made by laymen or well-wishers or "knowledgeable" relatives or religious functionaries or funeral directors, but by duly ordained rabbis, thoroughly steeped in the law and aware of the problems of the day.

Wearing Shoes

The comfort of wearing leather shoes is denied the mourner during *shiva*. As on Yom Kippur, when leather footwear may not be worn, the stockinged feet or the wearing of soft shoes during bereavement is symbolic of personal mortification and a disregard of vanity and comfort, in order better to concentrate on the deeper meaning of life. Thus, the prophet Ezekiel is told to remove his shoes while he is mourning. This act symbolizes for the Jew the formal acceptance of mourning.

1. Shoes made of materials other than leather *may* be worn, and it is not necessary to walk in stockinged feet. Shoes of cloth, reeds, hair, or wood, are permitted so long as they are not covered with leather and the soles are not made of leather. Rubber or synthetic plastic shoes may be worn even if the lace be made of leather, as it is not used to cover the foot. While shoes made of corfam or other imitation leather with rubber soles are theoretically permitted according to Jewish law, the appearance is similar to that of leather and, hence, might mislead people into believing that the mourner is not properly honoring the deceased. Such shoes should, therefore, be avoided if possible.

2. A pregnant woman, or a woman shortly after delivery, a sick person or one subject to illness because of the cold, certainly one who suffers from ailments of the feet, skin diseases, or one who has chronically weak feet so that he requires the support of structured leather, may wear leather shoes. Even in such cases it is preferable, if possible, not to wear shoes in the presence of those who come to visit during *shiva*.

3. One who is permitted to leave the house during *shiva* for official government business, or must make other important public appearances, *may* wear leather shoes while outside, but must remove them when he returns home. One

who has no *minyan* at home, and wishes to travel to services, may wear leather shoes in transit, if no other socially
acceptable, permissible shoes are available, but must remove
them at the synagogue and upon returning home. In all
these cases, a bit of earth should be placed inside the leather
shoes to keep the bereaved ever mindful that he is in mourning.

Greetings and Gifts

With the shocking disruption of normal life caused by a
death in the family, the standard forms of social intercourse,
its niceties and graces and minutiae of etiquette, are without significance. The mourning heart has no patience for
these formalities. Tradition, thus, scorns all types of greeting during *shiva*.

The sages, who consistently demand that one greet all
men graciously and courteously, regard greetings as out of
place when spoken by, or to, the mourner. It is absurd to
say to a man deep in anguish over someone he loved. "Hello.
How are you feeling today?" This is not only a question
that cannot be answered, it indicates a lack of compassion
and understanding. The *shalom aleichems* and the hellos
are hollow and purposeless, even offensive, to the despairing heart. Certainly, as Maimonides, the twelfth-century
sage, taught, we must strongly discourage the misplaced
small talk and lightheartedness of some mindless visitors.
The rejection of greetings at this time, far from betraying
a lack of cordiality, issues from a profound insight into
man's nature and a deep compassion for his predicament.
This law, as so many other laws of bereavement, originated
with Ezekiel. God tells Ezekiel (24:17) : "Sigh in silence."
Indeed, how can one mourn more eloquently than by "sigh-
ing in silence"?

The sages offer a second reason for avoiding the standard greeting of *"shalom." Shalom* is one of the names of

God, and greeting in the name of God at a time when God has taken a close relative could conceivably be, in the spirit of the mourner, an intimation of scoffing and an invitation to question God's justice, at a time when he is required to proclaim God's justice, as in the *tzidduk ha'din* prayer.

Traditionally, therefore, Jews do not extend greetings to the mourner. The visitor enters the door, usually left slightly ajar to avoid the first meeting and greeting, and sits down, without fuss and bother, to share the grief of his neighbor.

1. During *shiva*, the mourner should not extend greetings to others and others, naturally, should not bid him *shalom*.

2. When greetings *are* extended by visitors out of ignorance, the mourner, during the first three days, may not respond to the greeting. He should indicate, graciously, that he is a mourner and is not permitted to do so. After the three days he may respond to the greeting out of courtesy, but should do so in an undertone, to indicate respect to both the person and the tradition.

3. After *shiva* he may initiate the greeting and may respond to it. Customarily, however, the mourner is not greeted with *shalom* for the full year of mourning in the case of a parent's death, and for the 30 days after the death of other relatives.

4. If a large contingent of people visits as a group, such as, for example, representatives of an organization, he may bid them farewell. Special respect must be accorded to a large number of people.

5. On the Sabbath, the mourner may wish others *shabbat shalom*, and they may respond. As to whether others may initiate greetings, there is conflicting opinion, and the mourner should follow the practice of his own community.

6. May visitors greet each other in the house of mourning? It is considered in poor taste even to utilize the word *shalom* in the house of mourning, especially since one must

then differentiate between the greeting spoken to the bereaved and that spoken to the comforters.

7. Other forms of greeting to the mourner (not using the word *shalom*), such as "good evening," etc. should also be avoided. Merely sitting beside the mourner is sufficient. If one desires to approach the mourner directly, the mention of his name alone is indicative of both courtesy and the compassion for his bereavement. Visitors may greet each other without utilizing the word *shalom*.

8. The proper way to bid farewell is to use the Hebrew phrase, *ha'makom yenachem* (*otecha* for one male, *otach* for one female, *etchem* for many mourners, *etchen* for more than one female mourner) *b'toch she'ar avelai Tziyon vi'yerushalayim*. One may use the translation, as well: "May God comfort you among the other mourners of Zion and Jerusalem." Indeed, it is, after all, God alone who can provide the only valid, lasting comfort at this moment of anguish. God, in this phrase, is referred to as *Ha'makom*, which ordinarily means "the Place." It implies that the omnipresent God, who is everyplace at every time, was present at birth and is now present in the house of mourning—knows the grief that is suffered by the mourners. He is the God who will grant you comfort.

9. There is no reason why the visitors should not wish the mourner well: that he be blessed with good health and strength, that in the long future he be shielded from great sorrow, and that he be granted long life, or other appropriate blessings. By the same token, the mourner may extend these good wishes, or even *mazal tov* for some happy occasion, to those who visit. It is psychologically and spiritually valuable for the mourner to demonstrate concern for others—for their sorry plight or their good fortune, although he is himself steeped in the despair of his own difficulties.

10. To bring gifts of material things to the mourner is not only in poor taste, but in violation of the traditional custom. The avoidance of sending gifts is in the nature of

avoiding greetings. It expresses only the superficial joys of friendship at a time of profound personal disorientation. Traditionally, the meal of condolence was the proper gift of consolation. While, obviously, all visitors cannot provide this present, a gift to a charity in honor of the deceased is, instead, correct procedure. Thoughtful visitors will follow this course.

Personal Hygiene and Grooming

Bathing

As personal pleasures are denied the mourner in all his other activities during *shiva,* so the mourner may not bathe or shower for pleasure. The tradition of the Jew has always emphasized the urgent requirement of washing and it has never compromised its age-old insistence on the need for total cleanliness. But the sages of the Talmud realized that washing was also practiced for comfort, and this was not consistent with the spirit of mourning.

In having to judge where cleanliness ends and comfort begins, the sages maintained that the bathing of the whole body and the use of hot water were criteria of pleasure, and not essential to the basic cleansing process. While they prohibited washing of the whole at one time, as in a pool, or bath, or shower—and in hot water, they did permit the washing of separate parts of the body, or head and face, in cool water.

1. One who is ill, or a woman before or after giving birth, or anyone who feels his health requires him to bathe in warm water, may do so during *shiva* on the direct advice of a physician. He should prepare his bath, however, in as inconspicuous a manner as possible.

2. One who is inordinately delicate and who has accustomed himself to bathe or shower very frequently, may bathe, even during *shiva,* if he experiences severe discomfort. He should be careful to do so inconspicuously.

3. If one has become dirty he may remove the dirt with soap and water.

4. A woman should not perform the ritual of immersion in the *mikveh* during *shiva* since, in any case, she will be prohibited from marital relations during *shiva*, as will be noted below.

5. Children under Bar Mitzvah age may be washed, as they are not obligated to observe the laws of mourning.

The Use of Cosmetics

1. As mourners must refrain from bathing, so must they, male or female, refrain from the use of oils and soaps and perfumes, or colognes and hair cream, even if they be used only for individual parts of the body, or for the hair. Certainly, if soap or oil must be used to remove sweat or dirt, it is permissible. Rouge, powder, lipstick, mascara and nail polish should also be avoided, as these surely are for cosmetic purposes and not for cleanliness.

2. If the mourner is a bride, or is engaged to be married, or even keeping company with a man, and she feels that cosmetics are necessary for her appearance, she may use them even during this period of mourning, but she should exercise moderation.

3. If there are medical reasons for anointing oneself with oils or salves, they may of course be used.

Haircutting

The Talmud, in describing the origin of the prohibition of haircutting for the mourner, cites the command of God to the sons of Aaron that they should not prevent their hair from growing. From an analysis of the biblical text, we learn that the duration of the prohibition is 30 days.

Allowing the hair to grow is another indication of the withdrawal of the mourner from society. It is part of the general pattern of forsaking personal appearance and grooming, at a time of great personal loss. Indeed, one of

the prime characteristics of the hermit or the ancient Nazi-
rite, who was a spiritually-inspired rebel against the sinfulness of society, was the unrestrained growing of hair. It
expressed, evidently, a rejection of civility. Similarly, in our
day, many youngsters, not in the least spiritually-inspired,
demonstrate their rebellion by wearing their hair excessively long. It is, in a sense, an abandonment of, and withdrawal from, society which impels the mourner not to cut
his hair.

While the mourner is never asked to become a recluse—
religious or social—he is nevertheless in a state of social
withdrawal. He does not go to business or parties; he does
not even go out-of-doors. He does not wish to be bothered
with the social amenities of "hellos" and "goodbyes." He
allows his hair and beard and nails to grow in a spirit of
abandonment. He is disheartened by life's tragic twists and
turns. Only upon his emergence from deep despair, when
relatives or friends begin to comment upon his unkempt
appearance, does the mourner begin to groom himself again.

In ancient times, when the normal custom of society was
for all men to grow long beards, withdrawal from society
was symbolized by shaving, as in Jeremiah 41: "The people
came from Shechem . . . with shaven cheeks and rent clothing." Today, in the society of the clean-shaven, the mourner
withdraws by allowing his hair and beard to grow. As
noted in the chapter on personal hygiene, however, the
mourner is not expected to look unkempt and disheveled
and, may, therefore, comb his hair in accordance with the
minimum acceptable standards of social living.

From these principles the following traditions derive:

1. When mourning for relatives other than parents,
haircuts are not permitted until the end of the 30-day
period, the *sheloshim*.

2. Optimally, those in mourning for a parent should
not cut their hair for 12 months. However, the law provides
for the principle of "social reproach." This means that those

in mourning for parents may cut their hair after the 30 days at the first instance of even mild reproach or criticism by friends or neighbors. Immediately after this social reproach, the mourner is permitted to take a haircut. He may not do so before the thirtieth day after interment, even if he is reproached.

This reproach does not have to be articulated. If the length of the hair is so marked that one may be characterized as an eccentric, he is permitted to take a haircut.

3. A festival occurring after *shiva*, but during *sheloshim*, which ordinarily cancels the remainder of *sheloshim*, allows one mourning for relatives other than parents to take a haircut prior to the onset of the holiday, toward evening. On Passover this should be done before noon.

For mourners of parents, the festival before the end of *sheloshim* does not suspend the prohibition of taking a haircut. However, after the *sheloshim*, the festival takes the place of social reproach and allows the mourner to take the haircut toward evening before the onset of the holiday.

4. The onset of the Sabbath is not reason for the mourner to take a haircut.

5. The female mourner may set her hair and, if absolutely necessary, cut it. The sages were more lenient with regard to the woman's appearance because of her role as a fiancée or bride or wife. However, she should not take advantage of this permissiveness. The coloring and cutting of hair at the beautician's before the thirtieth day does not appear to be sufficiently important to exempt her from the laws of mourning. The washing and setting of hair at the beautician's, however, is permitted after *shiva*.

6. If the mourner is a political figure and must make an important appearance during the 30 days, he should consult his rabbi regarding the advisability of cutting his hair. Likewise, one who is compelled to appear in court, or before a distinguished gentile body, or before important business leaders who do not understand Jewish law, and his unkempt appearance would seriously damage his cause

or his business, should request rabbinic advice regarding his taking a haircut.

7. The moustache may be trimmed after *shiva* if its growth interferes with eating in any way.

8. Hair combing is entirely permissible during *shiva*, both for women and men. Neatness, as cleanliness, should not be ignored during *shiva*. It is entirely in keeping with the dignity of the deceased to honor him through the observance of the law, and also by a display of respectability and neat appearance despite the fact that he is in mourning and is not clean-shaven.

Shaving

Shaving follows the laws of haircutting: Theoretically, for relatives other than parents, shaving is permissible only after 30 days, and for parents, not until the mourner experiences the social reproach *after* the *sheloshim*. However, it should be realized that this law obtained in a predominantly beard-wearing society. In the modern, western world, where the clean-shaven face is standard, the estimated time for social reproach in regard to shaving can hardly be longer than a few weeks. After this time the excessive growth would surely cause the mourner anguish and shaving would be in order.

There is, however, less permissiveness to shave because of an appearance before a group of knowledgeable and observant Jewish people. So, too, if the mourner attends the circumcision of his son, there is no reason to violate the mourning practice of haircutting or shaving.

1. The occurrence of a festival after *shiva*, before the *sheloshim*, would permit the mourner for relatives, other than parents, to shave before the onset of the festival.

2. Even a mourner for parents, if he must represent the Jewish community in some endeavor, as was noted in the previous section on haircutting, may shave.

3. A groom, on the day of his wedding, may shave.

4. If the hair growth causes or aggravates a skin condition, the mourner may shave.

Nail Trimming

The male mourner may not trim his nails with scissors or nailfile during the *sheloshim*. However, if nail trimming is performed in a manner not normally used, such as the tearing of nails by hand, they may be torn even during *shiva*.

The female mourner who requires the trimming of her nails, such as for ritual immersion, or if they have grown to abnormal length, should preferably have her manicurist trim them after *shiva*. If she prefers to do them herself, she may do so, using file or scissors or other instruments.

Laundering and New Garments

The principle of avoiding pleasure during mourning also applies to the prohibition of laundering, or wearing freshly-laundered clothes during *shiva* and *sheloshim*. The mourner must deny himself certain pleasures while continuing to exercise normal standards of hygienic care and personal dignity.

One of the quiet, daily delights is the donning of laundered and pressed clothes. It is a feeling of refreshing newness that prepares one for the toil of the day. Being properly and carefully dressed creates a healthy frame of mind. Carlyle, the French essayist, maintained that the first impulse of man from ancient times is *"putz,"* ornamentation or dressing-up. Thus, the universal practice of dressing up for the Sabbath.

This spirit of newness and the fresh start is contrary to the mental attitude of the mourner. His mind is gripped by the "end of days," and times gone by. The mourner looks not forward, but backward to the past, one portion of which has just been closed shut. It is a past lived with one very close to him, with whom he was emotionally intertwined, who is now deceased. The days of mourning are filled with review, not with plans; with a relationship ended, not a new beginning; an era terminated without any recommencement in sight. In such a mood, the newly-pressed shirt is out of place. New clothes are a contradiction of the inner spirit.

While washed and tailored clothes for the mourning occasion surely may not be worn, the wearing of clean clothes is mandatory. If the only clothes available are soiled, they must be washed, and may then be worn. Tradition, thus, permits the mourner to wear freshly-washed garments for cleanliness only, but not for pleasure.

Laundering

Two laws are involved in the laundering of clothes during *shiva:*

1. The mourner may not wash clothes, even if only to soak them in plain water, or even in preparation for wearing them the week after, as this is considered "work" and prohibited during the *shiva.* The only exception is the case of an infant's clothes, when no one else is available to do them.

2. The mourner may not wear freshly-laundered clothes that have been washed either by someone else during *shiva,* or even before the demise. Thus:

   a. The mourner is not permitted to wear freshly-laundered or freshly-pressed clothes during the days of *shiva.* He should wear clean clothes that were worn to the funeral, or at any time previously, but by no means clothes that are soiled.

   b. If the clothing becomes soiled, he should wash the spot, and if that proves difficult he should change the garment.

   c. Shirts and blouses, trousers, underclothes, socks or stockings, or other garments that touch the body and are liable to absorb sweat and bodily odor, may be changed when necessary, even during *shiva*.

d. Handkerchiefs and bedsheets follow the law of underclothing referred to above. A freshly-washed tablecloth may be used for the Sabbath, but not for weekdays.

e. In honor of the Sabbath, a freshly-washed shirt and simple Sabbath outer garments may be worn. Undergarments, however, should not be changed on the Sabbath unless they are not clean. Publicly, the mourner dresses up for the Sabbath. Inwardly, he remains in mourning, even on the Sabbath.

f. New clothes may not be worn during *shiva*, even on the Sabbath.

g. After *shiva*, until *sheloshim*, the mourner may wash his clothes (without detergents) and press them. If a mourner wishes to wear new garments, he should have someone wear these particular articles of clothing for a short while so that they will no longer be considered new. Underclothes may be worn by the mourner without the above restrictions.

New Clothes

1. During *sheloshim* one may not wear new clothes, even if they are dyed, thus changing their original color.

2. Even mourners for relatives other than parents may not wear new clothes until after *sheloshim*. Exceptions may be made under certain circumstances which can be evaluated by a rabbi.

3. Technically, mourners for parents may don new clothes after *sheloshim*. However, common Jewish usage has urged them not to buy new clothes during the entire year. Therefore, if the mourner finds it *necessary* to buy

clothes, or if there has been a demonstration of social reproach (friends urging a change of wardrobe), or if a festival is approaching, the mourner may purchase new clothes. In this case, however, as in the case of mourners for relatives other than parents in the midst of *sheloshim*, one should have the new garment worn for a short while by a friend or relative.

Marital Relations

The principle of avoiding pleasure during mourning includes the act of sexual union during the observance of *shiva*. However, unlike the prohibition of cohabitation during the menstrual period and the seven days of purification which follow, when husband and wife must remain entirely separated according to Jewish law, the traditions of mourning prohibit only intercourse, but not other forms of intimacy and affection.

On the Sabbath, even while demonstrative public mourning practices are suspended, the prohibition of marital relations remains in force.

The prohibition holds also for festivals, even in the case of death occurring during the festival, when *shiva* does not begin until after termination of the holiday. Sexual congress is not permitted in that case from the time of death through the end of *shiva*, despite the fact that actual *shiva* begins later.

This law is based on the principle that on the Sabbath or holy days only *public* mourning practices, such as the wearing of shoes and the rent garment, are not permitted; the prohibition of *intimate* practices, such as marital relations, is, nevertheless, continued at all times. The joyous nature of the holy days does not alter the terrible shock of death which has struck in the soul of the mourner, although it requires of all Jews the face and the posture of spiritual delight in the eternal partnership with God, which the Sabbath celebrates.

Study of Torah

The study of Torah is not permitted during *shiva*, for it is considered a source of profound delight. As the Bible itself expresses it, "The laws of God are righteous and rejoice the heart." It becomes not only a source of joy, but a means of distraction to the mourner sunk in despair. Such enjoyment, even from a holy source such as Torah study, is prohibited during the initial mourning period. Thus, while the bereaved may not study the Bible and the Prophets, the Talmud and the Midrash, he may read the book of *Job*, the story of the classic mourner. He may also read the poetry of anguish, the book of *Lamentations* (that is read on the ninth of Av, when we commemorate the Temple's destruction), and also parts of Jeremiah that foretell doom. He may also read the laws of mourning and study books on ethical behavior.

However (and this is so very characteristic of the Jewish tradition of Torah learning), he should not study these in depth, for he may discover new understanding or glean new insights into the complex byways of talmudic logic, and this would bring him the sublime joy so well-known to those who have experienced the deep pleasures of scholarship.

An interesting exception to this law is cited in the Jerusalem Talmud which says that one who has an unquenchable desire to study may do so. But, the question is posed: The purpose of the prohibition is to deny the mourner the delight of learning which this man, who yearns for such study, will surely derive; should it certainly not be prohibited? The answer offered is that the exception is made for this man as it is made for one who might become ill from observing the laws of mourning and who is, therefore, exempt from these laws! The law forbids pleasure; it does not command pain. The Talmud recognized that it is entirely possible that the one who so deeply yearns to study may become physically ill when he is prevented from doing so. In such a case, it ruled, he is permitted to study.

Further, the question arose as to whether a scholar who finds a new interpretation, and is excited with his discovery, may put it into writing. The simple reply must be that writing is not a permissible form of work to the mourner, just as it is not permissible *chol ha'moed,* the intermediary days of Passover and Succot. However, in regard to writing down new insights into Torah, it is equated with a man who, normally forbidden to go to business during *shiva,* is permitted to do so if he will otherwise experience an irretrievable financial loss. By being prohibited from writing, the idea may be forgotten, and it is, therefore, considered an irretrievable loss.

"How goodly are thy tents, O Jacob, thy study halls, O Israel!" We should be constantly amazed at the rich tradition to which we are heir, and chagrined by its gross neglect in our times. Can such glorification of the mind and soul be found on any page of world literature? Are there Boswells sufficient to chronicle the biographies of so many poverty-stricken laborers who yearned for study? Are there historians wise enough to analyze the magnificent consolation the Torah brought to a people willing to endure any deprivation, even death itself, for its sake?

From the laws of mourning we catch a glimpse into the eternal law of Jewish life—the love of Torah.

May the mourner teach, if that is his profession? As indicated above, one who is needed to teach a group of people Torah, when there is no one to replace him, may continue to teach during *shiva.* Likewise, one may teach youngsters, if there is no other qualified teacher available, even on the very first day of mourning.

It is not permitted to keep students from study, even if the mourning laws must be temporarily suspended. Also, one who is accustomed to teach his own children should not sacrifice seven days of Torah study, but continue to teach them during *shiva*. While the mourner may teach in such circumstances, he should do so in as inconspicuous a fashion as possible, and should make some noticeable change of style which, while perhaps insignificant in itself, will convey the fact that he is making an exception to the laws of mourning.

Comforting the Bereaved
נחום אבלים

A sacred obligation devolves upon every Jew to comfort the mourners, whether he is related to them or not, and whether he was a close friend or a passing acquaintance. In Judaism, exercising compassion by paying a condolence call is a *mitzvah*, considered by some of our greatest scholars to be biblically ordained. The Bible records that God visited Isaac: "And it came to pass after the death of Abraham, that God blessed Isaac, his son" (Genesis 25:11). The sages infer from this verse that God Himself, as it were, was comforting the bereaved Isaac.

It is a man's duty to imitate God: as God comforts the bereaved, so man must do likewise. Consolation is considered a God-like action which all the children of Israel must perform. When, following the destruction of Jerusalem and the decimation of the Jewish people, Isaiah proclaimed God's message: "Comfort ye, comfort ye my people" (Isaiah 40:1), it indicated not merely a recommendation from on high, but a specific mandate obliging the prophet to bring consolation to his people.

The fundamental purpose of the condolence call during *shiva* is to relieve the mourner of the intolerable burden of intense loneliness. At no other time is a human being more in need of such comradeship. *Avelut* means withdrawal, the personal and physical retreat from social commerce and the concern for others. It is the loss that he alone has suffered. All the traditions of mourning express this troubled loneliness in diverse ways, covering the spectrum of social life—from the excessive growing of hair in indifference to social custom, to the avoidance of greetings, the minimum social courtesy.

Recognizing this state of mind, the visitor comes to the house of mourning, silently, to join the bereaved in his loneliness, sorrowfully to sit alongside him, to think his thoughts and to linger on his loss. The warmth of such human presence is inestimable. Practiced as the tradition prescribes it, true consolation is the distillation of empathy. The sum effect of the visitation of many friends and relatives, some long forgotten, others members of a community who may rarely have paid the mourner any attention at all, is the softening of loneliness, the relief of the heavy burden of internalized despair, and the affirmation that the world-at-large is not a hateful and angry place, but a warm and friendly one. It is a beckoning with open arms for the mourner to return to society. Comforting the mourners, says Maimonides, is *gemillat chasadim*, a genuine kindness to both the dead and the living.

The purpose of the condolence call is not to convince the mourner of anything at all. This is the time for accompanying him on his very own path, not for argumentation or debate. It is the time for the contemplation of disaster. While the mourner himself may wish to discuss it, it is not the prime purpose of this visit to relieve his fears for the future or his guilt for the past. It is not proper, say the sages (indeed it borders on sacrilege), to impress upon the mourner the inevitability of death, as though to doubt the true purpose and justice of a decree that God issued, but would change if only He were free to do so. It is not seemly, perhaps it is even entirely useless, to assure the mourner that others have suffered similar tragedies, or worse fates, as though by right he should be less despairing. "It could have been worse," is cold consolation. This is a time for subjectivity, for an intensely personal evaluation of life, and the mourners should not be deprived of even this indulgence. Some of the importuning of visitors that "life must go on," and that the mourner should be "thankful that worse did not occur," are well-meaning, but hollow and sometimes annoying expressions.

The strategy of true compassion is *presence* and *silence,* the eloquence of human closeness. Sad, muttered words are clumsy openers of the heart compared with the whisper of soft eyes. The comradeship demonstrated by the expression on the face speaks volumes that the ancient bards could not match with mere words, no matter how beautiful. It fulfills at once the mourner's desperate need for both *companion-ship* and *privacy.* It was, therefore, an old custom, unfortunately lost to our generations, for visitors to sit silently on the earth with, and like, the mourner. How magnificent an expression of compassion!

The first principle of comforting the mourners, found in the major codes of Jewish law, is that one should remain silent and allow the mourner to speak first. In many Jewish communities in olden days, the congregants accompanied the mourner as he walked home from synagogue on the Sabbath or holiday, and there they sat with him. How warm the mere physical presence of other human beings! How it relieves the sharp sting of tragedy! The classic mourner, Job, visited by three friends, sat with them for seven days and none uttered a sound. Ecclesiastes wisely notes that there "is a time to keep silent and a time to speak." The Midrash (Kohelet Rabbah on 3:5) records that the wife of Rabbi Mana died. His colleague, Rabbi Abin, came to pay a condolence call. Asked Rabbi Mana, "Are there any words of Torah you would like to offer us in our time of grief?" Rabbi Abin replied, "At times like this the Torah takes refuge in silence!"

It is in this spirit that Maimonides cautions visitors that they not speak overly much as, somehow, words have the tendency to generate a spirit of frivolity so contrary to the spirit of *shiva.* Indeed, the Talmud notes this when it remarks perceptively, "True reward comes to one who is silent in the house of mourning, and voluble in the wedding hall!"

It is true, of course, that it is exceedingly difficult to comfort with warmth and hope and compassion, while sitting relatively silent. Perhaps, that is the reason for the parting phrase of comfort, "May God comfort you among the other mourners of Zion and Jerusalem." For only God can truly comfort, even as He consoled Isaac after his father Abraham's death, and as He has comforted, through the ages, the other mourners of Zion after the tragic destruction of the ancient Temple, and has comforted the exiled, and those who suffered in pogroms and crusades. If the visitor feels uncomfortable in the tension of silence, he may of course converse with the mourner, but—little and wisely.

When to Pay the Shiva Call

1. One may visit the mourner by day or by night.

2. If possible, it should be delayed until the third day after interment. This advice is given because the mourner's wound is fresh, and the deceased is constantly in his mind. However, if for some reason this cannot be arranged, the visit may be made even on the very first day. Comforting the bereaved actually begins at the cemetery when the mourners leave the grave passing through parallel rows of friends and relatives.

3. Visitors do not customarily pay condolence calls on the Sabbath or holidays, as these are days when one should not mourn publicly. However, the mourner may receive company and condolences on these days. There may be *shiva* visitation on *chol ha'Moed,* Rosh Chodesh, Purim and Hanukkah.

4. If one did not visit during *shiva,* he should express condolences anytime during the 12 months upon meeting those bereaved of parents, and during the first 30 days for those bereaved of other relatives.

5. Condolence calls may be paid mourners who have returned to business during *shiva* (if it was religiously permissible to do so) the same as to other mourners. If the mourner returned to work in violation of the tradition, he need not be visited. He has denied himself the solace of religious consolation.

Etiquette at the House of Mourning

1. There should be no greeting, either of welcome or farewell. Details of this law may be found above.

2. It is not customary to speak until the mourner does. One should not speak too much and monopolize the discussion. Conversation in the house of *shiva* should be in the nature of response to the mourner.

There is really no need in these pages to chastise those who believe that joking and humorous remarks or frivolous tales will relieve the bitterness of the mourner's feelings. This all-too-prevalent type of "socializing" in the house of mourning is a constant reminder that coarse souls know no bounds.

The purpose of the visitor's presence and speech during the *shiva* should not be designed to distract the bereaved. It is altogether fitting, and entirely proper, to speak of the deceased, his qualities, his hopes, and his loved ones. Far from recalling the anguish which surely has not been forgotten, it gives the bereaved the opportunity to reminisce and to express his grief aloud. Psychologists assure us that the mourner very often desires to speak of his loss. Dr. Eric Lindemann, in his *Symptomatology and Management of Acute Grief,* says: "There is no retardation of action and speech; quite to the contrary there is a push of speech, especially when talking of the deceased." Both the mourner's words and his tears should not be avoided or suppressed. It is analogous to the world of nature, where animals frequently use these means to heal themselves; they recover by licking their wounds.

3. One should not urge the mourner to "sit" on the *shiva* stool, as this innocent remark may imply to the mourner that he "remain" in grief. It may possibly cause resentment.

4. The visitor should, by all means, be sensitive to the mourner's feelings. There is a time for all things, the Bible tells us, and surely there is a time for *leaving* the house of the bereaved. Visits should never be unduly prolonged, mistakenly believing that one's presence brings an unusual degree of relief.

5. Upon leaving, the visitor should recite the phrase in Hebrew or in English or both: *Hamakom yenachem et'chem b'toch she'ar avelai Tziyon Vi'yerushalayim.* (The varied Hebrew text for the second person, masculine and feminine, singular and plural, is found in an earlier section.) "May God comfort you among the other mourners of Zion and Jerusalem."

Behavior During the Condolence Call

1. Greetings should not be answered during the first three days. (See chapter on Greetings and Gifts, above.)

2. The mourner should sit when people comfort him as they are about to leave. However, especially during prolonged visits, he need not sit all the time, but may stand and walk as he desires.

3. The mourner need not rise before any guest, no matter what his stature.

4. At mealtime, in the company of guests, the mourner should sit at the head of the table on a lower stool.

Psychological Symptoms of Grief

For a clearer and deeper understanding of the dynamics of grief, the visitor should be familiar with the results of a psychological study of bereavement. Below is the Lindemann report excerpted and abbreviated by Geoffrey Gorer in his book, *Death, Grief and Mourning*. Dr. Lindemann describes here the symptomatology of normal grief.

> The picture shown by persons in acute grief is remarkably uniform. Common to all is the following syndrome: sensations of somatic distress occurring in waves lasting from 20 minutes to an hour at a time, a feeling of tightness in the throat, choking with shortness of breath, need for sighing, and an intense subjective distress described as tension or mental pain. The patient soon learns that these waves of discomfort can be precipitated by visits, by mention of the deceased, and by receiving sympathy. There is a tendency to avoid the syndrome at any cost, to refuse visits lest they should precipitate the reaction, and to keep deliberately from thought all references to the deceased.

> Another strong preoccupation is with feelings of guilt. The bereaved searches the time before the death for evidence of failure to do right by the lost one. He accuses himself of negligence and exaggerates minor omissions.

> In addition, there is often a disconcerting loss of warmth in relationship to other people, a tendency to respond with irritation and anger, a wish not to be bothered by others at a time when friends and relatives make a special effort to keep up friendly relationships.

> These feelings of hostility, surprising and quite inexplicable to the patients, disturbed them and were again often taken as signs of approaching insanity. Great efforts are made to handle them, and the result is often a formalized, stiff manner of social interaction.

> The activity throughout the day of the severely bereaved person shows remarkable change. There is no retardation of action and speech; quite to the contrary there is a push of speech, especially when talking about

the deceased. There is restlessness, inability to sit still, moving about in an aimless fashion, continually searching for something to do. There is, however, at the same time, a painful lack of capacity to initiate and maintain organized patterns of activity. What is done is done with lack of zest, as though one were going through the motions. The bereaved clings to the daily routine of prescribed activities; but these activities do not proceed in the automatic self-sustaining fashion which characterizes normal work but have to be carried on with effort, as though each fragment of the activity became a special task. The bereaved is surprised to find how large a part of this customary activity was done in some meaningful relationship to the deceased and has now lost its significance. Especially the habits of social interaction—meeting friends, making conversation, sharing enterprises with others, seem to have been lost.

These five points: 1) somatic distress, 2) preoccupation with the image of the deceased, 3) guilt, 4) hostile reactions, and 5) loss of patterns of conduct, seem to be pathognomic of grief. There may be added a sixth characteristic, shown by patients who border on pathological reactions . . . this is the appearance of traits of the deceased in the behavior of the bereaved.

The duration of a grief reaction seems to depend upon the success with which a person does the grief work, namely emancipation from the bondage of the deceased, readjustment to the environment in which the deceased is missing, and the formation of new relationships. One of the big obstacles to this work seems to be the fact that many patients try to avoid the intense distress connected with the grief experience and to avoid the expression of emotion necessary for it. The men victims after the Cocoanut Grove fire appeared in early psychiatric interviews to be in a state of tension with tightened facial musculature, unable to relax for fear they might "break down." It required considerable persuasion to yield to the grief process, before they were willing to accept the discomfort of bereavement.

End of Shiva

It was noted above that just as at the commencement of *shiva*, the tradition considers a portion of the day as a full day, so at its conclusion the *shiva* terminates in the morning, although it is only a small portion of the seventh day. Thus, if interment took place on Tuesday before dark, *shiva* ends on Monday morning. The mourner must wait, however, until after the morning service. He then receives consolation and arises.

If interment took place on Sunday, the *shiva* technically should end on the Sabbath morning. So, indeed, the private observances of mourning terminate on the Sabbath morning after services. Thus, too, the mourner should not accept a Torah honor until the late afternoon Sabbath service. However, the public observances of *shiva* end on Friday, prior to the onset of the Sabbath. For details as to exactly when it ends see the section of "The Sabbath During *Shiva* and *Sheloshim*," above.

Many follow the custom of having all mourners walk together, for a short distance. This symbolizes the return to the society from which the *avel* has withdrawn.

Sheloshim Observances
שלשים

The *sheloshim*, or 30-day period, constitutes the full mourning for all relatives other than father and mother. Mourning for those bereaved of their parents terminates at the end of 12 Hebrew months.

The counting of *sheloshim* follows the principles used in counting *shiva,* as detailed above.

1. A portion of a day is equal to the full day. Thus, *sheloshim* ends after the synagogue service on the morning of the thirtieth day.
2. The period technically commences after interment, not after death. Thus, for example, if burial took place on Monday afternoon, *sheloshim* ends four weeks later on Tuesday morning.
3. Unlike *shiva,* a festival does not cancel the *sheloshim* period unless the observance of *shiva* had already ended prior to the onset of the holiday.

Following is a brief review of the *sheloshim* observances. (For details see the pertinent chapters above.)

1. The following practices are observed only during *shiva,* and are not practiced during *sheloshim:*
   a. Sitting on a low stool
   b. Remaining indoors
   c. Wearing of non-leather shoes
   d. Abstention from marital relations
   e. Prohibition of work
   f. Prohibition of studying Torah

2. The following prohibitions continue in force and are to be observed during *shiva* and during *sheloshim* under normal circumstances:
   a. Haircutting, shaving, nailcutting, bathing, and the wearing of new clothes or newly laundered clothes
   b. Getting married
   c. Attending parties
   d. Greetings may be extended by the mourner, but others should not inquire after his *"shalom"* as, obviously, he is not experiencing peace. So gifts, including Purim gifts, are not to be sent to the mourner. On Purim, however, the mourner is obligated to send gifts to others, as prescribed by tradition.

Purim and Hanukkah Observances

Purim

Purim does not cancel *shiva*. There is a de-emphasis of public mourning as on the Sabbath (some hold there is no mourning at all), but private mourning must be observed. Thus, sitting on the low stool and the removal of regular shoes are not required on Purim. Similarly, Purim observances, such as the festival meal (the meat and wine, but without the rejoicing) and the sending of gifts—*mishlo'ach manot*—are obligatory upon the mourner as upon all Jews. Also the mourner should attend the Megillah reading at the synagogue, and if he is the only person capable of reading it publicly, he is obliged to do so. Wherever possible, though, the mourner during *shiva* should not read publicly or lead services on Purim. Shushan Purim, celebrated the day following Purim, should be observed as Purim proper only when the mourner has always observed it as festive day.

Hanukkah

Hanukkah, too, does not cancel *shiva*. Indeed, while important religious authorities held that there is no mourning on Purim, and surely no public mourning, Hanukkah provides no such relief, and all mourning observances must be kept. Hanukkah festival observances, such as the kindling of candles, is obligatory; and the mourner, but not the *onen*, should recite all three blessings including *shehecheyanu*, the prayer to God for sustaining us in life "unto this time." However, he should not kindle the menorah in behalf of the congregation, and in so doing publicly proclaim these words, since the joy it naturally evokes is not in harmony with this period of distress in his life. The mourner does not recite the Hallel prayer in the house of *shiva* because these are psalms of joy. He should, however, absent himself briefly so that the other worshippers may recite it as required. In the synagogue proper, the mourner should recite the Hallel. Other Hanukkah procedures are discussed elsewhere in this book.

4✧ Year-long Mourning Observances

Counting the Twelve Months

THE 12-MONTH PERIOD concludes the full mourning period for those who are bereaved of their parents just as the thirty days concludes the mourning for other relatives. It should be noted that the counting of the 12 months does *not* follow the rules used in the counting of *shiva* and *sheloshim*.

Following are the differences:

1. When counting the 12 months we do not follow the principle that a portion of the day is equal to a full day and that, therefore, a portion of a month is equal to a full month. We must count 12 full months.

2. The counting of the 12 months begins from the day of *death*, *not* as in counting *shiva*, from the day of interment. Thus, one who died on the first day of the Hebrew month of Tevet is mourned until the end of the first day of Tevet of the following year. If death occurred on the second day, he is mourned through the second day of the next year, and so on.

3. The duration of mourning observances is not one

147

year, but 12 months. Thus, on leap year, when the Hebrew calendar adds one full month, called Adar Sheni, only 12 months are observed, but not the thirteenth that is added to make the leap year. This applies to all mourning observances except Kaddish, which is recited only 11 months, as will be described in the next chapter.

Survey of Observances

Following is a brief survey of the observances of the 12-month period:

1. Haircutting, technically prohibited for 12 months, is permitted upon the occasion of social reproach after the *sheloshim*, as indicated above.

2. Similarly, the wearing of new clothes is permitted upon "social reproach" after the *sheloshim*, and after being worn for a brief period of time by others, although technically it is a twelve-month observance.

3. The mourner should change his usual seat in the synagogue at prayer. On the Sabbath he may sit in his usual place.

4. The mourner should, in general, pay closer attention to educational, charitable and religious matters for these, say the sages, are most eloquent tributes to the teachings of the deceased parent. Thus, it is customary for the mourner to study a portion of the Torah before or after daily services. He should also learn to lead all or part of the congregational services.

5. Regulations pertaining to the recital of Kaddish, and participation in joyous celebrations, will be treated in the following chapters.

THE KADDISH
Transliteration and Translation
קדיש

יִתְגַּדַּל וְיִתְקַדַּשׁ שְׁמֵהּ רַבָּא בְּעָלְמָא דִי בְרָא כִרְעוּתֵהּ,
וְיַמְלִיךְ מַלְכוּתֵהּ בְּחַיֵּיכוֹן וּבְיוֹמֵיכוֹן וּבְחַיֵּי דְכָל בֵּית יִשְׂרָאֵל,
בַּעֲגָלָא וּבִזְמַן קָרִיב, וְאִמְרוּ אָמֵן.

יְהֵא שְׁמֵהּ רַבָּא מְבָרַךְ לְעָלַם וּלְעָלְמֵי עָלְמַיָּא.

יִתְבָּרַךְ וְיִשְׁתַּבַּח, וְיִתְפָּאַר וְיִתְרוֹמַם, וְיִתְנַשֵּׂא וְיִתְהַדָּר,
וְיִתְעַלֶּה וְיִתְהַלַּל שְׁמֵהּ דְּקֻדְשָׁא, בְּרִיךְ הוּא, לְעֵלָּא מִן כָּל
בִּרְכָתָא וְשִׁירָתָא, תֻּשְׁבְּחָתָא וְנֶחֱמָתָא, דַּאֲמִירָן בְּעָלְמָא,
וְאִמְרוּ אָמֵן.

יְהֵא שְׁלָמָא רַבָּא מִן שְׁמַיָּא, וְחַיִּים, עָלֵינוּ וְעַל כָּל יִשְׂרָאֵל,
וְאִמְרוּ אָמֵן.

עֹשֶׂה שָׁלוֹם בִּמְרוֹמָיו, הוּא יַעֲשֶׂה שָׁלוֹם עָלֵינוּ וְעַל כָּל
יִשְׂרָאֵל, וְאִמְרוּ אָמֵן.

Mourner: *Yisgadal v'yiskadash shmai raba.* Magnified and sanctified be His great name.

Cong: Amen.

Mourner: *B'olmo deev'ro chir'usai,* In this world which He has created in accordance with His will, *v'yamlich malchusai, b'chayechon u'vyomechon,* may He establish his kingdom during your lifetime, *u'vchayai d'chol bais Yisroel,* and during the life of all the House of Israel, *ba'agolah u'vizman koriv, v'imru amen.* Speedily, and let us say, Amen.

Mourner: *Y'hai shmai rabah m'varach, l'olam u'lalmey olmaya!* Let His great name be blessed for ever and to all eternity!

Cong: (Repeats above verse.)

Mourner: *Yisborach v'yishtabach v'yispa-er v'yisromam;* Blessed, praised, glorified and exalted; *v'yisnasai v'yishadar v'yisaleh v'yis-halal,* extolled, honored, magnified and lauded, *shemei d'Kudsha, b'rich Hu.* Be the name of the Holy one, blessed be He.

Cong: *B'rich Hu.* Blessed be He.

Mourner: *L'aila min kol birchasa v'shirasa, tushbechasa v'nechamasa,* He is greater than all blessings, hymns, praises and consolations, *da'amiron b'olmo; v'imru, Amen.* Which can be uttered in this world; and let us say Amen.

Cong: Amen.

Mourner: *Y'hai shlama raba min shmaya,* May abundant peace from heaven descend upon us, *v'chayim alenu v'al kol Yisroel; v'imru amen.* And may life be renewed for us and for all Israel; and let us say, Amen.

Cong: Amen.

Mourner: *Oseh shalom bimeromav, Hu ya'aseh shalom,* He who makes peace in the heavens, may He make peace, *alenu v'al Kol yisroel; v'imru amen.* For us and for all Israel; and let us say, Amen.

Cong: Amen.

History of Kaddish

The Kaddish is a vigorous declaration of faith. It is one of the most beautiful, deeply-significant and spiritually-moving prayers in the Jewish liturgy. It is an ancient Aramaic prose-poem, a litany whose word-music, strong rhythms, stirring sounds, and alternating responses of leader and congregation, cast sheer hypnotic power over the listeners. It has well been noted that the Kaddish is the echo of Job in the prayerbook: "Though He slay me, yet will I trust in Him." It is a call to God from the depths of catastrophe, exalting His name and praising Him, despite the realization that He has just wrenched a human being from life. Like the *Kol Nidre* prayer of the Day of Atonement, the significance of Kaddish is usually taken for

granted. It is a response from the sub-vaults of the soul—
almost a primitive, mesmerized response to the sacred
demand to sanctify Almighty God. Its passionate recitation
has inspired a "healthy, cheerful manliness" in a time of
deep sorrow.

The Kaddish appears in the traditional service no less
than 13 times. It is recited at the conclusion of all the
major prayers and at the conclusion of the service. It also
serves as a transition recital at every minor turning-point
in the service. It is recited after a Talmud study period,
at the cemetery after burial, at services during the year of
mourning, and at every *yahrzeit*. These sages said that one
who recites the Kaddish with all his inner power and conviction will merit the abolition of any severe Divine decree
directed against him. In fact, they contended that the whole
world itself, as it were, is maintained because of its recital,
and that it redeems the deceased, specifically from perdition.

The Kaddish was considered so vital to the religious
life of the Jew that it was recited in Aramaic, the spoken
tongue of the Jewish masses in ancient times, so that every
individual would understand it. In testimony to its continuing power, it is recited in that language to this very
day. Another reason suggested for the use of the common
Aramaic language is that it functioned as an educational
device. It taught that the daily, secular life must be infused
and interpenetrated by holiness, the epitome of which is
expressed in the Kaddish. Inevitably, the Kaddish became
so very popular that the sages actually had to forewarn
the people lest they come to rely on it as on some magical
power, and lest they increase the number of recitations,
possibly leading to the undesirable consequence that a
prayer for the dead might become central to the worship
service.

For all its majesty and grandeur and importance, the
origins of the Kaddish are beclouded in the obscurity of
our ancient religious tradition. From the sparse, brief, yet
emphatic, references to the Kaddish in the Talmud, it is

evident that the recitation of the essence of the Kaddish:
Yehai shmai rabbah, "May His great name be blessed"—
was so well-established a custom that its origin and significance were simply taken for granted. It is probable
that the Kaddish was formulated after the destruction of
the first Temple and was recited primarily after a lecture
or discourse on a Torah theme. It then slipped easily into
the worship service into which its themes and responses
fitted admirably.

There arose five variations of the basic Kaddish which
embodied the *yehai shmai rabbah,* the central core of every
Kaddish.

1. The abbreviated form, called the "Half Kaddish," is
used as a transitional theme following minor portions of
the service.

2. The "Complete Kaddish" is used to terminate major
parts of the service and, thus, includes the prayer, *titkabel,*
asking God to accept the heartfelt prayers just uttered.

3. The "Rabbi's Kaddish" is used as an epilogue to the
study of rabbinic literature, and contains the rubric *al
Yisrael,* a prayer for the welfare of students of Torah—
and of all Israel—in the hope that they may devote themselves uninterruptedly to their sacred tasks.

Until this point in its history the Kaddish was considered highly important, but its significance was appreciated only by scholars and students who understood the
deeper meaning of the prayers. In the tractate *Soferim,*
an early medieval *geonic* document, we are told that it
soon came to be used as a solemn recitation at the end of
the *shiva* period, when mourning the death of a scholar.
The Kaddish began to ride the crest of popularity when, in
order to avoid embarrassing distinctions between scholar
and layman, it came to be used for all who died and by all,
especially youngsters, who did not know how to recite the
prayers or study the Oral Law. It then began to engage the

minds of all Jews, knowledgeable or illiterate, and it was recited at the closing of every Jewish grave.

4. Thus, a fourth form of Kaddish arose, the "Burial Kaddish," which adds one paragraph referring to the resurrection of the dead and the restoration of the Temple. (For transliteration of the Burial Kaddish, see below.) It thus became associated with the deepest emotions of man.

5. The service itself soon incorporated a fifth form of Kaddish, the "Mourner's Kaddish," which was recited for the first year after interment, making it the primary prayer for the Jewish bereaved of every age. While there remains nothing explicit in the Mourner's Kaddish that refers to the grave, or the dead, or to life after death, the recitation of the Kaddish was so well patterned to the mood of the mourner that it became a cherished part of the Jewish people, regardless of denominational attachment.

The Function of the Kaddish

The Mourner's Kaddish performs two pragmatic functions: 1) It blends in with the internal spirit of the mourner, imperceptibly healing his psychological wounds, and 2) it teaches the mourner vital and profound lessons about life and death, and the conquest of evil. It is therefore, no accident of spiritual history that the Kaddish has become so important to those stricken with grief, and that, in the course of time, it became the hallmark of bereavement.

The Kaddish as Consolation

As far back as ancient times, the Kaddish was associated, albeit indirectly, with consolation, *nechamah*. In the earliest source dealing with the Mourner's Kaddish we find that the leader of the service proceeded to the rear of the synagogue where the mourners were congregated, and publicly

comforted them with the mourner's blessing and the Kaddish. It should be noted that the Kaddish recitation coin-
cides, and is precisely coterminous, with the length of
time during which tradition enjoins the Jew to comfort
mourners bereaved of their parents, namely, 12 months.
(Only later did the tradition reduce this period to 11
months.)

In a spirit of consolation and surrender this beautiful
litany begins with the admission that the world that is
known only to Him, the Omniscient Creator of the universe,
remains mysterious and paradoxical to man. It ends with
an impassioned hope, expressed in the words of the friends
of Job as they sought to comfort him, *oseh shalom bimeromav*, that He who is sufficiently mighty to make peace
among the celestial bodies may also bring peace to all
mankind.

Finally, we pray to achieve, in the words of the Kaddish,
the *nechemata*, the consolation of all of the Jewish people,
not only for their dead, but for the destruction of their
ancient Temple and their holy city, Jerusalem. Indeed,
many rabbis maintain that the Kaddish finds its origin in
the prayer composed by the men of the Great Assembly,
specifically for the consolation of the population following
the destruction of the first Temple and their subsequent
exile. It is, in fact, in response to this historic tragedy
that Ezekiel first cries out the words from which tradition
has drawn the opening words of the Kaddish: "I have
exalted and sanctified My name and I have made it known
in the eyes of all the nations, and they shall know that I
am the Lord." The Master of all will bring His people
salvation.

Besides the *concepts* found in the Kaddish, the very
words offer implicit comfort. Because of the accentuation
and repetition of the positive thoughts of "life" and "peace,"
these values become impressed upon the bewildered, and
those with saddened hearts. It transfers, subliminally, the
fixed, inner gaze of the mourner from the departed to the

living, from crisis to peace, from despair to hope, from isolation to community.

Indeed, the very crucial moment when man's faith is most shaken, when very likely he feels rebellious against God for the death that has befallen him, he rises to recite the praises of the Creator: *Yisgadal v'yiskadash* . . ., magnified and sanctified be He who created the universe . . . All the laws of nature operate in accordance with His own will. Just at the time when man's focus is on the Kingdom of Heaven, the world of the dead, the destination of his beloved, the Kaddish quietly, and almost imperceptibly, transfers his gaze to God's kingdom on earth, among the living—*v'yamlich malchusai b'chayechon u'vyomechon*, "May He establish His kingdom during your lifetime and in your days." When man's vision is blurred with images of a breathless frame, with shrouds and coffin and grave, with the ultimate decay and decomposition of the human being, the Kaddish fills the mind of the mourner with "life" and "days" and "this world," by the constant, hypnotic repetition, morning and night, of the words *chayim* and *yamim* and *olam*. When the mourner experiences disorientation and disruption, a sense of agitation and conflict and guilt, the Kaddish mesmerizes him with thoughts of eternal rest and quiet, and emphasizes over and over again the peace that God made in the heavens, and the *shalom* that He brings to people on earth.

One other major technique of consolation in the Kaddish is the insistence, because it is a prayer of holiness, that it be recited only in public quorum, never privately. The recitation, usually made alongside other mourners, creates a fellowship of the bereaved in a time of profound loneliness and helplessness. It teaches, implicitly, that others have experienced similar pains; that death is a natural, if often untimely, end to all life; that the rhythm of man has followed the same beat since the days when Adam refused to eat from the Tree of Life.

The Kaddish is, thus, a comforting prayer, grandiose in

its spiritual conception, dramatic in its rhythms and word-music, and profound in its psychological insights.

When Mourners Console the Master

A great hasidic sage noted that the death of every one of God's creatures causes a gap in the armies of the exalted King. The Kaddish, he said, is recited in the hope that that gap will be filled. It was left to Israel's poet laureate, S. Y. Agnon, to interpret this with a beautiful analogy.

The King of Kings, Almighty God, is not like a human king. When a king of flesh and blood orders his armies into battle, he sees only the large effects, the massive logistics and the great goal. He does not know the individual men. They are not distinguishable one from the other. They are human machines that carry rifles, and perform a function. If he loses half a regiment, he sincerely regrets the mass death. But he mourns no individual human being.

Not so is the King of Kings. He is Master of the world, yet he cares for each individual life. Men are not machines or ciphers. They are human beings. When God's soldiers die He mourns, as it were, each man. When a man dies, His own Name is diminished, His own sanctity lessened. His Kingdom experiences a terrible vacancy. God suffers, as it were, just as the human mourner suffers.

When we recite the Kaddish, we offer God consolation for His loss. We say *yisgadal:* Thy name has been diminished; may it be magnified. *Yiskadash:* Thy sanctity has been lessened; may it be increased. *Yamlich malchusai:* Thy kingdom has suffered a sudden loss, may it reign eternally.

This astonishing interpretation of the Kaddish—which sees it as the mourner's attempt to offer consolation to the Master of all men—is itself a consolation to the bereaved. The knowledge that God cares for every man, and that He suffers in the loss of every one of His creatures made in His own image, is a source of warmth and comfort.

THE KADDISH AS EDUCATION

Beneath the surface, the Kaddish declaration expresses a thought basic to an understanding of the Jewish attitude towards life: the acceptance of seemingly undeserved pain and unreasonable tragedy in life as being the just—even if paradoxical—act of an all-wise God. The Kaddish prayer is, thus, found in ancient sources bracketed with the *tzidduk ha'din*, the prayer justifying God's edict. This prayer is recited at the moment of burial, and proclaims, "The Lord hath given and the Lord hath taken. May the name of the Lord be blessed."

The Kaddish echoes this theme: "May His great name be blessed for ever and ever." It is the spirit of recognition that Almighty God knows our innermost secrets; that He reliably and justly rewards and punishes us; that He knows what is best for mankind, and that all His doing is for the eventual benefit of the whole human race. It is only by virtue of this acceptance of death as the just and inexorable terminus of life that life can be lived to its fullest. It is only through the difficult, but necessary, acknowledgement that only the Creator of the universe understands the design of His creation, that we avoid becoming disabled by the dogged questioning of imponderables that can wear out our very existence. Thus do we recite in the words of the Kaddish, "Magnified and sanctified be His great name, in the world which He created according to His will." It is a world whose ways bypass our understanding and conform only with His will. How can our limited intellects fathom His exalted greatness or plumb the endless depths of the Divine mind? If tragedy strikes, if our families are beset by evil circumstances, we have faith that the just God has acted justly.

The Significance of Kaddish

A Reflection of Parental Esteem

The true function of the Kaddish goes even deeper. Beyond the psychological healing which it encourages, beyond educating the mourner to adjust to tragedy, is there not some mysterious influence, some wondrous power that affects so marvelously the soul of the mourner? How is the Kaddish related to mourning for parents?

Put simply: the Kaddish is a spiritual handclasp between the generations, one that connects two lifetimes. What better consolation is there for the mourner than the knowledge that the ideas and hopes and concerns and commitments of the deceased continue on in the life of his own family? The son's recitation of Kaddish represents a continuation of that life; it snatches the deepest worth of the individual from the cavernous jaws of death.

How does that happen? Jewish tradition recognizes the important influence of the father upon the son during the lifetime of the parent. The "merit of the Fathers" is a bold and important theme in rabbinic literature. It should be remembered that collectively, the Jew asks God for mercy in recognition of the righteous deeds of the patriarchs of old whose descendants we are. Tradition also recognizes that the sins of the parents—impure motives, ill-begotten wealth, purposeless living, and so on—may make themselves felt in the lives of the children for many generations. The child's psyche indelibly bears the imprint of the parent, whether we think it just or not. For all that, however, Jewish thought never considered the parent able to redeem an erring son by virtue of his own good deeds before God. Abraham could not save his wayward son, Ishmael. Isaac could not save his avaricious son, Esau.

Curiously, though, in the complicated calculus of the spirit, the reverse *is* possible! The deeds of the child *can* redeem the life of the parent, even after the parent's death!

It is a neat reversal, a "merit of the *children.*" The ethical, religious and social virtues of children place haloes on their parents. The Talmud declares, *bera mezakeh aba,* the *son* endows the *father.* Elsewhere, Rabbi Simeon bar Yohai says, *mah zar'o bachayim, af hu bachayim,* so long as his children live, so long does the parent live. They who leave worthy children do not die in spirit. Their mortal remains are interred in the earth, but their teachings remain among men.

While it is true that no individual can intervene with God in behalf of the life of another—neither parent for child, nor child for parent—a person may surely modify the significance of another person's life and grant it meaning and value. As the tree is judged by its fruit, and the artisan by his product, so a parent achieves personal significance by the moral success of his child. Of David, who had left a son worthy of himself, the Talmud refers to his death as he "slept," indicating the continuity of life. Of Joab, who had no son who could inherit his greatness, it says "he died," implying finality. The reflection of the child upon the parent is true in life, and it is true after death as well.

It is precisely in this regard that the Kaddish reaches its deepest value. The Kaddish serves as an epilogue to human life as, historically, it served as an epilogue to Torah study. Was that life marked primarily by goodness and dignity and nobility, or by shame and disgrace, by folly and weakness? In either case the Kaddish is effective. The sages state that the son's recitation of Kaddish confirms a parent's life of goodness on one hand, and effects repentance for a parent's life of sin, on the other.

Indeed, the rabbis declare that one is obligated to honor parents in death as well as in life. The Kaddish is the verbal demonstration of the deep and abiding honor that Jews were bidden to give parents since the day the fifth commandment was pronounced on Sinai. The very duration of the Kaddish recitation for parents is ample testimony to that respect. Because the wicked soul is said to undergo judgment for a full year, the child, in reverence for his parent, ends the Kaddish at eleven months, bearing witness, in one month's eloquent silence, to the goodness of those who bore him.

It is not the recitation of Kaddish alone that is emblematic of the parent's teaching, but also the fact that the mourner elicits a response of holiness from others, causing others to proclaim the greatness of God with him—which the sages term, *Kiddush Ha'Shem*, sanctification of the Name. The mourner announces, "Magnified and sanctified be His great name," and his neighbors respond, "Let His great name be blessed for all eternity." The mourner continues, "Blessed, praised, glorified, exalted; extolled, honored, magnified and lauded be the name of the Holy One, blessed be He," and the congregation replies, "Blessed be He." The Kaddish is, thus, a public sanctification of God's name. It is a self-contained, miniature service that achieves the heights of holiness, and it is this great spiritual triumph that reflects on the life of mother and father, and confirms the correctness of their teachings.

If, on the other hand, parents have strayed or sinned, and have desecrated the name of God (*chilul ha'Shem*), the Kaddish which is the sanctification of the name, (*kiddush ha-shem*), is considered true repentance for the deceased, and it redeems them from retribution. The Kaddish is not an explicit prayer for this redemption of parents, but its recital is an indication that good has come forth from them, and it is thus redemptive.

The fundamental and most frequently recorded incident regarding Kaddish is the mystical vision of the great sage, Rabbi Akiba. This incident is found in numerous sources: the Talmud, Midrash, Zohar, and other literary works, which attests to its wide acceptance and its popularity. Rabbi Akiba had a vision of a well-known sinner who had died and was condemned to intolerable punishment. The sinner informed the rabbi in the vision that only if his surviving son would recite the *Barchu* and Kaddish would he be redeemed. The rabbi proceeded to teach the youngster these prayers. When the youngster recited the Kaddish, he saved his father from perdition. The child endows the parent!

Moreover, this concept of the "merit of the children" is associated historically with the central core and response of the Kaddish. Tradition records a dialogue between the aged patriarch, Jacob, and his 12 sons. Jacob had been anxious about the future. He was not sure whether some of his children might not follow in the wicked footsteps of their uncle, Esau, or their great-uncle, Ishmael. Will one of his sons defect from the faith of his fathers? When in great consternation he confronted his sons, they declared together, "Hear O Israel (Jacob), the Lord our God, the Lord is one." With great relief at being assured of the merit of his children, Jacob responded in full gratitude, "Blessed be His name whose glorious Kingdom is forever and ever." This response has been enshrined as the verse immediately following the *Shema, Baruch shem k'vod mal-chuto le'olam va'ed.* In its Aramaic form it is almost identical with the central response of the Kaddish, *yehai shmai rabbah mevarach le'olam le'olmai olmaya,* "May His great name be blessed forever and ever." The Kaddish is a firm handclasp between the generations!

When death stalks our homes it brings an end to physical life. The current is cut off. That is all. But the spirit is mightier than the grave. The thoughts and emotions, the ideals and attitudes of the heirs attest to the undying influence of the dead. The recitation of the Kaddish is a public demonstration that a parent's life was not lived without furthering, in some sense, the cause of the good. It is no exaggeration to say that the spiritual handclasp of the Kaddish has helped assure the continued survival of the Jewish people, the Jewish religion, the synagogue and its major institutions.

Kaddish Observances

The Time for Kaddish

The Kaddish is recited at every service, morning and evening, Sabbath and holiday, on days of fasting and of rejoicing.

1. While Kaddish must be recited on these days, the mourner may not violate basic religious practices in order to say the Kaddish. Thus, if one is not within walking distance of a synagogue, and must ride in violation of the Sabbath, it is more valuable, in terms of both respect for the deceased and of keeping of the law, to pray at home, although the Kaddish will have to be omitted for lack of the necessary quorum. Indeed, some congregations do not permit the recitation of the mourner's Kaddish on Sabbaths and holidays precisely to discourage travelling to the synagogue for that purpose. Compared with the Sabbath, a foundation of Judaism, Kaddish is of lesser value. Respect for parents and concern for them, even in death, while highly commendable, should not impel one to violate ancient and hallowed religious tradition. The mourner may not determine which is the more sacred observance. Tradition performs that all-important task of balancing, sensitively, the scale of religious values man lives by, and this detailed and carefully worked-out balance has secured the eternity of the Jewish religion.

2. The Burial Kaddish recitation begins immediately following the closing of the grave. The mourner's Kaddish begins at the first service, usually the *minchah* prayer, recited upon returning from the interment.

3. The period that the mourner recites the Kaddish for parents is, theoretically, a full calendar year. The deceased is considered to be under Divine judgment for that period. Some communities, therefore, adhere to the custom that Kaddish be recited for 12 months in all cases. However, because the full year is considered to be the duration of

judgment for the wicked, and we presume that our parents do not fall into that category, the practice in most communities is to recite the Kaddish for only 11 months. Even on leap years, which last thirteen months, the Kaddish is recited for only 11 months. We subtract one day, so that we terminate the Kaddish in time to allow a full 30 days before the end of the 12-month period. Thus, if we begin on the eighth day of the Hebrew month of Cheshvan, we end on the seventh day of Tishre.

4. If a parent insists on the child's reciting Kaddish for the full 12 months, there is surely no reason not to obey him. If children feel this might bring public dishonor to their parent, they should recite only the Rabbi's Kaddish in the twelfth month, despite his request. This is a practice worthwhile encouraging in every case for all parents.

5. The 11-months-minus-one-day are calculated from day of death. However, if one wishes to count from the day of burial, if burial occurred many days after death, he may do so.

6. On the last day of Kaddish recitation, the mourner should receive an *aliyah*, a Torah honor.

7. Kaddish for relatives other than parents, for whom one is obliged to mourn: son, daughter, brother, sister, and spouse—is recited for 30 days according to the custom in some areas.

Requirement of a Minyan

The Kaddish is to be recited only in the presence of a duly-constituted quorum which consists of 10 males (including mourners) above the age of Bar Mitzvah. If there are only nine adults and one minor present, it is still not considered a quorum for a *minyan*. However, many commentators hold that in certain circumstances, when there is no other opportunity for its recitation, and the minor himself is the mourner, he may be counted toward completing the *minyan*.

While the Kaddish is an intensely personal tribute

spoken in respect to one's own parents, it may not be said privately. And while it is true that the individual is accorded great value in Jewish ethics, and it is the individual who is commanded, "Be ye holy, for I the Lord your God am holy," this service of holiness must be recited only in public, eliciting the response of a congregation. The Jewish experience has taught that such values as peace and life, and the struggle to bring heaven down to earth, of which the Kaddish speaks, can be achieved only in concert with society, and proclaimed amidst friends and neighbors of the same faith. If the Kaddish were solely an expression of personal remembrance for the deceased it would be logical to recite it privately—as the *yizkor* may be recited. But, as it is an adoration of God, it must be prayed at a public service in the midst of a congregation of adult thinking and believing men.

Indeed it is because of this age-old insistence on a congregational presence for the Kaddish that *minyanim* have been convened in the most unlikely places; that travelers could find Jewish communities all over the world; that, indeed, Jewish communities have remained united in all the ages of the dispersion. Such has been the effect of these religious laws that the recitation of the Kaddish has united the generations in a vertical chain, father to son, while the requirement to gather the *minyan* for Kaddish has united Jews on the horizontal plane. It has brought together parents and children and also man and his neighbors.

Mourners Obligated to Say Kaddish

The primary obligation to say Kaddish falls upon the son of the deceased. It is he who is required to recite it—he and not his sister; he and not his relatives; he and not someone paid to substitute for him. The son brings merit to the father. In the vision of Rabbi Akiba, it was the son's recitation that saved his father, and it was he who had to learn it for that reason. Not even the Kaddish of Rabbi Akiba himself, the spiritual giant of the age, could serve as a substitute. The traditional selection of the son is not a matter of personal preference depending on the family situation and the parent-child relationship. It is a clearly-defined obligation placed upon him by tradition, and he may not shirk this sacred duty. Indeed, in past generations, an only son was frequently referred to by his parents as the *kaddishel*. One simply may not delegate an agent to fulfill a personal religious obligation. As one may not ask a relative, or pay a stranger to fulfill the obligations of the fifth commandment, to honor his own parents, so may one not recite the Kaddish for parents after death through a hired medium. The prayer without the person is bare.

If the Son Is a Minor

This obligation to recite Kaddish devolves upon the son even though he be a minor (not having reached Bar Mitzvah age). It is worthwhile to emphasize, *especially* if he is a minor. There is every indication that the Kaddish was intended precisely for those who could not, or did not know how to, lead services. This simple recitation, learned easily in one sitting, enabled the youngster to lead the congregation in hallowing the name of God. The Kaddish is also an appropriate psychological method for the child to express his grief and thereby to receive consolation that is gradual and lasting, one that will bind him closely to the synagogue for the remainder of his life. The minor, however, should not be asked to conduct services whether or not he knows how. Whether the child is old enough to recite Kaddish at services is a relative matter, and is best decided by the family in conjunction with the rabbi.

The Adopted Son

It is entirely proper, though not religiously mandatory, for a son to say Kaddish for a foster parent, especially if he has been raised by that parent for many years. An adopted son, naturally, should not be compelled to do so if there was no filial sentiment between them. There is a stronger plea for the adopted son to say Kaddish, however, if there are no natural sons who survive the parent.

The Daughter

The obligation to recite Kaddish is placed upon the son, not upon the daughter. The sages, in their infinite wisdom, deep human compassion, and sharp insight into man realized only too well that the Kaddish which must be recited at services before breakfast and at dinner time, could not be made compulsory for women—mothers and wives who must attend to their families. It was not prejudice, but down-to-earth practicality that insisted that daughters be exempt. It should be noted that the sages did not, thereby, imply that there is a difference in the degree or quality of compassion and respect between son and daughter, or that the son and not the daughter could bring merit to the parent. Indeed, it is a common observation that women, usually, are closer to parents. For this reason, sons *and* daughters must observe all the mourning obligations equally, with the one exception: the Kaddish recitation.

The sages appreciated full well the equality of male and female in the realm of emotion and love, but saw the folly of legally requiring a woman, whose primary vocation is the home, to attend services morning and night. This being the case they required *no* woman, regardless of her individual circumstance, (even if she could manage the obligation) to recite the Kaddish. However, it is entirely in keeping with the spirit of the mourning laws for the daughter to attend Sabbath services regularly, to pay special attention to the words of the Kaddish, and to respond fervently with the "amen," with the specific intention of recalling her parent. The emphatic "amen" pronouncement, say the rabbis, is equivalent to the full recitation of Kaddish. Depending on the custom of the synagogue, also, she may rise with the other mourners for the Kaddish prayer. The daughter, especially if there is no son, may recite the Kaddish quietly to herself.

Is the Kaddish Obligation Transferrable?

Relatives or friends may not relieve the son of his obligation whether or not an uncle attends services regularly, or a brother was closer to the deceased than the son. It is the son who must recite the Kaddish, even though it be irregularly, or even unconscientiously, performed. There is no doubt that the daily recitation of the Kaddish may become burdensome, but it is a burden that must be borne and, like other vital burdens of life, cannot be delegated.

No person may be hired to say Kaddish instead of a surviving son, whether the designated person be very pious or moral or scholarly, or a rabbi, cantor or sexton, whether or not he is a better person than the son. The Kaddish is not a magical incantation, some exalted abracadabra that opens the gates of Heaven and that needs saying, no matter by whom. The son's *paying* for the Kaddish, rather than *praying* it, defeats every conceivable purpose of the sacred prayer. No value can be achieved by transferring this personal religious responsibility to a paid emissary. There is no possibility for a "merit of the children"; there is no personal relationship to the tragedy; there is no respect paid the deceased; there is no psychological healing; there is no sanctification of the name of God; there is, in sum, nothing religious about the whole matter. It is another unfortunate consequence of the prevalent utilitarian idea that everything in this world can be bought. "Merit of the children" must be deserved; it cannot be bought. A bought Kaddish will only reflect adversely on the parent whose child has no time or patience for the reverence he should give his parents.

If No Son Survives

Without a surviving son, the primary obligation to recite the Kaddish has dissolved, but arrangements for its recitation should, nevertheless, be made, if at all possible. As to who must bear this secondary responsibility there is much discussion in the tradition. Some maintain that this obligation should devolve first upon a younger brother of the deceased, as traditional religious mandate requires him to render respect to an elder sibling as to a parent. Others maintain that the obligation is upon the son-in-law who is likened to a son, or upon grandchildren, who are biblically referred to as sons. There is substantial opinion that would place the obligation upon the father, if he is alive, much as David prayed for his errant son, Absalom.

Clearly, in our day it would depend on which of these relatives feels closest to the deceased, or finds it easier to accomplish the task of reciting Kaddish, or feels religiously more impelled to do so. Indeed, a friend may wish to say it out of love or loyalty. In fact, a sharing of the responsibility may be more effective. Whoever does undertake to say the Kaddish, however, should be one who is himself orphaned from one of his parents, or he should obtain his parents' express consent.

If relatives cannot, for one reason or another, accept the full obligation for reciting Kaddish, should a stranger be hired to do so? In the absence of a son, or a personal reliable substitute, Jewish families, traditionally, have paid a sexton or another synagogue functionary to say the Kaddish. They felt that it was better to pay for this service, than to receive it free, as they were then able to consider the agent a personal emissary, and were, thus, assured of its recitation. The person who is thus engaged should not, by right, be saying the Kaddish for many others, as it will then lose all personal bearing to the deceased.

It must be noted that this custom, while practiced sincerely and conscientiously, has unfortunately brought a host of evil consequences in its train. It has caused people to think of respect for the dead only in material terms. It has engendered the feeling that somehow the Kaddish is a sort of credit system that can be manipulated financially. It has encouraged people, ultimately, to "pay" for all other services, so that they soon seek to "hire" a *yahrzeit* or *yizkor* or a *malei* prayer at the grave, a practice which is reprehensive to the religious spirit. In a larger sense, people come to believe that paying is more important than praying, and begin to consider the synagogue a celestial supermarket. They substitute the bank for the Bible, and believe that they can erase all personal vices by contributions to charity. The harm this practice has caused far outweighs the good it has innocently sought to instill. As such, it should be minimized, if not totally abandoned.

There is, however, a wise recommendation, in this regard, made by some of our greatest scholars: To contribute to a religious academic institution—a Yeshiva or Day School or home for elderly people—to enable one man to study Torah or Talmud every day, and to recite, at the end of the study period, the Rabbi's Kaddish, in honor of the dead. This is a personal memorialization, a "Merit of the Children" that includes study and prayer, Torah and Kaddish, in a dignified and worthy manner. In fact, this was practiced by some leading Torah scholars even though they were survived by pious sons who undoubtedly recited the Kaddish regularly.

For Whom Kaddish Is Said

Kaddish is said for the deceased father or mother, regardless of how intimate or strained the relationship between deceased and bereaved. While the primary obligation is towards father and mother, it is also said, according to the custom of some communities, for other close relatives: brother, sister, son, daughter, and wife, for the 30-day period.

Kaddish may be recited for Torah scholars and for Jews killed in war or at other times, who died *al kiddush hashem*, for the sanctification of the name of God. It may be recited for a close friend and also at the graveside of a worthy gentile, providing a duly-constituted *minyan* is present.

Age of the Deceased

Customs differ as to how old a deceased must be for Kaddish to be recited for him. Some communities set the minimum age at 20, others at Bar Mitzvah, still others at approximately eight or nine years, depending on the maturity of the child and whether he can be considered *bar da'at*, knowledgeable and aware of basic religious requirements. There are some who maintain that a normal child who lived beyond 30 days deserves to have the Kaddish recited for him. While each case depends largely on community custom, it is generally held that Kaddish be said for a child who has reached a degree of maturity even though he is younger than Bar Mitzvah age. If the father insists it may be said for an infant of 30 days.

Suicides

Suicides, especially when one is not sure of the motive, are honored with the recitation of Kaddish by their survivors. Mourners should be encouraged to recite it for the distinct spiritual benefit of the suicide who, if the act was intentional, was guilty of a heinous crime. Indeed, it is recommended for this reason, that they recite it for the full year rather than for the customary 11 months. See the special chapter on Suicides, below.

Transgressors

Those who sinned in public or private, out of spite or passion, and those who denied their faith or even who converted to other religions, are subjects of much scholarly controversy in regard to the requirement of saying the Kaddish. The majority of opinions tend toward permitting the Kaddish to be said for them. In fact, considering that even wicked parents, technically, deserve the child's respect, and considering that the Kaddish is designed to relieve the Divine punishment inflicted on perpetrators of evil, and also taking into account the religious good that accrues to the living through identification with God, the synagogue and fellow Jews, Kaddish should be recited for 12 months. The denial of the Kaddish for children of such individuals is one that can hardly be acceptable in the modern day.

Persons Missing and Assumed Dead

Such cases are extremely difficult to judge (especially when there are no reliable witnesses to the death) and competent, rabbinic authority must be consulted. Generally, for all persons excepting married men, the Kaddish may be recited when the missing person is assumed, beyond doubt, to be dead, even though the body has not been found. Married men assumed dead present a difficult problem. The recitation of the Mourner's Kaddish for them might lead others to consider the surviving widow to be of legally marriageable status, but this is religiously questionable. In such cases, and after due consultation with proper authorities, it might be advisable to have the son recite the Rabbi's Kaddish, not the Mourner's Kaddish, during services. If the body is found later, Mourner's Kaddish merely need be continued for the balance of the 11 months for parents.

When Kaddish Is Said at Services

1. *The Burial Kaddish*   קדיש דאיתחדתא

This Kaddish is not said at synagogue services, it is recited only immediately after the closing of the grave.

This is a special prayer which contains a special paragraph at the beginning. It is never added, except at this tragic moment. It is recited, on this occasion, on all days excepting those on which *tzidduk ha'din* and *tachanun* are not recited. Following is the additional introductory paragraph of the Burial Kaddish which includes the reverence for the dead and the consolation for the destruction of Jerusalem and the Sanctuary:

Yisgadal v'yiskadash shmai rabbah.
Magnified and sanctified be His great name.

B'olmo d'hu asid l'is-chadosho,
In the world which He will renew,

U'lachay'o maisayo, ul'asoko yos'hone lechayai olmo,
Reviving the dead, and raising them to life eternal,

*U'lemivnai karto d'yerushalem, u'leshachlel hechalai
    b'gavah;*
Rebuilding the city of Jerusalem, and establishing
    therein His sanctuary;

U'lemekar pulchana nuchro'o me'aro,
Uprooting idol worship from the land and,

V'la'asovo pulchono d'shmayo le'asrei—
Replacing it with Divine worship—

V'yamlich kudsho b'rich hu b'malchusai vikorai
May the Holy One, blessed be He, reign in His majestic
    glory.

(The regular Mourner's Kaddish is continued from this point, beginning with *b'chayechon* . . .)

2. *The Mourner's Kaddish*   קדיש יתום

This is recited primarily after *alenu*, and also after the Psalm of the Day. It is also recited in the early morning

service after the psalm, *Mizmor shir chanukat habayit le'
David.* At the *minchah* and *ma'ariv* services, it should be
recited after *alenu,* which concludes the service.

3. *The Rabbi's Kaddish*   קדיש דרבנן

In all cases, the recitation of the longer Rabbi's Kaddish
is considered of greater importance than the others. This
is the Kaddish after *ain k'elokenu* and the morning sacrifices
section, both of which contain portions from Torah and
Talmud. The mourner may also say the Kaddish following
the Torah reading.

As noted above, it is preferable for the mourner who
cannot lead the full service to lead, at least, the concluding
portion of the morning service (which is quite easy to
learn), from *ashrai* and *u'va le'tziyon* through Kaddish and
alenu.

Posture of Kaddish Recitation

The mourners must rise for the Kaddish and may say
it in unison with the other mourners of the congregation,
although it was originally intended as an individual prayer,
recited responsively with the whole congregation. The Kaddish, being a prayer of holiness, must not be interrupted.
Indeed, the core response, "Let His great name be exalted,"
is considered important enough for the congregants to
interrupt any of their own prayers in order to respond.
The conclusion of the Kaddish is a quotation from the book
of Job asking God who makes peace in the heavens to bring
peace to all of us. This verse concludes the Kaddish. As
the mourner ends his confrontation with God, he customarily retreats three short steps, symbolizing the conclusion
of his audience with God, and then returns to his original
stance.

If Parent Requests Kaddish Be Not Said

In the case where a parent demands that his children should not recite Kaddish for his deceased mate, he is not to be obeyed. The Kaddish is expressive of a relationship between parent and child, and the surviving parent may not interfere with this life-long relationship.

If the deceased left instructions that no Kaddish should be recited after his *own* death, then one should examine the reason for the request. If it was to avoid inconvenience for his children, his request can be set aside by the children, and they can allow themselves to be inconvenienced. If the motive is a lack of belief in the purpose of the Kaddish itself, the children may use their own judgment in deciding whether or not it should be recited. Knowing their parent, if they feel the recitation represents a principle he strongly opposed, he should be obeyed.

When Mourner Cannot Attend Services

Although we live in an unstable age when the press of emergency transactions, business or personal circumstances, or illness, may prevent one from attending one of the services, the Kaddish may not be recited privately. It is a public prayer and simply must be recited in a quorum.

What should be done, in such cases, is what the Kaddish itself seeks to do: enhance the "Merit of the Children." The mourners should read a portion of the Bible—a chapter from the Five Books of Moses or the Prophets—or, if he is able, study a *mishnah* or page from the Talmud. This is a constructive and entirely valid substitute for the Kaddish, when one finds it extremely difficult to attend one of the services.

Tradition recommends other ways to glorify a parent's teaching. Children should make a standard practice of contributing to charity in their parents' memory. Even more effective and more beautiful, mourners should strive to adopt one *mitzvah*, one special deed, which they will take to heart and practice regularly as a memorial tribute. This custom adds life to the influence of a parent who has passed on and builds a future life for those who survive.

How magnificent is the tradition that has transformed a potential faith-shattering tragedy into faith-building future, and that has taught, unwaveringly, that the only valid expression of grief is the ethical and religious betterment of oneself.

Joyous Occasions During Mourning
שמחה

The observance that most affects the daily life of the mourner during the 12-month period is the complete abstention from parties and festivities, both public and private. Participation in these gatherings is simply not consonant with the depression and contrition that the mourner experiences. It borders on the absurd for the mourner to dance gleefully while his parent lies dead in a fresh grave. Thus, the sages decreed that while complete physical withdrawal from normal activities of society lasts only one week, withdrawal from joyous, social occasions lasts 30 days in mourning for other relatives, and one year (12 Hebrew months) in mourning for one's parents. Joy, in terms of the mourning tradition, is associated largely with public, social events rather than with personal satisfactions.

The Definition of Joy

The difficult problem, however, is which social occasion is to be defined as *joyous*, and thus prohibited the mourner. There are, on one hand, social gatherings, such as friendly get-togethers, parties, community meetings, pleasure-trips and cruises, business gatherings, synagogue-sponsored events, and so on. On the other hand, there are religious celebrations, such as *b'rit,* Bar Mitzvahs and weddings. Which are considered "joyous" in terms of the mourning tradition? What criteria are to be used in making the determination? Clearly, the law cannot determine "joy" arbitrarily, by the frequency of smiles or by some computerized meter of internal jollity.

The sages, through the centuries, have established general criteria of "joyous" occasions. The first consideration was whether the party was religious or social. On this point the great teachers were divided. The majority, and largely the prevailing attitude, was that only "true-joy" was prohibited. True-joy is that which goes to the roots of the person, his in-depth relationship to God and to his family. This is what the Talmud had in mind when it prohibited the mourner from entering a wedding hall to participate in the gala dinner. The occasion of celebrating the observance of a *mitzvah,* such as a wedding or Bar Mitzvah, struck true-joy in the heart of the person, and this the mourner was not permitted to experience.

The establishment of this criterion is far from arbitrary. Rather it is a consequence of the Jewish spiritual world-concept. Man finds genuine happiness in the fulfillment of his obligations to God. His deep satisfactions come not from the distractions of the entertainment media and the superficial frivolities of the age, the games and contests of society at play. It is true that fellowship gatherings grant unmistakable and positive joy, and many are the encomia offered by the sages for the comradeship characteristic of friendly social occasions. Yet the delight that is derived is not nearly so profound as the true-joy of the religious occasion.

Thus, these scholars maintained that the primary prohibition was the *simchah shel mitzvah,* the *religious* celebration, and the archetype of this true-joy festivity was the wedding ceremony and feast. Only secondarily was the *social* occasion prohibited.

A minority view, held by some of the most esteemed thinkers in Jewish life, maintained that tradition primarily prohibited the *simchat mera'im*, the purely social joys, the gaieties of the hail-fellows, and the round of parties that often mark life. Any occasion celebrating the observance of a commandment surely could not be prohibited to the mourner wishing to observe the commandment! Can these joys mar the spirit of the bereaved? Can they bring shame to the deceased? Can it be said that participation in religious family festivities distracts one's mind from the dead?

Committed Jews, eager to keep the law, anxious to do full honor to parents, and relatively unconcerned with the number of affairs they attend during the year, keep both views, and sedulously avoid both the religious and the social festivities, as a general rule. Exceptions to this custom were enumerated in the tradition. These will be discussed below.

Other obvious criteria of what constitutes joy were established. Music, especially dance music, and especially that which is enjoyed in the company of others, is a clear mark of gaiety. Another criteria is the festive dining with a celebrant. A sumptuous celebration dinner surely is a joyous occasion. There are moments, at a wedding reception or on a pleasure cruise, for example, when simply being present in a hall for dancing and dining, without participating in either, is not permitted the mourner. It is a spirit of public light-heartedness that is to be avoided. It should be noted that the joy that is prohibited the mourner is commensurate with the degree and period of mourning, and also with the relation to the deceased. Thus:

1. During *shiva* the mourner must refrain from doing those things which even possibly evoke joy, such as the recitation of certain joyous verses from the prayerbook, or excessive playing with the children, or even indulging heatedly in discussions with the visitors to the house of mourning. These latter were considered *s'chok,* pleasantries,

unbecoming the bereaved and prohibited during all of the stages of mourning. Ecclesiastes says, "There is a time for wailing (*bechi*), and a time for laughter (*s'chok*)." As mourning is surely the time for wailing, excessive laughter is not permitted.

2. Before *sheloshim*, which ends the mourning observance for those bereaved of relatives other than parents, joyous religious and social occasions under normal circumstances are prohibited. After *sheloshim*, all festivities are permitted these bereaved.

3. For those who mourn parents, the *sheloshim* period requires a more intense restraint from joy than the remaining months of the year. For example, the bereaved are permitted to attend a Bar Mitzvah party (all may obviously attend the synagogue service) during *sheloshim* (after *shiva*) together so long as they avoid listening to the instrumental music and participating in the dinner together with the celebrants. After *sheloshim*, and for the balance of the year, however, they may participate fully in the dinner if the Bar Mitzvah lad speaks on some Torah subject, making the celebration a truly religious function.

Following are some of the details of the law that derive from these concepts. In difficult situations one should discuss the particulars with the rabbi so that he may decide any question of law. Below are guidelines that mark the rule, and its exceptions, in the prohibition of attending joyous occasions during mourning.

Social and Business Gatherings

1. Community business meetings, such as synagogue or fraternal organization membership meetings, are permitted the mourner after *shiva*.

2. Social dinners, even though no music is played, and even though they are held for charitable causes, are not to be attended by mourners for parents for 12 months, and other mourners for 30 days.

3. Pleasure cruises and group tours are somewhat similar to social dinners in the eyes of the law, even though the meals are eaten privately. These are considered truly to be "joy rides," and should be discouraged during the 30 days at least.

4. Large house parties also are to be discouraged the mourner for parents for 12 months, and other mourners for 30 days, even though no full meal is served. There is no stricture against get-togethers, inviting a few friends or relatives at a time. The important consideration to be remembered is that these events must not develop into social "occasions." Fellowship is fine, but festivities are not appropriate.

5. Business parties, where gaiety and shoulder-rubbing is the method, and business achievements the goal, should also be avoided during the full mourning period. If absence at such events might cause financial loss, a rabbi should be consulted. Business conventions are, similarly, to be avoided in normal situations. However, if attendance is mandatory, or economically beneficial, the mourner may attend but should not be present during music and dancing periods. He should take his meals privately, or with several friends, unless the purpose of the meal is purely business, in which case he is permitted to dine with the convention, after the *sheloshim* period.

6. Professional musicians who derive all, or part of, their livelihood from playing at joyous occasions, may do so after *shiva*, as they are not playing for joy. If they are financially able, they should avoid playing during the *sheloshim*.

7. Attendance at operas and concerts, theaters and movies is to be discouraged. Listening to radio and television, depends on the above-mentioned criteria of joy. Generally, sports events and broadcasts over radio and TV of news and sports are permitted.

Religious Celebrations
סעודת מצוה

B'rit

The mourner who has just become a father may attend the *b'rit* of his son even the very first day after interment. He may dress in Sabbath clothes. He may help prepare and eat the festive meal, even (perhaps preferably) in his own home. If it is not in his own home, he may travel to the location of the *b'rit*. However, immediately after the *b'rit*, he should return to continue the *shiva* at the house of mourning.

The *mohel*, if there is no other competent one available, may perform the *b'rit*, even during his *shiva*. He should not participate in the festive meal during *sheloshim* if he is mourning a parent, but may do so (after *shiva*) if he is mourning other relatives.

The *sandek* (who is a mourner) may attend the *b'rit*, but should not participate in the festive meal during *shiva*, as previously noted for the *mohel*. He may wear shoes and dress for the occasion. However, it is not considered entirely proper to invite a mourner to be the *sandek* in the first place.

Pidyon Ha'ben

The laws of *pidyon ha'ben* are similar to those of *b'rit*. The Kohen, in this instance, is permitted those matters which the *mohel* may do in performing the *b'rit*.

Bar Mitzvah

A parent in mourning may prepare the Bar Mitzvah party even during *sheloshim*, so long as it is after *shiva*. He should not, however, eat the meal with the guests. He may eat in another room, and socialize with the guests during the meal proper, without music.

Such a parent may also dress for the occasion. The Bar

Mitzvah lad himself, if he is in mourning for one of his parents, may dress in his full Sabbath best. The religious ceremony of Bar Mitzvah is not cancelled even if the boy is in mourning. All mourners, whether or not they are related to the Bar Mitzvah, may attend the celebration during *sheloshim,* but should avoid eating at the dinner or listening to music. After *sheloshim,* the mourner for parents may attend and participate in the meal if the celebrant speaks on matters of Torah, thus indicating that it is a *simchah shel mitzvah,* a religious occasion.

The Ceremony At the Wedding

1. If the ceremony takes place in a catering hall or similar place where music is played, the general rule is that mourners for parents should not attend for 12 months and for other relatives 30 days.

2. In the catering hall proper, if the orchestra is not present, mourners for parents may attend after *sheloshim.*

3. If the wedding takes place in a synagogue, where customarily there is only vocal but no instrumental music, the mourner for parents may attend after *shiva.* After the *sheloshim,* in such case, the mourner for parents may even participate in the recital of the blessings at the ceremony and dress up for the occasion. If there is instrumental music he may not attend at all until the end of the year.

4. If the mourner (even for parents) makes the tenth for the *minyan,* and there are no other available men to constitute a quorum, he may attend the wedding and eat the meal even during the *sheloshim.*

5. If the absence of the mourner will cause a delay in the wedding date, and there is a possibility that the delay might cause one of the couple to withdraw from the marriage, the mourner may attend at any time and under any conditions.

6. If the rabbi is a mourner, he may perform a wedding after *shiva,* but should avoid listening to the music.

7. When mourners do attend at such times that are not normally permissible, they must perform some useful function:

a. Relatives who attend after *shiva* (during *sheloshim*), must serve as ushers or helpers at the ceremony, even if they are not mourning parents. These mourners, of course, may attend after *sheloshim* without this requirement.

b. Close friends of the celebrant who are in mourning should not attend the wedding ceremony during *sheloshim*. However, if they feel that their absence will cause the bride or groom remorse or pain, they may attend as assistants before the ceremony. After *sheloshim*, if they are mourning parents, these friends may attend the affair if they asist before the ceremony.

The Dinner

Dining at a festive meal with friends and relatives falls directly within the category of *simchah*, joy, and should be avoided by the mourner until after 12 months when mourning for parents, and 30 days when mourning for other relatives. In pressing circumstances, mourners should proceed as follows:

1. Father and mother, brother and sister, and children of the bride or groom, may attend the ceremony and eat at the dinner during *sheloshim* even if they are in mourning for parents. They should, however, be of some help in the preparation or service at the meal, or in the serving of drinks, and so on.

2. Other relatives of the couple may join the wedding reception after *sheloshim*, if they mourn parents, (other mourners after *shiva*) but should help in serving.

Celebration of the Talmud

At the conclusion of a tractate of the Talmud a celebration (*siyyum masechet*) is usually held (such as that attended by first born who, otherwise, would be required to fast before Passover). Such celebrations may be attended by mourners, and they may participate in the meal that follows the talmudic discourse. The festive meal at Hanukkah and at a housewarming are in the same category providing that they partake of the character of religious celebration through a Torah discussion or with religious songs and praise of God.

Festivities on the Sabbath

The Sabbath is a day when public mourning is avoided (even though personal mourning prohibitions remain in force). May one attend a public, joyous occasion on the Sabbath?

The general rule is that the Sabbath only adds to the *simchah* that is coincident with it, and hence should make it doubly prohibitive. At the same time, however, if the community would ordinarily expect the mourner to attend, his absence would appear to be public mourning which is not permitted on the Sabbath. The following procedures, therefore, should be followed:

Post-wedding festivities (*sheva berachot*) held every evening for seven days after the wedding, should not be attended even on the Sabbath until after *sheloshim* for mourners for parents, and after *shiva* for other mourners. The same is true for *b'rit, shalom zachar* (celebrated on the first Friday night following the birth of a son), and for a mother returning to the synagogue for the first time after childbirth, if a party is customarily made in her honor.

However, the above is intended for friends and distant relatives of the celebrant. Close relatives of the immediate family and prominent individuals, ordinarily expected to attend, may attend these celebrations and join in the meal. Their absence clearly would be an indication of mourning in public, which is prohibited on the Sabbath.

The Mourner and Marriage

The quintessence of all joyous occasions, in the Jewish view of life, is the wedding. When the sages wished to convey the idea that happiness may be found everywhere, they said "all the world is a wedding." To the relatives, friends and well-wishers, joy at the wedding is defined in material terms, such as dining and dancing. Thus, the mourner may attend the ceremony if there is no music and if he does not participate in the banquet. But to the couple being married, the food and music are ancillary, merely incidental accompaniment to the significant moment under the canopy. For them the definition of joy is the spiritual personal bond that unites them. Were the wedding shorn of the material goodies, the smiles and the tinsel, and only the couple, the two witnesses, the *minyan* and the rabbi were present, the wedding ceremony would still be the memorable peak of joy. The thrilling sounds of *mazel tov*, the beauty of flowers and music would be gone, but the essence would remain for a lifetime.

Thus, for the mourner himself, marriage should be prohibited. But this is not a light matter. One may refrain from celebrations and music for a year, but marriage is of the fabric of life itself, and life inevitably must go on. And so all mourners, for parents or other relatives, while being prohibited from marrying during *shiva*, were permitted to marry after *sheloshim*. (The laws of marriage *during sheloshim* will be considered later.) The wedding can be held in the presence of the full complement of friends and material abundance and beauty and music and gaiety. It is, after all, the festival of festivals and, therefore, shaving, haircutting, washing and dressing in the finest apparel are permitted.

The mourning laws relating to marriage affirmed the need for life to go on and to be lived to its fullest, but they also considered that, nonetheless, a close relative has just been taken from life. The glorious union of marriage and the bitter severance of death are two contrasting threads, and the tradition understood the needs of both.

Following are the laws that flow from this understanding of human need at the rare moment of the coincidence of such paroxysms in life.

1. *When Marriages May Take Place:*

a. Mourners should not be married during *sheloshim,* and certainly not during *shiva,* even without pomp and music and sumptuous reception. Engagements may not be contracted or announced during this period.

b. *After* the *sheloshim,* the wedding may proceed with all the adornments, the music and the food, and the bride and groom, and their parents may dress for the occasion, without showing any evident signs of mourning.

c. During *sheloshim* (after *shiva*) there are exceptional circumstances when marriages may be contracted:

—*If the groom is the mourner:*
If he is childless, and preparations had been made, such as: the date set, the arrangements contracted for, and the food bought, so that postponing the wedding would incur a severe financial loss, or cause a large group of people to be absent.

If the date had *not* been set, but for some cogent reason, such as military draft, it must be held during *sheloshim,* the couple may marry, but not live as man and wife until after *sheloshim.*

—*If the bride is the mourner:*
The marriage may take place during *sheloshim* only if she had already been engaged, the preparations made and the groom is childless.

2. *When Remarriages May Take Place:*

a. *If the wife died:*

The husband must wait for the passing of the three

major festivals (Passover, Succot and Shavuot) before he remarries. Rosh Hashanah and Yom Kippur do not count as festivals for this purpose. Shemini Atzeret may be counted as a festival in certain cases involving the family's urgent personal circumstances. The ostensible reason for this delay is the hope that the duration of three separate holidays and the cycle of seasons would temper his despair, and he would not enter a second marriage with the first love still fresh in mind. This time-span may be as long as a year if death occurred soon after Succot, or only a few months if death occurred immediately prior to Passover.

There are notable exceptions to this general rule:

—If the husband did not sire children, marriage may be held after *shiva* and they may live as husband and wife.

—If he has small children who need to be cared for, marriage may be held after *shiva,* but marital relations must be postponed until after *sheloshim.*

—If he cannot bear to live alone, for whatever reason (this is not an infrequent occurrence), he may be married, but may have no marital relations until after *sheloshim.*

If the husband died:

The wife may remarry after three months, a considerably shorter time than the three-festival duration for a man. Evidently, the wife was considered better able to control her emotions, having to be more concerned with the rearing of her children than with her own feelings. The reason for the three-month delay is that it must be evident that she is not bearing a child from a deceased mate. Under exceptional circumstances to be judged by competent rabbinic authority, if it is known medically that she could not possibly be pregnant, and if her fiance is childless, she may be granted permission to remarry after *shiva.* Also, if she finds unusual hardship in supporting her orphaned children, and it can be determined absolutely that she is not pregnant, she may be granted permission to remarry immediately after *shiva.*

3. *Becoming a Mourner after the Ceremony*

a. If one of the seven close relatives of the bride or groom died after the ceremony, but before the marriage was consummated, the couple must live apart until after *shiva.*

b. If the relative died after the consummation of the marriage, the mourning is postponed until after the full week of wedding celebration. During this time, the mourner may care for personal hygiene and grooming, and may experience all the joys of living. When the week is over, however, the garment of the mourner is rent and *shiva* begins in full, as noted above.

5. ◇ Post-Mourning Practices and Procedures

The Monument
מצבה

"And Rachel died and was buried on the way to Ephrath, which is Bethlehem. And Jacob erected a tombstone on Rachel's grave" (Genesis 5:19-20). Erecting a monument is a very ancient tradition. Whether the stone is placed directly over the grave, as a footstone or headstone, the monument serves three purposes:

1. To mark the place of burial, so that priests may avoid defilement from the dead—a ritual impurity that the Bible prohibits. For this purpose only a simple marker would be required.

2. To designate the grave properly, so that friends and relatives may visit it. For this, what is required is only the name of the individual on a modest stone.

3. To serve as a symbol of honor to the deceased buried beneath it. For this purpose one should erect as respectable a monument as the heirs can afford, avoiding unnecessary ostentation.

Type of Monument

The expense for the monument is technically considered part of the burial costs. Thus, it is an obligation that the heirs assume, whether or not funds were left for this purpose. Even if the decedent willed that no stone be erected, his behest is not heeded. The cost, the size, shape and lettering of the monument should be determined by the monies available to the family and the type of monument generally used on that particular cemetery. One should do honor to the deceased, but one should not use funds for the monument which are needed for living expenses.

While the form of the marker is of little religious significance, what is important is that there be a clear, visible demarcation of the gravesite. For example, there are cemeteries that utilize small, flat stones that are flush with the earth, and it is difficult to determine whether they are footstones or headstones. These are not generally desirable, unless the whole outline of the grave is clearly evident. If only footstones are permitted by the cemetery, they may be used and the small size is not considered a belittling of the deceased. In the case of a youngster, or of a public charity case, a small permanent marker may be used. Even for stillbirths and infants not surviving 30 days, markers must be used. The purpose is so that the area will be recognizable, and priests will avoid contact with ritual impurity.

Double monuments are frequently used by man and wife, two unmarried sisters, mother and daughter, father and son, or two brothers. Caution should be taken, however, before ordering them. Might the surviving spouse remarry? If she does, will she unquestionably desire to be buried next to the first mate? Will one of the unmarried sisters remarry? Will the survivor desire to be buried in the Holy Land? Is a long-distance move contemplated? In the moment of grief, there are feelings of guilt and love that are not always sustained in the future. Great care should be taken before finally ordering the double monument. (Which plot a remarried spouse should occupy is considered above in Cemetery Plots.)

When to Erect the Monument

It is popularly assumed that the monument must be erected approximately 12 months after death. In reality, only few scholars hold this view, and it is not customary to follow their recommendation. There is every reason, based on major commentaries and numerous sources and long tradition, to arrange for the tombstone to be built as soon after *shiva* as possible. For the reasons enumerated above, especially in order to honor the deceased, one should erect the tombstone immediately after *shiva*. The sages considered this so important that, in certain cases, they even permitted the mourner to leave the house of mourning *during shiva* to make the necessary arrangements. This was considered an integral part of the burial arrangements.

The reason usually given for waiting 12 months is that the tombstone serves as a reminder, and that for the first 12 months the deceased is remembered, in any case, by the recitation of Kaddish and the avoidance of joyous occasions. Despite the rationale, however, the honoring of the dead should take priority over his being remembered, and arrangements for the stone should be made immediately. Indeed, it is not appropriate to recite a eulogy, even for the very righteous, after 12 months have passed.

If it is not possible to arrange for the monument soon after *shiva*, it may wait until *sheloshim*, or immediately thereafter. Naturally, monument-makers require much time to cut the stone, but the honor to the deceased derives from the fact that the family orders it promptly. In addition, the days of *shiva* are probably an opportune time to discuss the tombstone, since the entire family is gathered together and consultation among members of the family is simplified.

The family should be advised to take great care in selecting a monument maker. Recommendations of friends, and suggestions by the cemetery owners, should be sought. Members of the family should inspect the erected monument before scheduling the unveiling, to check the wording and spelling, and the proper location of the stone.

Inscription and Style

Good taste, quiet dignity, and the avoidance of ostentation are the only guidelines for selecting the monument. The cost of the monument will be determined usually by the lettering, carving, ornamentation and the finish, rather than by size alone.

Inscriptions, in past years, used to occupy the entire slate and often abounded in well-intentioned exaggerations, sometimes to the point of utter and barefaced falsehoods. Many phrases that were used could be applied only to the most righteous of men. This is no longer the type of inscription used. What is recommended is a short *Hebrew* descriptive phrase, in addition to the Hebrew name of the deceased and his father's Hebrew name, the full English name, and the Hebrew and English dates of birth and death. It may contain all of these or only the names. It is most appropriate, however, to include the Hebrew dates whenever Christian dates are inscribed. An additional name, given in times of illness, is used in the inscription only if it was in use for more than 30 days, and if the deceased had recovered from that illness.

Styles of monuments vary. The particular shape is of no consequence to the tradition. However, sculptured animals, or the face of the deceased, if carved in relief, are out of place in Jewish cemeteries. Photographs mounted on monuments are not in good taste. Some authorities maintain that they are prohibited. It does seem that a person should be remembered without having his portrait to stare at. If already erected, however, these tombstones should cause no disputes, and are better left to stand as they are.

Following are facts you should have ready when preparing to purchase a monument:

—The name of the cemetery and the *exact* location of the plot.

—The full English name.

—The full Hebrew name of the deceased and his father.

—The birthday (this may be omitted).
—The date and approximate hour of death.
—The relationship to family: mate, parent, grandparent, friend, etc.
—Jewish status: Kohen, Levi or Israelite.

Grave Visitations and Prayers

The traditional attitude of Judaism was not to encourage excessive grave visitation. The rabbis were apprehensive that frequent visiting to the cemetery might become a pattern of living thus preventing the bereaved from placing their dead in proper perspective. They wanted to prevent making the grave a sort of totem, at which the mourner would pray to the dead rather than to God, and thereby be violating one of the cardinal principles of Judaism: that God is One and that there are no intermediaries between a man and his God.

Proper Times for Visiting

Various customs have arisen regarding the proper times for visiting the graves of dear ones:

1. Propitious times to visit the grave are on days of calamity or of decisive moments in life: on the concluding day of *shiva* and *sheloshim*, and on *yahrzeit*; on fast days, such as Tisha B'Av, or before the High Holy Days; on *erev* Rosh Chodesh, the day prior to the first days of the months of Nissan and Elul. One or another of these days seems proper for families to visit their beloved dead. There is no rule of thumb as to the annual frequency of such visitation, excepting that people should avoid the extremes of constant visitation on the one hand, and of complete disregard on the other.

2. Visitation should not be made on *chol ha'moed*—the middle days of Passover and Succot—nor on Purim, as these are holy days of joy.

3. There is dispute regarding the propriety of visiting at certain other times, such as Rosh Chodesh, Hanukkah and *erev* Purim, Lag B'omer, the days in Nissan which precede Passover, and other days on which *tachanun* is not recited. Consequently, these days should be avoided for visitation and unveiling if at all possible. If for some reason, whether it is because members of the family must leave town, or will be visiting from out-of-town at certain other times, or because a mate wishes to be remarried following the unveiling and insists upon waiting until that time, or some other cogent reason (and not mere arbitrariness), the visitation may be held at those times. If held on these days the rabbi will avoid provoking unnecessary tears and, therefore, will not recite the *malei* memorial prayer. He should temper his eulogy so as not to bewail, but rather to praise the dead. These days are days of national joy and the spirit of total tragedy should not prevail. However, the psalms and Kaddish may be recited.

Personal Prayers and Devotions

1. If one has not visited a cemetery in 30 days he should recite the following blessing addressed to the deceased: *Baruch ata adonai Elo-kenu melech ha-olam asher yatzar etchem badin, v'dan v'chilkail etchem badin, v'hemit etchem badin, v'yode-ah mispar koolchem badin, v'atid l'ha-chazir ul-ha-chayot etchem badin. Baruch ata adonai-m'chayeh hametim.*

"Praised be the Eternal, our God, the Ruler of the Universe who created you in judgment, who maintained and sustained you in judgment, and brought death upon you in judgment; who knows the deeds of everyone of you in judgment, and who will hereafter restore you to life in judgment. Praised be the Eternal who will restore life to the dead."

2. It is entirely proper for learned Jews to study the *mishnah* for several minutes at graveside.

3. Several chapters from the Book of Psalms are usually recited. Also Psalm 119, whose verses are grouped according to the alphabet, may be read, selecting those portions which begin with the letters of the name of the deceased. These Psalms may be recited as close to the grave as desired. Some people customarily place their hand on the tombstone during the recitation.

4. Much care must be taken to direct one's personal prayers at graveside to God. To pray to the deceased, or to speak directly to him in the form of prayer, borders on blasphemy. It is sheer necromancy, outlawed by the Bible (Deut. 18, 11) along with sorcerers, soothsayers and enchanters. Not all the good intentions in the world can justify praying to the dead as intermediaries. That is an abomination to a people that has based its faith on the unity of God, and has abhorred spiritualizing via ghosts and wizards. Better no visitation to the cemetery at all than one which induces "inquiring of the dead."

Memorial Prayer

The *malei rachamim*, is a memorial prayer of undetermined origin that has been taken to heart by all Jews. Its ubiquitous appeal and profound emotional effect has caused it to be chanted at funerals and unveilings, at every visitation to the cemetery, and in the synagogue on Sabbaths before *yahrzeits*, and at *yizkor* services. This prayer may be recited in English without any loss of religious significance.

The Unveiling

The service of commemoration or unveiling is a formal dedication of the monument. It is customary to hold the unveiling within the first year after death. It should be held at anytime between the end of *shiva* and the *yahrzeit*.

Unveilings are held on those days when grave visitations may be made, as outlined in the previous chapter. They are held in all weather and, in our day, precisely on time. With the shortage of available rabbis, and the large number of unveilings concentrated in the spring or fall, it is clearly advisable to call the rabbi six or seven weeks in advance, and to set the date after consulting with him.

The unveiling is the formal removal of a veil, a cloth, or handkerchief draped over the stone. It symbolizes the erection of the tombstone. The unveiling may be executed during the service by anyone the family designates.

The service consists of the recitation of several Psalms, the eulogy, the removal of the veil, the *malei rachamim*, and Kaddish. For purposes of reciting the Kaddish, a *minyan* is required. In the *minyan* are included all adults present. If no *minyan* is available, the unveiling may be held, but the Kaddish may not be recited.

The rabbi will frequently suggest placing pebbles on the monument. This custom probably serves as a reminder of the family's presence. Also, it may hark back to biblical days when the monument was a heap of stones. Often, the elements or roving vandals dispersed them, and so visitors placed other additional stones to assure that the grave was marked.

It is advisable, if the rabbi was not personally acquainted with the deceased, to outline, before the service, his life and goals. If the family is enthusiastic in its admiration, rather than bored and indifferent, the eulogy will reflect this sincerity and devotion.

Unveiling cards are usually sent to friends and family two or three weeks in advance of the date. One should be sent to the rabbi as well. Care should be taken to record the precise location of the grave, and specific and clear instructions on how to reach the cemetery and the gravesite.

Eating and drinking on the cemetery are in poor taste. They desecrate the cemetery, and reflect shame upon the deceased. In previous ages a snack may have been required because of the long trip a cemetery visit may have required. Or, perhaps, the reason is that in raising the glass of wine, we say *l'chayim*, "for life," implying "not for death." Today drinking is associated with socials and bars, and the spirit of levity usually prevails. This custom should be discouraged.

Yizkor: Recalling the Dead
יזכור

Recalling the deceased during a synagogue service is not merely a convenient form of emotional release, but an act of solemn piety and an expression of profound respect. The *yizkor* memorial service was instituted so that the Jew may pay homage to his forbears and recall the good life and traditional goals.

This memorial service is founded on a vital principle of Jewish life, one that motivates and animates the Kaddish recitation. It is based on the firm belief that the living, by acts of piety and goodness, can redeem the dead. The son can bring honor to the father. The "merit of the children" can reflect the value of the parents. This merit is achieved, primarily, by living on a high ethical and moral plane, by being responsive to the demands of God and sensitive to the needs of fellowman. The formal expression of this merit is accomplished by prayer to God and by contributions to charity.

It is understandable, therefore, that when the *yizkor* was first introduced into the service, probably during the massacres of the Crusaders and the early medieval pogroms, it was natural to be recited during the Day of Atonement. On that holiest day of the year, when Jews seek redemption from their sins, they seek atonement as well for members of the family who have passed on. "Forgive Thy people, whom Thou hast redeemed," says the Bible in Judges, chapter 21. Say the sages: "Forgive Thy people," refers to the living; "Whom Thou hast redeemed," refers to the dead. The living can redeem the dead. Atonement must be sought for both. One scholar even suggests that the term *Yom Ha'Kippurim*, the technical name for the Day of Atonement, is written in the plural, "atonements," because on that day the Jew must seek atonement for both those who are present and those who sleep in the dust.

But even prayer is not sufficient for a dignified and meaningful memorial. It must be accompanied by charity, as the personal, material demonstration of kindness. Thus, *yizkor* came to be recited on major holidays when Deuteronomy 15-16 is read, and which contains the phrase, "Each man shall give according to his ability." Those chapters command man to be charitable, to support the poor, the orphan, the widow, and the Levites who depend on his graciousness. They emphasize that on the three pilgrim festivals of Passover, Shavuot and Succot no man may appear at the Temple empty-handed. Each man must be generous according to his ability. Accordingly, the proper memorial service contains a phrase denoting a sum of charity that is being pledged. This statement should not be taken lightly; it is not a mere liturgical formula. If no charity will be given it should not be included. It is preferable not to promise than to renege on a vow. Thus, the *yizkor* service recited on Yom Kippur, Passover, Shavuot and Succot, includes both prayer and charity.

The Rubric of the Memorial Service

There are two distinct prayers that are traditionally referred to as *hazkarat neshamot*, recalling of the dead. First is the *malei rachamim*, recited by the rabbi or cantor publicly at funeral and unveiling services, at holiday *yizkor* services, and after the Torah readings on Monday and Thursday mornings, and on Saturday afternoons for *yahrzeit*. The second *hazkarat neshamot* prayer refers to the synagogue *yizkor* service. This is designed to be read by

the individual congregant, silently, on Yom Kippur and
the three pilgrim festivals, mentioned above.

Yizkor Prayer for a Male Deceased

יִזְכּוֹר אֱלֹהִים נִשְׁמַת _____ שֶׁהָלַךְ לְעוֹלָמוֹ.
בַּעֲבוּר שֶׁאֲנִי נוֹדֶרֶת צְדָקָה בַּעֲדוֹ, בִּשְׂכַר זֶה, תְּהֵא נַפְשׁוֹ
צְרוּרָה בִּצְרוֹר הַחַיִּים עִם נִשְׁמוֹת אַבְרָהָם יִצְחָק וְיַעֲקֹב,
שָׂרָה רִבְקָה רָחֵל וְלֵאָה, וְעִם שְׁאָר צַדִּיקִים וְצִדְקָנִיּוֹת שֶׁבְּגַן
עֵדֶן. וְנֹאמַר אָמֵן.

Merciful God in Heaven, grant perfect repose to the
soul of .... who has passed to his eternal habita-
tion; and in whose memory, the members of his family
pledge charity. May he be under Thy divine wings among
the holy and pure who shine bright as the sky; may his
place of rest be in paradise. Merciful One, O keep his soul
forever alive under Thy protective wings. The Lord being
his heritage may he rest in peace; and let us say, Amen.

Yizkor Prayer for a Woman Deceased

יִזְכּוֹר אֱלֹהִים נִשְׁמַת _____ שֶׁהָלְכָה לְעוֹלָמָהּ.
בַּעֲבוּר שֶׁאֲנִי נוֹדֵר צְדָקָה בַּעֲדָהּ, בִּשְׂכַר זֶה, תְּהֵא נַפְשָׁהּ
צְרוּרָה בִּצְרוֹר הַחַיִּים עִם נִשְׁמוֹת אַבְרָהָם יִצְחָק וְיַעֲקֹב,
שָׂרָה רִבְקָה רָחֵל וְלֵאָה, וְעִם שְׁאָר צַדִּיקִים וְצִדְקָנִיּוֹת שֶׁבְּגַן
עֵדֶן. וְנֹאמַר אָמֵן.

Merciful God in Heaven, grant perfect repose to the
soul of .... who has passed to her eternal habita-
tion; and in whose memory, the members of her family
pledge charity. May she be under Thy divine wings among
the holy and pure who shine bright as the sky; may her
place of rest be in paradise. Merciful One, O keep her soul
forever alive under Thy protective wings. The Lord being
her heritage, may she rest in peace; and let us say, Amen.

One general *yizkor* prayer may be recited for all one's deceased, citing the individual names in the spaces indicated. Or, one prayer may be recited for each deceased, if so desired, or separate paragraphs for males and females. One must be sure that the Hebrew text is worded in the plural or singular, male or female. Prayerbooks usually indicate whom the *yizkor* paragraph is intended for. The *yizkor* may be read in translation.

The name should be recited in Hebrew, giving both the name of the deceased and the name of the deceased's father. The Sephardic tradition uses the mother's name instead of the father's, as, for example, *Shmu'el ben Channah*. The bereaved should learn and remember these names. If they are absolutely not ascertainable, the English names may be used.

For Whom Yizkor Is Recited

Yizkor may be said for all Jewish dead: parents, grandparents, mates, children, family and friends. It may be recited for suicides and for sinners. A question of propriety usually arises regarding *yizkor* for a deceased first mate after remarriage. The only reason it would not be said is the hurt it might cause the present mate. Being that the *yizkor* is recited silently, there can be no such fear and the prayer may be recited.

When Is Yizkor Recited?

1. Despite the common practice, *yizkor* should be recited beginning with the very first holiday after death. There is widespread belief that *yizkor* may not be recited during the first year. This is an unfounded belief which may well be discarded. Precisely because *yizkor* is a redemptive prayer for the dead is reason enough for it to be recited during the first year, when the soul is said to be judged. There is no legitimate religious reason to delay it. Great

scholars have noted the erroneous practice and have strongly decried it.

2. There is also current a belief that *yizkor* is recited only for 50 years after death. This is totally without foundation. *Yizkor* is recited through all of one's lifetime. The memory of the departed does not end in a particular year. It is retained forever.

3. *Yizkor* is recited after the morning Torah reading on Yom Kippur, on the last day of Passover and Shavuot, and on the seventh day of Succot, called Shemini Atzeret. It is recited on these days even if they fall on the Sabbath at which time memorials are, otherwise, inappropriate to the festive nature of the holiday. In most synagogues it is recited after the rabbi's sermon.

The Requirement of a Minyan

Yizkor should be recited at synagogue services. If one cannot possibly attend these services because of illness, or because there is no *minyan* available, one may recite *yizkor* privately at home, although it is distinctly and unquestionably preferable to recite it at a public synagogue service. In this respect, it is unlike the Kaddish which may not be recited privately, under any circumstances.

Candle Lighting for Yizkor

It is an ancient custom, on the four holidays when *yizkor* is recited, to kindle *yahrzeit* candles for the departed. It is best that the lights be flaming wicks, as the flame and candle symbolize the relation of body and soul. However, if this is not available, electric bulbs or gas light may be used. For *yizkor* memorial purposes, one light will serve adequately to recall all the departed.

Yahrzeit: Memorial Anniversary

Despite the Germanic origin of the word *yahrzeit*, the designation of a special day and special observances to commemorate the anniversary of the death of parents was already discussed in the Talmud. This religious commemoration is recorded not as a fiat, but as a description of an instinctive sentiment of sadness, an annual rehearsing of tragedy, which impels one to avoid eating meat and drinking wine—symbols of festivity and joy, the very stuff of life.

Tradition regards this day as commemorative of both the enormous tragedy of death and the abiding glory of the parental heritage. It was a day set aside to contemplate the quality and life-style of the deceased, and to dwell earnestly upon its lessons. It is a day when one relives the moment of doom, perhaps even fasts to symbolize the unforgetable despair. It is a day conditioned by the need to honor one's parent in death as in life, through study and charity and other deeds of kindness. It is also conditioned by the non-rational, but all-too-human feelings that it is the day itself which is tragic, one which might bring misfortune with every annual cycle, and for which reason one slows one's activities and spends a good part of the day safely in the synagogue.

Yahrzeit may be observed for any relative or friend, but it is meant primarily for parents. Its observance takes place in three locations: the home, the synagogue and the cemetery.

Yahrzeit Home Observances

1. *Fasting.* It was customary for some mourners to fast on the *yahrzeit* for parents from the time of the *minchah* service of the previous day until dark on the day of *yahrzeit*. If one has committed himself to this custom of fasting on every *yahrzeit*, it becomes a sacred obligation to continue

the practice at every *yahrzeit* in the future. If one cannot fast, either because of weakness, or for any other cogent reason, he should at least try to avoid eating meat and wine and participating in festivities. If *yahrzeit* occurs on a holiday, or on other days of public joy on which the *tachanun* prayers are not recited, one should not fast, as it conflicts with the joyous spirit of the day.

2. *Yahrzeit Candles.* The kindling of the *yahrzeit* candle is a custom dating back to very early times, and is observed by almost all Jews. The kindling takes place at dark on the evening before the anniversary, and on Sabbaths and holy days *before* the regular candle-lighting. It is customary to allow the lights to extinguish themselves, rather than to put them out after dark at the end of *yahrzeit*. If there is any real danger of fire, one should extinguish them directly. If one forgets to light candles on the evening before, he should do so in the morning. On the Sabbath this may, of course, not be done, as it is biblically ordained that one may not make fire (put on the lights) on the Sabbath.

If the holiday had begun when he recalled that he had *yahrzeit* he may kindle it by taking the light from another flame. If one forgot to light candles and *yahrzeit* had passed, it would be advisable to make some contribution to charity.

The lights should be candles of wick and paraffin. If these are not available at all, gas or electric lights are permitted. As the flame and wick symbolize soul and body, it does appear significant to use the candle, rather than a bulb, if at all possible.

If all the children are in one house during *yahrzeit*, one candle suffices. It is preferable, however, in terms of respect for the deceased parent, for each child to light his own candle. If they are in different homes, separate candles are, of course, required. In commemorating the *yahrzeit* of several people at once, there should be a candle for each deceased. The candle is not a fetish, but a symbol, and overindulgence, by lighting numerous candles for every deceased one remembers, is not desirable.

3. *Torah Study and Charity.* One should make donations to religious schools or synagogues, to medical institutions or to the poor, on behalf of the deceased on *yahrzeit.* One should also make every effort to study some aspect of religious life on this day. It may be *mishnah,* which is the traditional *yahrzeit* study, or if one is not able to do so, a chapter of the Bible, in English or Hebrew.

Synagogue Yahrzeit Observances

On the Sabbath prior to *yahrzeit,* the *malei rachamim* memorial prayer is recited after the Torah reading at *minchah.* If possible, the mourner should chant the *maftir* portion and should lead the Saturday night *ma'ariv* service. He should, in any case, receive an *aliyah,* a Torah honor. This *aliyah* is considered a "required" honor. The synagogue usher should be made aware of the *yahrzeit.*

On the day of *yahrzeit* one should lead, if at all possible, all synagogue services. Those who cannot, would do well to learn at least the *minchah* service, which is brief and simple. The rabbi will be delighted to teach the mourner, or direct him to the cantor or sexton or lay teacher. He should recite the Kaddish at every service. In addition, there is usually a Psalm added to the morning service so that the *yahrzeit* observer may recite at least one Kaddish without the accompaniment of other mourners.

It is customary, though by no means mandatory, to bring some slight refreshments—liquor and cake—to the synagogue for all to partake of after early morning services, to toast *l'chayim,* "to life." This slight repast should not, of course, be allowed to develop into a full-fledged party.

Cemetery Yahrzeit Observances

The annual visit to the grave at *yahrzeit* is a traditional custom. At graveside one may recite the Psalms, selections of which are indicated in the chapter on unveilings, and then the *malei rachamim* prayer in Hebrew or English. It is far better, as mentioned above, to recite the prayer oneself than to hire a medium or proxy. *Mishnah* should be studied at the graveside, if at all possible. The Hebrew or English text may be used.

The Date of Yahrzeit

1. The date of *yahrzeit* during the first year *and* on all subsequent years, is one full Hebrew year from the date of *death*. If it is a Hebrew leap year, which numbers 13 months, it is commemorated thirteen months later. While the Kaddish is recited for 11 months, and other mourning observances are kept for 12 months, *yahrzeit* is judged not in terms of months, but years. Thus, if a parent died on the fourth day of Elul, 5718, *yahrzeit* is observed on the fourth day of Elul, 5719. This applies even if the burial took place several days after death, or if the deceased was buried overseas even one week later, or if the remains were missing, and then found and buried many months later. Many authorities maintain that in case of long delay between death and burial, *yahrzeit* on the *first* year be commemorated on the anniversary of burial.

2. The question does arise regarding the *yahrzeit* date when the death or *yahrzeit* falls on leap year, or on a Rosh Chodesh of one or two days. In order to clarify this matter it is necessary to understand the following:

a. The Hebrew lunar calendar, in a regular year, has 12 months. They are: Tishre, Chesvan, Kislev, Tevet, Shevat, Adar, Nissan, Iyar, Sivan, Tammuz, Av, Elul.

b. On leap years, an extra month is added, termed Adar I, and inserted prior to the regular Adar, which then becomes Adar II.

c. Each month has either 29 or 30 days. The first day of the month is called Rosh Chodesh, or new moon. In months that have 30 days, two consecutive days of Rosh Chodesh are celebrated—one on the thirtieth day of the previous month, the other on the first day of the next month. The months of Kislev and Tevet sometimes have two and sometimes one day of Rosh Chodesh.

The principle followed is that the *yahrzeit* is always observed in the *same month* and on the *same day*. Hence, if death occurred in Adar I of leap year, in regular years it is observed in Adar, but in leap years in Adar I. The same is true if it falls in Adar II of leap year—that is when it is observed.

If death occurred in Adar of a regular year, the *yahrzeit* in leap years is customarily observed in Adar I. Some insist on both Adar I and II being observed. Certainly, this latter custom should be observed if possible.

If death occurred in leap year, on the first of the two days of Rosh Chodesh Adar I (the 30th day of Shevat) or of Adar II (30th day of Adar I) the *yahrzeit* in regular years remains the first day of Rosh Chodesh Adar. If death occurred on Rosh Chodesh Kislev or Tevet, in a year when it is celebrated *one* day (which is really the first day of the month), if *yahrzeit* falls in a year when Rosh Chodesh Kislev or Tevet is celebrated two days, it is observed on the *second* day of Rosh Chodesh (really the first day of the month).

If death occurred on the first day of a *two*-day Rosh Chodesh (Kislev or Tevet), and the next year Rosh Chodesh is only *one* day, *yahrzeit* is observed on the 29th day of the previous month, the true month in which death occurred. If the next year (if the *first* yahrzeit) was also a *two*-day Rosh Chodesh, he should establish every *yahrzeit* on Rosh Chodesh Kislev or Tevet, whether one or two-day celebration.

3. When not sure of the day of death, or if it is not possible to determine it accurately, the mourner should choose a date. Out of respect to the deceased, it should not be the same date as the *yahrzeit* for the other parent. If in doubt between one day and the next, as the fifth or sixth

day of Elul, he should choose the earlier date, reasoning
that if it is the true date it is fine, and if it is not, then
he has merely anticipated, which also indicates a fine degree
of respect.

4. If death occurred a great distance from the location
of the mourners, and the time difference establishes different dates of death, we generally observe *yahrzeit* according to the date of the city where death occurred.

5. If death occurred at dusk, it is best to consider the
following day as *yahrzeit*.

6. When *yahrzeit* falls on Sabbath or holidays candles
must be kindled *before* the onset of evening. The cemetery
may be visited either one day before or after the holiday.
The *yahrzeit* fast, if that is observed, should be delayed
until the day after the holiday. All other synagogue ceremonies can be observed on the Sabbath or holiday.

7. One who has forgotten to observe *yahrzeit* on the
proper date should observe it as soon as he remembers. If
he cannot find a *minyan* on that day he may recite Kaddish
at the next *ma'ariv* service.

8. If he is sick, or disabled, or is otherwise prevented
from observing any of the *yahrzeit* tradition, he may depu-
tize a friend, or the sexton, to observe it for him. "A man's
messenger is as himself." This should be resorted to *only*
in emergency circumstances. What was written above with
regard to paying for the Mourner's Kaddish applies equally
to the one-day-a-year *yahrzeit* observance.

Memorial by Proxy

The annual display of respect manifested by the holiday-
season-visitations to the cemeteries is very impressive. However, it is frankly appalling to see the impudent public display of Jewish ignorance that accompanies these visitations.
As the masses swarm over the graves and are greeted by
the omnipresent "rabbis" who hawk the *malei*, the beautiful Hebrew memorial prayer to the compassionate God, the
scene smacks of religious decadence, of a bankruptcy of

mind and soul, of a topsy-turvy view of Judaism, and an unimaginably absurd concept of what constitutes respect for the dead. This charge does not refer solely to the ubiquitous *malei*-makers. Many of them are observant, learned, and dignified Jews, certainly qualified to receive compensation for the service they perform. But some, it must be admitted, are crude and uncomely hucksters. This charge does not refer, also, to many of those mourners who request the service of the *malei*-makers because they sincerely desire to pay *additional* religious tribute to their beloved by recitation of a prayer in the language of the *Siddur*.

What is of concern to the thinking Jew is the reason for the nightmarish situation which is unquestionably a blight on American-Jewish living. The cause is not difficult to find, although it is enmeshed in a sack of unsavory symptoms—the superstitious, "not-taking-any-chances" payoff to dear father; the preposterous notion that two dollars to a bearded Jew will somehow placate a God he hasn't ever cared to know; the impersonal "respect-paying"; the sad, momentary flick-of-the-memory that in a fleeting moment is expected to cover a multitude of travesties inflicted during life. What is the most evident cause in this whole unappetizing syndrome is the ignorance of the dynamic, brilliant faith that was our ancestors'; the unconcern for the meaning of our parents' Jewishness; the indifference even to the prayer that is recited, so long as it is couched in holy-sounding phrases. It is this festering on the open sores of the Jewish cranium that is so appalling.

If it were not so tragically serious, the cemetery scene, and the grotesque chant and talk that fills it, would provide scenario, score and script for a side-splitting comedy. Only with universal and intensive Jewish learning will we be able to avoid the debacle of the holiday cemetery scene. Only with the attitude that will derive from the study of the sources and wellsprings of Jewish life will we be able to look forward to a true holy day spirit, not only in the public places, but in the homes of Jews throughout the land.

6. Special Situations

Delayed News

IN OUR WORLD of instant global communication, extended delay in receiving news is relatively rare. Even without benefit of electronics, evil tidings seem to have an unfailing homing device and always find their mark. Yet, often bad news must be withheld so as to protect the ill and weak, or because families are dispersed to distant corners of the globe, or because people simply have lost touch, especially today when the "extended family"—cousins, uncles and aunts—are no longer closely-knit. What are the mourning laws in such cases of delayed news? The tradition divides delayed news into two categories: news that arrived before or after 30 days from day of death.

Brief Delay   שמועה קרובה

The "brief delay" refers to news that arrived *within* 30 days of the day of *death,* but after *shiva* has begun. In such instances the mourner observes the mourning practices from the time of hearing the news and follows all the laws as though he had just returned from the cemetery.

If news came during the first week he must observe *shiva* from the moment of hearing the news. In special circumstances he need not observe the full *shiva*, but may join other mourners and rise from *shiva* whenever they do, even though it be only for one hour of the last day. In order to do this, four conditions must be satisfied:

1. He must not have begun to observe mourning *before* meeting the other mourners.

2. The "Primary Mourner" must be present. A Primary Mourner is one who was responsible for the funeral arrangements, or for disposal of the deceased's belongings, and who is considered to be the head of the family, whether that person be the spouse, child, or sibling of the deceased. He must be older than 13. If responsibility is shared equally among the mourners, any one of them may be considered a Primary Mourner.

3. The other mourners must be sitting *shiva* in the city where either death or burial occurred.

4. He is not too distant from the other mourners (more than one day's travel time by any means of transportation).

If news came late on the thirtieth day it is considered a brief delay even though other relatives have completed the *sheloshim* that morning. The thirtieth day must have passed for the news to be considered "extended delay." The unusual circumstance of news coming precisely on the thirtieth day from the day of burial and the thirty-first from the day of death is a subject of dispute in the law. Therefore, if *shiva* can be observed, it should be done. If there are difficulties attendant upon doing so this may then be considered an "extended delay" and the procedure outlined in the next section should be followed.

If news arrived on the Sabbath or holiday which happens to be the thirtieth day it is considered extended delay.

If a holiday occurred between the time of death and the arrival of the news, this does not have the effect of suspending *shiva* or *sheloshim*, as the mourners had not as yet acknowledged the mourning.

If news arrived during a holiday, mourning begins on the night following the end of the holiday. The days of holidays are counted toward *sheloshim,* but only the last day of the holiday is counted toward *shiva.*

If news arrived on the Sabbath, only personal mourning observances should be followed, as outlined above, and the Sabbath is counted as the first day of *shiva.* After the Sabbath the mourner rends the garment and accepts full mourning. If a holiday occurs immediately after the Sabbath, the *shiva* is suspended.

Upon hearing the news, in the case of brief delay, the mourner must rend the garment and recite the "Righteous Judge" blessing. He does not don *tefillin* on that day. Neighbors are obligated to provide him with the customary meal of consolation.

The question has arisen in religious literature as to whether one may intentionally withhold the news of death from the mourner until after the thirtieth day. While this may be required in instances of those who are sick, or weak, or mentally ill, these cases should be decided by competent doctors or by the considered and informed judgment of the family. In ordinary, uncomplicated situations, the rule generally to be followed is that news may be withheld from all relatives other than son and daughter.

Extended Delay   שמועה רחוקה

"Extended delay" is defined as news that arrived *after* the thirtieth day from the day of death. Thus, if death occurred on a Wednesday, *sheloshim* is completed on Thursday, four weeks later. Thursday night is the beginning of extended delay.

The length of time that has elapsed since the death is considered as mitigating the severity of grief. The mourner, therefore, practices only a token observance. It is sufficient for him to remove his shoes and sit on a low stool, and stop all work and study for approximately an hour. He need not desist from washing and working beyond that time. For relatives, other than parents, the mourner need not stop working at all if it proves difficult for him to do so.

For parents, at any time, whether after 30 days or after the full year, he must rend the garment and recite the mourner's benediction, "the Righteous Judge."

As for other relatives for whom one is obligated to mourn, he need not rend the garment after 30 days, but he should recite the benediction on that day. If it is not recited on the day of the arrival of news, it is not recited at all.

For parents, while the laws of *shiva* and *sheloshim* are suspended, the mourning practices of the full year obtain until 12 months from the day of burial. If news arrived after one year, all mourning is suspended. However, if the mourner desires to recite Kaddish he should not be denied this privilege.

The Kohen
כהן

To be able to accept the fact of death is a blessing; to respect the dead is an act of devotion. But to *love* death is wicked; to *worship* the dead is a monstrous blasphemy. For there is a balance—a delicate, sensitive balance—between accepting death and loving it, between honoring the dead and worshiping at their graves. The consequence of this difference is a wide conceptual chasm between the faith which affirms life and also expects immortality beyond the grave, and the faith which denies the value of life as it seeks and strives for the beyond with all its power.

Judaism has taught, through its laws and traditions of mourning, the proper respect and honor for those who have passed on. Man must accept the inevitable and undeniable end of life. But the end of life must not be his conscious goal. "Choose life." "The dead do not praise the Lord." Judaism taught, through detailed levitical regulations, that the dead defile the living. The dead must be buried for their own honor. But they may not be handled excessively, dressed lavishly, held up for view, mummified and masked, primped and painted. *The dead defile the living.*

Judaism emphasizes life, and demonstrates this emphasis in the beautiful, though complicated, fabric of the laws of ritual impurity. Leviticus 21 commands the priests, servants at the sanctuary, "None shall defile himself for the dead among his people." Those whose lives are dedicated to maintaining the holiness of the Temple will be profaned by contact with the dead. The sanctity of the priesthood is easily blemished.

Further, the greater the level of sanctity during life, the greater the intensity of defilement in death. Animals that die defile in a relatively minor way. Pagans who die defile—but only on direct contact with the corpse. Jews who die defile the entire domain in which they rest. The *Kohen*, with certain exceptions, may not enter the building that contains the dead. "Behold," declares the Talmud, "the bones of the donkey render only purity. The house of Johanan, the High Priest, renders impurity. For in accordance with the degree of their belovedness is their defilement."

The laws of defilement prevented the all-too-common worship of the dead, affirmed the holiness and sacred value of life.

The laws of defilement of the *Kohen* had been given to a people only recently liberated from Egypt where the primary concern of the priesthood was death, burial, embalming. The Egyptian priest was a sort of undertaker, and the priesthood a cadaverous profession. The Jewish *Kohen* must be contrasted with this picture of morbidity. His concern was exclusively "life," and his service was only for the living. The Bible had to expressly permit the *Kohen* to attend the corpses of his seven close relatives. Following is a sketch of the laws of priestly purity:

Degrees of Defilement

The male *Kohen* may be rendered disqualified from service in our day, as in ancient times, if he is defiled by the dead—by the corpse of a human being older than 40 days, or even by any limb separated from a human being. The defilement may be contracted in one of two ways:

1. *Defilement by direct contact* effected either by touching, carrying, or moving the corpse, which the *Kohen* is prohibited from doing; or

2. *Defilement of domain,* which refers to the *Kohen's* being present in the same enclosure with the corpse while it rests there. While the deceased is present, the entire house—all its rooms and floors—is considered levitically impure. Hence, the *Kohen* may not enter the house of the deceased. If the corpse is already there, he must leave at once. Even if the common cover for the *Kohen* and the corpse is only a roof extension or beam, lattice work, a bridge, or even a tree, it is considered a common domain and it defiles.

When the Kohen Must Defile Himself

While the *Kohen* may not compromise the sanctity of his priesthood by contact with the dead, the Bible specifically commands him to prepare, handle, and concern himself with the bodies of his seven nearest relatives: wife, father, mother, son, daughter, brother (but not if he is a brother only from his mother's side), and unmarried sister. The Bible does not give mere *permission* to defile in these cases, it *commands* him to do so—even if others are available to make arrangements. The *Kohen* should stay in the domain of the deceased. This command of defilement prevails until the closing of the grave, but not one moment longer. Immediately after the filling of the grave, he may not wait even for the Burial Kaddish, but must depart quickly.

Met Mitzvah

For a corpse left unattended even the High Priest must defile himself and provide for its proper burial. Such a corpse is termed *met mitzvah,* and requires singular devotion and care.

In our days, the rule of *met mitzvah* would apply to the deceased who does not have a sufficient number of Jews to serve as pall-bearers or care for other burial arrangements. In such a case the *Kohen* may not move from the corpse's side even to find another Jew to serve in his stead. He is under biblical obligation to remain with the corpse and honor him.

The Kohen at the Chapel

The *Kohen* may not enter the chapel or any one of its rooms if the deceased (not one of the seven relatives) is housed there. However, the *Kohen* may stand outside the chapel, close to the wall, to hear the funeral service. Families of the deceased will usually understand the absence of the *Kohen* if they are given even the simplest explanation. One need not consider himself overly-pious or very religious in order to preserve the privileged heritage that his father and faith have conferred upon him.

The Kohen at the Cemetery

There are two rules of thumb the *Kohen* must follow when accompanying any corpse out-of-doors:

1. He must not approach by less than six feet any grave on the cemetery. In difficult circumstances some contend that four and one-half feet is sufficient, since the casket is buried deep in the earth. The *Kohen* should certainly not touch the tombstone.

2. If the casket is not yet interred, it being either in procession, or at the graveside before burial, the *Kohen* may come as close as one and a half feet from it. He should take care not to touch it, carry it, or be pushed against it.

The Kohen at Unveilings

The *Kohen* may not attend the unveiling of even close relatives for whose burial he was commanded to defile himself, unless he can be assured that he will not need to walk within six feet of any grave. If this is possible, or where the grave is at the edge of the cemetery, he may attend. Of course, in such instances, he may not personally unveil the monument even for his parents. The sister, wife, or mother of the *Kohen* may do this for him.

The Family of the Kohen

Wives and daughters of the *Kohen* are not bound by the laws of defilement and are permitted to practice all regular procedures applicable to all Jews.

Sons of the *Kohen* are themselves *Kohanim*. A child, as soon as he is capable of being educated in these matters, should be taught the laws of the *Kohen*. This, surely, should not wait until Bar Mitzvah, the age when he is obligated to fulfill the laws.

Suicides

Man is the magnificent creation of an all-wise and all-merciful God. The awesome determination of life and death is not given to man. As it is God's prerogative to grant life, so it is His sole decision to take life: "Perforce were you born," say the rabbis of the Talmud, "and perforce must you die" (*Ethics of the Fathers*, chapter 4). One who takes his own life is a murderer, as is one who takes another's life. "I will seek your blood for your souls," is applied by the *midrash* to one who destroys his own soul. The suicide, in effect, denies the lordship, the supreme mastery of God, when he decides that he is the lord of his own soul. He is then committing not only an act of violence; he is guilty of sacrilege.

Suicide is considered by many thinkers to be an even more heinous crime than murder itself. The murderer has the possibility of recanting his vicious deed. Not so the suicide. Death is considered a punishment that atones for evil committed in life. But the suicide has used this very act of atonement in order to commit his terrible crime.

The horror of this act in the eyes of men, however, is not primarily theological—the blasphemy of God, but moral —the betrayal of family and friends. It is a default of all responsibility, leaving children, a mate or parents staring vacantly at the end of a broken chain, betrayed and bewildered, a lingering *Gotterdammerung* with a vision of doom to haunt them all the days of their life.

What leaves one incredulous at the sight of a suicide is not only the betrayal, but the ultimate uselessness of this irretrievable decision. Say the sages in the fourth chapter of the *Ethics of the Fathers:* "Do not allow your natural impulse to convince you that the grave is a refuge, for perforce were you formed; perforce were you born; perforce do you live; perforce shall you die; and perforce are you destined to give an account and reckoning before the supreme King of Kings, the Holy One, blessed be He." There is no refuge in death. Death brings surcease from anxieties and despair and conflict, but not oblivion. The dead shall rise to be judged.

It is the enormity of this crime that gave rise to the oft-quoted folk-phrase: "Suicides do not receive a share in the world to come." Ostensibly, this is because they have refused the rightful share of their duties in this world. They cannot receive Divine reward as they have denied the very rule of the Divinity.

The Definition of a Suicide

What is a true suicide? Which man can be considered a normal individual who coolly and intentionally plans and commits an act of suicide? Who can, with any reliable degree of accuracy, determine the nature, motivation and purposeful quality of this heinous act? What mysterious force has impelled this man to perform an act so contrary to human nature?

Because of these difficult problems, the rabbis have sought to deal leniently in their treatment of the suicide. Suicide has a strict, legal, religious definition in Judaism that does not always accord with the off-hand general conclusion made by neighbors and relatives. The determination of suicide must be made by a qualified rabbi, using criteria of religion. It is not to be decided on the basis of police or court reports or analyses alone. There must be taken into consideration the question of insanity, intoxication or drug influence, the motivation of the act, the possibility of a last-minute change-of-heart, the complex problem of whether or how this was planned. It is surely no decision that can be made easily, least of all by those not acquainted with both the letter and the spirit of *Jewish* law.

The rabbi, in cooperation with psychiatrists and law enforcement agencies, will have to determine the following questions before rendering his decision:

1. Is there even a remote possibility that this was murder, and not suicide? Is the determination of suicide a probability or a certainty?

2. Might the deceased have been insane, to any degree, even temporarily? Might he have been under the influence of liquor, or narcotics, or other barbiturates?

3. Was the deceased motivated by extreme suffering, by enormous fear of punishment—either at the hands of God or of society, or by terrible anxiety?

4. Was the act of suicide planned in advance? Was that plan expressed verbally or committed to writing? How long before the suicide was it made? Could it have been merely an exercise in emotional exaggeration as exasperated people are sometimes wont to do? Did self-destruction come as was planned?

5. Did death come instantly or did the deceased linger, during which time he might have tried to alter the course of events, or repent of the crime?

6. Was the final act the result of some cruel, fashionable game or fancy, or in the spirit of reckless abandon? Was it a result of anger or hatred?

With these facts available, the rabbi will be able to decide the mode of burial and the procedures for mourning. It should again be emphasized that this decision is *not* a police matter and, certainly, it should not be made by the layman.

Mourning Traditions for the Suicide

The principle followed in these laws is that no honor is to be paid the suicide because the crime deserves only rebuke. However, respect for the bereaved family must be scrupulously considered, as they are the sufferers and not the perpetrators of the act. All aspects of the mourning traditions, therefore, which affect the honor of the living are to be observed, while those laws devised solely for the honor of the dead are suspended.

Aninut

The period between death and burial, *aninut,* which exempts the mourner from performing the positive commands (as outlined in an earlier chapter) is based upon two needs: one is the time-consuming concern for the details of the burial arrangements and the mental anguish attendant upon it; the other is the need to honor the deceased which preoccupies the mind of the bereaved. While the second principle does not apply to the intentional suicide (there is no honor in self-destruction), the first obviously does, as burial is required. The period of *aninut,* therefore, extends from death only to the time when all arrangements have been completed with the undertaker and cemetery, and not, as is customary, until the interment.

Burial

The procedure for *taharah* (purification rites), and requirements for shrouds, casket and grave are the same as for other Jewish dead. The only difference is the location of the grave. If the suicide is definitely an intentional suicide, he is to be buried at least six feet from surrounding graves. Sometimes cemeteries reserve a special section for suicides. Otherwise, it is usually located near the fence or border of the cemetery.

Rending the Clothing

While commentators dispute this matter in halachic literature, the opinion generally followed is that mourners do rend the garment, even for intentional suicides.

Eulogy

No eulogy should be made for an intentional suicide, despite any good qualities he may have demonstrated in life, as it is in his very death that he committed this sacrilege. Eulogizing these dead would constitute an act of hypocrisy. The erection of the monument and its unveiling should be performed by the recitation of Psalms, but without benefit of eulogy.

Mourning Observances

If there is even a remote possibility that the family's honor would be compromised if no mourning laws were to be observed, they should be followed in every detail. This applies even where the deceased is technically considered an intentional suicide.

Kaddish

While the Burial Kaddish at graveside is not recited, the Mourner's Kaddish is recited regularly, morning and night. Although the Mourner's Kaddish is normally recited for 11 months, if the deceased is beyond doubt an intentional suicide, it should be recited for the full year, as he certainly requires the full redemptive effect of the Kaddish.

Comforting the Bereaved

While the deceased may not be specially honored and should receive no public recognition, the family of the deceased must be given every courtesy. The mourners should be accompanied to the cemetery and should be visited at home. These mourners, perhaps more than any others, require the healing comfort of understanding friends and neighbors. Great care should be taken during the hours of consolation. The rabbinic dictum that the bereaved should be allowed to open the conversation while visitors listen attentively, seems to be the best advice for this tragic moment.

Yizkor and Yahrzeit

Yizkor should be recited at the regular time for intentional suicides, and no variations are to be made in the prayers. *Yahrzeit* is observed as for other relatives.

7 ✧ The World Beyond the Grave

Life After Death

MAN HAS HAD AN abiding faith in a world beyond the grave. The conviction in a life after death, unprovable but unshakeable, has been cherished since the beginning of thinking man's life on earth. It makes its appearance in religious literature not as fiat, commanded irrevocably by an absolute God, but rather arises plant-like, growing and developing naturally in the soul. It then sprouts forth through sublime prayer and sacred hymn. Only later does it become extrapolated in complicated metaphysical speculation. The after-life has not been "thought up"; it is not a rational construction of a religious philosophy imposed on believing man. It has sprung from within the hearts of masses of men, a sort of *consensus gentium*, inside out, a hope beyond and above the rational, a longing for the warm sun of eternity. The after-life is not a theory to be proven logically or demonstrated by rational analysis. It is axiomatic. It is to the soul what oxygen is to the lungs. There is little meaning to life, to God, to man's constant strivings, to all of his achievements, unless there is a world beyond the grave.

The Bible, so vitally concerned with the actions of man in this world, and agonizing over his day-to-day morals, is relatively silent about the world-to-come. But, precisely, this very silence is a tribute to the awesome concept, taken for granted like the oxygen in the atmosphere. No elaborate apologia, no complex abstractions are necessary. The Bible, which records the sacred dialogue between God and man, surely must be founded on the soul's eternal existence. It was not a matter of debate, as it became later in history when whole movements interpreted scripture with slavish literalism and could not find the after-life crystallized in letters and words, or later, when philosophers began to apply the yardstick of rationalism to man's every hope and idea and sought empirical proof for this conviction of the soul. It was a fundamental creed, always present, though rarely articulated.

If the soul is immortal then death cannot be considered a final act. If the life of the soul is to be continued, then death, however bitter, is deprived of its treacherous power of casting mourners into a lifetime of agonizing hopelessness over an irretrievable loss. Terrible though it is, death is a threshold to a new world—the "world-to-come."

A Parable

An imaginative and telling analogy that conveys the hope and confidence in the after-life, even though this hope must be refracted through the prism of death, is the tale of twins awaiting birth in the mother's womb. It was created by a contemporary Israeli rabbi, the late Y. M. Tuckachinsky.

Imagine twins growing peacefully in the warmth of the womb. Their mouths are closed, and they are being fed via the navel. Their lives are serene. The whole world, to these brothers, is the interior of the womb. Who could conceive anything larger, better, more comfortable? They begin to wonder: "We are getting lower and lower. Surely if it continues, we will exit one day. What will happen after we exit?"

Now the first infant is a believer. He is heir to a religious tradition which tells him that there will be a "new life" after this wet and warm existence of the womb. A strange belief, seemingly without foundation, but one to which he holds fast. The second infant is a thorough-going skeptic. Mere stories do not deceive him. He believes only in that which can be demonstrated. He is enlightened, and tolerates no idle conjecture. What is not within one's experience can have no basis in one's imagination.

Says the faithful brother: "After our 'death' here, there will be a new great world. We will eat through the mouth! We will see great distances, and we will hear through the ears on the sides of our heads. Why, our feet will be straightened! And our heads—up and free, rather than down and boxed in."

Replies the skeptic: "Nonsense. You're straining your imagination again. There is no foundation for this belief. It is only your survival instinct, an elaborate defense mechanism, a historically-conditioned subterfuge. You are looking for something to calm your fear of 'death.' There is only *this world*. There is no world-to-come!"

"Well then," asks the first, "what do you say it will be like?"

The second brother snappily replies with all the assurance of the slightly knowledgeable: "We will go with a bang. Our world will collapse and we will sink into oblivion. No more. Nothing. Black void. An end to consciousness. Forgotten. This may not be a comforting thought, but it is a logical one."

Suddenly the water inside the womb bursts. The womb convulses. Upheaval. Turmoil. Writhing. Everything lets loose. Then a mysterious pounding—a crushing, staccato pounding. Faster, faster, lower, lower.

The believing brother exits. Tearing himself from the womb, he falls outward. The second brother shrieks—startled by the "accident" befallen his brother. He bewails and bemoans the tragedy—the death of a perfectly fine fellow. Why? Why? Why didn't he take better care? Why did he fall into that terrible abyss?

As he thus laments, he hears a head-splitting cry, and a great tumult from the black abyss, and he trembles: "Oh my! What a horrible end! As I predicted!"

Meanwhile as the skeptic brother mourns, his "dead" brother has been born into the "new" world. The head-splitting cry is a sign of health and vigor, and the tumult is really a chorus of *mazel tovs* sounded by the waiting family thanking God for the birth of a healthy son.

Indeed, in the words of a contemporary thinker, man comes from the darkness of the "not yet," and proceeds to the darkness of the "no more." While it is difficult to imagine the "not yet" it is more difficult to picture the "no more."

As we separate and "die" from the womb, only to be born to life, so we separate and die from our world, only to be re-born to life eternal. The exit from the womb is the birth of the body. The exit from the body is the birth of the soul. As the womb requires a gestation period of nine months, the world requires a residence of 70 or 80 years. As the womb is *prozdor*, an anteroom preparatory to life, so our present existence is a *prozdor* to the world beyond.

The Concept of Immortality

The conception of an after-life is fundamental to the Jewish religion; it is an article of faith in the Jews' creed. The denial of the after-life constitutes a denial of the cornerstone of the faith. This concept is not merely an added detail that may lose its significance in some advanced age. It is an essential and enduring principle. Indeed, the Mishnah (*Sanhedrin* X, 1) expressly excludes from the reward of the "world beyond" he who holds that the resurrection of the dead is without biblical warrant. Maimonides considers this belief one of the 13 basic truths which every Jew is commanded to hold.

The concept of after-life entered the prayerbook in the philosophic hymns of *Yigdal* and *Ani Ma'amin*. Centuries later, hundreds of thousands of Jews, packed in cattle-cars, enroute to the crematoria, sang the *Ani Ma'amin*, the affirmation of the coming of the Messiah.

Philosophers, such as Hasdai Crescas in the fourteenth century, changed the formulation of the basic truths, but still kept immortality as a fundamental principle without which the Jewish religion is inconceivable. Simon Ben Zemah Duran, in the early fifteenth century, reduced the fundamentals to three, but resurrection was included. Joseph Albo, in the same era, revised the structure of dogmas, and still immortality remained a universally binding belief. No matter how the basic principles were reduced or revised, immortality remained a major tenet of Judaism. Indeed, we may say of immortality what Hermann Cohen says of the Messiah, "If the Jewish religion had done nothing more for mankind than proclaim the messianic idea of the Old Testament prophets, it could have claimed to be the bed-rock of all the world's ethical culture."

Strange as it may appear, despite the historic unanimity of scholarly opinion on the fundamental belief, the practical details of immortality are ambiguous and vague. There is no formal eschatology in Judaism, only a traditional concensus that illuminates the way. The veil has never been pierced, and only shadowy structures can be discerned. But, as a renowned artist remarked, the true genius of a painting can be determined at dusk when the light fades, when one can see only the outline, the broad strokes of the brush, while the details are submerged in darkness. The beauty of the concept of immortality and its enormous religious significance does not lie in details. Maimonides denies that man can have a clear picture of the after-life and compares earth-bound creature with the blind man who cannot learn to appreciate colors merely by being given a verbal description. Flesh-and-blood man cannot have any precise conception of the pure, spiritual bliss of the world beyond. Thus, says Maimonides, the precise sequence in which the after-life will finally unravel is not a cardinal article of the faith, and the faithful should not concern themselves with the details. So it is often in Judaism that *abstract* principles must be held in the larger, conceptual sense, while the formal philosophic details are blurred. Contrariwise, pragmatic religious ideals—the observances of the faith—are worked out to their minutest detail, although the basic concept behind them may remain unknown forever.

For all that, there is a consensus of belief based on talmudic derivations from the Torah and philosophic analyses of statements uttered by the sages. The concept is usually discussed under the headings of "Messiah" and "Resurrection of the Dead." (Concepts such as *Ge-hinnom* and *Gan Eden* are too complicated for discussion in this work.) The term, *olam ha'ba*, the "world beyond," while relatively unclear, seems to have encompassed the two basic concepts of Messiah and Resurrection. Maimonides lists these two as cardinal principles of the Jewish creed.

Messiah
משיח

The generic term, Messiah, means "anointed one." Kings and priests were anointed in ancient times to set them apart as specially designated leaders of society. The anointed one will bring redemption to this world. It will be a time of true bliss, unparalleled in our own existence. It will not be a *new* world, a qualitatively *different* world, rather will it be this world brought to perfection. Universal peace, tranquility, lawfulness, and goodness will prevail, and all will acknowledge the unity and lordship of God.

Will the Messiah be a specific person, or will he only *represent* an era of perfection—the "days of Messiah?" Traditional Judaism believes, without equivocation, in the coming of an inconceivably great hero, anointed for leadership—a descendant of the House of David, who will lead the world out of chaos. He will be of flesh and blood, a mortal sent expressly by God to fulfill the glory of His people. The traditional belief is that man must work to better the world and help bring on the Messiah. It believes the idea that mankind *by itself* will inevitably progress to such an era to be unfounded optimism. A supernatural gift to mankind, in the person of the Messiah, will be required to bring the world to this pinnacle of glory. God will directly intervene to prevent the world from rushing headlong into darkness, and will bring the redemption through a human personality. The personal Messiah, supernaturally introduced to mankind, will not, however, be a Divine personality. He will only bring about the redemption that is granted by God. The Messiah will have no ability to bring that redemption himself. He will have no miraculous powers. He, himself, will not be able to atone for the sins of others. He will have no superhuman relationship to God. He will be an exalted personality, of incomparable ability, who will usher in the rehabilitation of the Jewish people and the subsequent regeneration of all mankind.

How the Messiah will come, and how we will be able to identify him has aroused the magnificent imaginative inventiveness and poetic fancy of masses of Jews in every age. Many of these ruminations are contradictory. Some are founded in biblical interpretation, some on traditional beliefs handed down from father to son, while others are flights of folkloristic fancy.

The time of the coming of the Messiah has aroused such fantastic conjecture by so many who confidently predicted specific dates and signs, causing so much anxiety and unreasonable anticipation, and culminating in such heartbreaking and spiritually-shattering frustration, that the sages have had to chastise severely those who "count the days" to "bring near the end" of redemption.

While some theologians have sought to dispute the supernatural introduction of the Messiah, or to denigrate

the idea of a personal Messiah, there is no *a priori* reason
to deny either. On the other hand, however, there does stand
a millennium of unwavering conviction on the part of our
most profound scholars and the great masses of Jews to
affirm it. The authority of hundreds of generations will
withstand superficial rational analysis, let alone the metaphysical misgivings and begrudging consent of contemporary, sophisticated theologians.

The Resurrection of the Dead
תחיית המתים

The body returns to the earth, dust to dust, but the soul
returns to God who gave it. This doctrine of the immortality
of the soul is affirmed not only by Judaism and other religions, but by many secular philosophers as well. Judaism,
however, also believes in the eventual resurrection of the
body, which will be reunited with the soul at a later time
on a "great and awesome day of the Lord." The human
form of the righteous men of all ages, buried and long since
decomposed, will be resurrected at God's will.

The most dramatic portrayal of this bodily resurrection
is to be found in the "Valley of Dry Bones" prophecy in
Ezekiel 37, read as the *Haftorah* on the Intermediate Sabbath of Passover. It recalls past deliverances and envisions
the future redemption of Israel and the eventual quickening
of the dead.

> The hand of the Lord was upon me, and the Lord
> carried me out in a spirit, and set me down in the midst
> of the valley, and it was full of bones; and He caused
> me to pass by them round about, and, behold, there were
> very many in the open valley; and, lo, they were very
> dry. And He said unto me: "Son of man, can these
> bones live?" And I answered: "O Lord, God, Thou
> knowest." Then He said unto me: "Prophesy over these
> bones, and say unto them: 'O ye dry bones, hear the

word of the Lord: Thus saith the Lord God unto these bones: Behold, I will cause breath to enter into you, and ye shall live. And I will lay sinews upon you, and will bring up flesh upon you, and cover you with skin, and put breath in you, and ye shall live; and ye shall know that I am the Lord.' " So I prophesied as I was commanded; and as I prophesied, there was a noise, and behold a commotion, and the bones came together, bone to its bone. And I beheld, and, lo, there were sinews upon them and flesh came up, and skin covered them above; but there was no breath in them. Then said He unto me: "Prophesy unto the breath, prophesy, son of man, and say to the breath: 'Thus saith the Lord God: Come from the four winds, O breath, and breathe upon these slain, that they may live.' " So I prophesied as He commanded me, and the breath came into them, and they lived, and stood upon their feet, an exceeding great host. Then He said unto me: "Son of man, these bones are the whole house of Israel; behold, they say: 'Our bones are dried up, and our hope is lost; we can clean cut off.' Therefore, prophesy, and say unto them: 'Thus saith the Lord God: Behold, I will open your graves, and cause you to come up out of your graves, O my people; and I will bring you into the land of Israel. And ye shall know that I am the Lord, when I have opened your graves, and caused you to come up out of your graves, O My people. And I will put My spirit in you, and ye shall live, and I will place you in your own land; and ye shall know that I the Lord have spoken, and performed it, saith the Lord.' "

The power of this conviction can be gauged not only by the quality of the lives of the Jews, their tenacity and gallantry in the face of death, but in the very real fear instilled in their enemies. After destroying Jerusalem and callously decimating its Jewish population, Titus, the Roman general, returned home with only a portion of his Tenth

Legion. When asked whether he had lost all of his other men on the battlefield, Titus gave assurance that his men were alive, but that they were still on combat duty. He had left them to stand guard over Jewish corpses in the fields of Jerusalem because he was sincerely afraid that their bodies would be resurrected and they would reconquer the Holy Land as they had promised.

The belief in a bodily resurrection appears, at first sight, to be incredible to the contemporary mind. But when approached from the God's-eye view, why is rebirth more miraculous than birth? The adhesion of sperm and egg, the subsequent fertilization and development in the womb culminating in the birth of the astoundingly complex network of tubes and glands, bones and organs, their incredibly precise functioning and the unbelievably intricate human brain that guides them, is surely a miracle of the first magnitude. Curiously, the miraculous object, man himself, takes this for granted. In his preoccupation with daily trivia, he ignores the miracle of his own existence. The idea of rebirth may appear strange because we have never experienced a similar occurrence, for which reason we cannot put together the stuff of imagination. Perhaps it is because we can be active in creating life, but cannot participate with God in the recreation of life. Perhaps it is becuase, scientifically, recreation flies against any biological theory, while we are slowly coming to know how life is developed, and our researchers are about to create life in the laboratory test tube. But, who has created the researching biologist? And, can we not postulate an omnipotent Divine Biologist who created all men? Surely resurrection is not beyond the capacity of an omnipotent God.

The sages simplified the concept of bodily resurrection by posing an analogy which brings it within the experience of man. A tree, once alive with blossoms and fruit, full of the sap of life, stands cold and still in the winter. Its leaves have browned and fallen, its fruit rots on the ground. But the warm rains come and the sun shines. Buds sprout.

Green leaves appear. Colorful fruits burst from their seed. With the coming of spring, God resurrects nature. For this reason the blessing of God for reviving the dead, which is recited in every daily *Amidah,* incorporates also the seasonal requests for rain. When praying for the redemption of man, the prayerbook uses the phrase *matzmi'ach yeshuah,* "planting salvation." Indeed, the talmud compares the day of resurrection with the rainy season, and notes that the latter is even more significant—for resurrection serves only the righteous while the rain falls indiscriminately on all men.

This is one, supplementary reason why the body and all its limbs require to be interred in the earth and not cremated, for it expresses our faith in the future resurrection. Naturally, the all-powerful God can recreate the body whether it was buried or drowned or burned. Yet, willful cremation signifies an arrogant denial of the possibility of resurrection, and those who deny this cardinal principle should not share in the reward for its observance. The body and its limbs—whether amputated before death, or during a permissible post-mortem examination—have to be allowed to decompose as one complete organism by the processes of nature, not by man's mechanical act.

Resurrection: A Symbolic Idea

Some contemporary thinkers have noted that the physical revival of the dead is symbolic of a cluster of basic Jewish ideas:

First, man does not achieve the ultimate redemption by virtue of his own inherent nature. It is not because he, uniquely, possesses an immortal soul that he, *inevitably,* will be resurrected. The concept of resurrection underscores man's reliance on God who, in the words of the prayerbook, "Wakes the dead in great mercy." It is His grace and His mercy that rewards the deserving, and revives those who sleep in the dust.

Second, resurrection is not only a private matter, a bonus for the righteous individual. It is a corporate reward. *All* of the righteous of *all* ages, those who stood at Sinai, and those of our generation, will be revived. The *community* of the righteous has a corporate and historic character. It will live again as a whole people. The individual, even in death, is not separated from the society in which he lived.

Third, physical resurrection affirms unequivocally that man's soul *and* his body are the creations of a holy God. There is a tendency to assume that the affirmation of a spiritual dimension in man must bring with it the corollary that his physical being is depreciated. Indeed, such has been the development of the body-soul duality in both the Christian tradition and in Oriental religions, and accounts for their glorification of asceticism. Further, even the Greek philosophers who were enamored of the beauty of the body, came to denigrate the physical side of man. They crowned reason as man's noblest virtue. For them the spiritual-intellectual endeavor to perceive the unchanging truth was the highest function of man. Man's material existence, on the other hand, was always in flux, subject to change and, therefore, inferior. Thus, they accepted immortality of the soul—which to the Greeks was what we call mind—which survives the extinction of his physical being. But they could not understand physical resurrection because they did not, by any means, consider the body worthy of being reborn.

To the contrary, Judaism has always stressed that the body, as the soul, is a gift of God—indeed, that it belongs to God. *Ha'neshamah lach ve'haguf pa'alach*, the Jew declared, "The soul is yours, and the body is your handiwork." To care for the body is a religious command of the Bible. The practice of asceticism for religious purposes was tolerated, but the ascetic had to bring a sacrifice of atonement for his action. Resurrection affirms that the body is of value because it came from God, and it will be revived by God. Resurrection affirms that man's empirical existence is valuable in God's eyes. His activities in this world are significant in the scheme of eternity. His strivings are not to be deprecated as vain and useless, but are to be brought to fulfillment at the end of days.

The concept of resurrection thus serves to keep God ever in man's consciousness, to unify contemporary and historic Jewry, to affirm the value of God's world, and to heighten, rather than to depress, the value of man's worthy strivings in this world.

Which specific virtues might guarantee a person's resurrection is a subject of much debate. The method of resurrection is, of course, an open question that invites conjecture, but which can offer no definite answer.

While the details of the after-life are thus very much a matter of speculation, the traditional consensus must serve to illuminate the dark path. In the words of Rabbi Joshua ben Chanania (*Niddah* 70b) : "When they come to life again, we will consult about the matter."

Life After Death: A Corollary of Jewish Belief

The existence of a life after death is a necessary corollary of the Jewish belief in a just and merciful and ethical God.

God Is Just

The Jew is caught in a dilemma: He believes that God is righteous and just—He rewards the good and punishes the wicked. Yet, for all the strength of his belief, he lives in a world where he sees that life is unfair. He sees all too often the spiritual anomaly of *zaddik vera lo, rasha vetov lo,* the righteous who suffer and the wicked who prosper. The sages answer by saying that there is *spiritual* reward and *spiritual* punishment. The answer that religion gives is that the good, just, and eternal God revives the righteous dead, while the wicked remain in the dust. It is in life-after-death at which time the just God balances the scales and rewards or punishes those who truly deserve it. This doctrine of resurrection is, thus, a necessary corollary of our belief in a just God.

God Is Merciful

But if we ask of God only that He be just, can we expect that we ourselves will be resurrected? Who is so righteous as to be assured of that glorious reward? Hence we call upon God's *mercy* that He revive us. The concept of resurrection is an affirmation of His mercy. Thus, Joseph Albo, a fifteenth-century philosopher, notes that in the prayerbook the concept of resurrection is associated with *rachamin rabim,* "*great* mercy," whereas God's gift of life and sustenance are considered only *chen, chessed* and *rachamim,* "grace, kindness and mercy." Says Rabbi Albo: "The life of man is divided into three portions: The years of rise and growth, the middle years or the plateau, and the years of decline." These are described by the three adjectives— grace, kindness and mercy. While one is young and vigorous one does not require an *extra* measure of assistance from God in being nourished. All that he needs is *chen,* Divine grace. In the second portion of life, man grows older, but he is still able and strong. He needs more than just Divine grace, he needs God's kindness, *chessed.* In the declining years, he is weak, dependent on others, and in desperate need of more than grace and kindness. He now needs *rachamim,* God's mercy. But there is also a fourth portion of life: life after death. For this man requires more than grace, kindness and mercy. He needs *rachamim rabim,* "great mercy"! Thus, in Albo's scheme, resurrection is only a natural, further development of God's providence. In the words of the prayerbook: *Mechalkel chayim bechessed, mechayeh metim berachamim rabim.* "He sustains the living with kindness and revives the dead with *great mercy.*"

God as an Ethical Personality

The concept of life-after-death also follows from a belief in God as the God of goodness. A great teacher of our generation supports this by citing the *amidah* prayer in the daily prayerbook, "You support the *falling*, and heal the *sick*, and free those who are *bound up*, and keep your faith with those who *sleep in the dust*." The prayerbook lists a series of evils that befall man, and asserts that God will save man from them. Those who "fall" suffer financial failure, a defect in the structure of society. We believe that God who is good will overcome that defect. He will "support the falling." Worse than that is sickness, which is a flaw in the physical nature of man. We believe that God is good and will not tolerate such an evil forever. He will heal the sick. Worse yet is the disease of slavery, the sickness which man wishes upon his fellowman. God will overcome this, too, for He not only supports the falling and heals the sick, He is the great emancipator of man. The worst evil of all, however, the meanest scandal, the vilest disgrace to that being created in the image of God, is death, the end to all hope and all striving. But we believe in an ethical and good God. As He prevailed over the evils of lifetime, so will He prevail over the final evil, that of death. Thus, we conclude, you who support and heal, and free, will also keep your faith with those who are dead.

The Meaning of Death

What is death? Is it merely the cessation of the biological function of living? Is it but the tragedy to end all other tragedies? Is it simply the disappearance of the soul, the end of consciousness, the evaporation of personality, the disintegration of the body into its elemental components? Is it an end beyond which there is only black void? Or, is there a significance, some deep and abiding meaning to death—one that transcends our puny ability to understand?

With all of modern man's sophistication, his brilliant technological achievements, the immense progress of his science, his discovery of new worlds of thought, he has not come one iota closer to grasping the meaning of death than did his ancient ancestors. Philosophers and poets have probed the idea of immortality, but stubbornly it remains, as always, the greatest paradox of life.

In practice, however, we must realize that what death means to the individual depends very much on what life means to him.

If life is a stage, and we the poor players who strut and fret our hour upon the stage and then are heard no more; if life is a tale told by an idiot, full of sound and fury, signifying nothing; if life is an inconsequential drama, a purposeless amusement—then death is only the heavy curtain that falls on the final act. It sounds its hollow thud: *Finita la comedia,* and we are no more. Death has no significance, because life itself has no lasting meaning.

If life is only the arithmetic of coincidence, man a chance composite of molecules, the world an haphazard conglomeration without design or purpose, where everything is temporal and nothing eternal—with values dictated only by consensus—then death is merely the check-mate to an interesting, thoughtful, but useless game of chance. Death has no transcendent significance, since nothing in life has had transcendent significance. If such is the philosophy of life, death is meaningless, and the deceased need merely be disposed of unceremoniously, and as efficiently as possible.

If life is only nature mindlessly and compulsively spinning its complicated web, and man only a high-level beast, and the world—in Shopenhauer's phrase—*eine grosse shlachtfeld,* a great battlefield, and if values are only those of the jungle, aimed only at the satisfaction of animal appetites—then death is simply a further reduction to the basic elements, progress an adventure into nothingness, and our existence on this earth only a cosmic trap. In this scheme, life is surrounded by parentheses, dropped or substituted without loss of meaning to nature. Death, in this sense, is the end of a cruel match that pits man against beast, and man against man. It is the last slaughter. Furtively, irrevocably, despairingly, man sinks into the soil of a cold and impersonal nature, his life without purpose, his death without significance. His grave need not be marked. As his days were as a passing shadow, without substance and shape, so his final repose.

If life is altogether absurd, with man bound and chained by impersonal fate or ironbound circumstances, where he is never able to achieve real freedom and only dread and anguish prevail—then death is the welcome release from the chains of despair. The puppet is returned to the box, the string is severed, the strain is no more.

But if life is the creation of a benevolent God, the infusion of the Divine breath; if man is not only higher than the animal, but also "a little lower than the angels"; if he has a soul, as well as a body; if his relationship is not only the "I-it" of man and nature, but the "I-Thou" of creature with Creator; and if he tempers his passions with the moral commands of an eternal, transcendent God—then death is a return to the Creator at the time of death set by the Creator, and life-after-death the only way of a just and merciful and ethical God. If life has any significance, if it is not mere happenstance, then man knows that some day his body will be replaced, even as his soul unites with eternal God.

In immortality man finds fulfillment of all his dreams. In this religious framework, the sages equated this world with an ante-room to a great palace, the glorious realm of the future. For a truly religious personality, death has profound meaning, because for him life is a tale told by a saint. It is, indeed, full of sound and fury which sometimes signifies nothing, but often bears eloquent testimony to the Divine power that created and sustained him.

The rabbis say *hai alma k'bei hilula damya,* this world can be compared to a wedding. At a wedding two souls are united. In that relationship they bear the seed of the future. Ultimately, the partners to the wedding die—but the seed of life grows on, and death is conquered, for the seed of the future carries the germ of the past. This world is like unto a wedding.

Death has meaning if life had meaning. If one is not able to live, will he be able to die?

APPENDIX

The Preparation of the Remains:
A Guide for the Chevra Kadisha*
חברה קדישא

This guide is *not* intended for the general reader. The layman may find the details of *taharah* too morbid for casual reading soon after the death of a relative. It is solely for the use of the prospective member of the Chevra Kadisha who is required to study and review the laws of *taharah*. The lay reader is advised to omit this Appendix.

Man is created in the image of God, and thus possesses dignity and value. Because God has created him, he is endowed with sanctity. To destroy man is to commit not only an offense against man, but sacrilege—the desecration of the Name of God. An indignity inflicted on man is a profanation of the name of God. The body that housed the soul is sanctified by Judaism. It is a gift of Almighty God, and the sanctity adheres to the body even after the soul has left.

The care and consideration and respect that are bestowed upon the living must be accorded the dead as they are attended, prepared and escorted to their final abode on earth. To assist in the preparation and burial of the dead is one of the greatest *mitzvot* in our faith.

---

* Much of the text of this Appendix is based on a paper prepared by Rabbi Solomon Sharfman of Brooklyn, New York.

239

The association that is organized to perform this service is appropriately named Chevra Kadisha, the Holy Society. It was one of the first associations to be established in the traditional Jewish community of the past. Membership in the Chevra Kadisha has always been accounted a unique privilege. The members must be Sabbath observers, of high moral character, and conversant with the laws and customs that are the responsibility of the office they occupy.

The Jewish communities in America have developed in haphazard fashion and few are fortunate to have an active and well-informed Chevra Kadisha. The terrible abuses that have been perpetrated upon the dead are largely a result of a lack of dedicated volunteers who are willing to ignore the uncomeliness and bother of such work in order to prepare and bury the dead with honor and dignity. As the American communities become better organized, there is increased recognition of the need for a Chevra Kadisha. But as charity becomes more impersonal and help and kindness more aseptic, such service becomes as rare as true saintliness.

The rules and regulations that govern the activities of the Chevra Kadisha are widely scattered in the literature of Jewish law. Customs have been transmitted by word of mouth from generation to generation and they frequently vary in details from country to country and community to community. No single outline of procedures can possibly reconcile all the differences, most of which have some valid basis in Jewish law and tradition. The following general outline embraces the procedures that are followed in most Jewish communities. It may serve as a guide for the newly-organized Chevra Kadisha that has no traditional custom of its own.

The Chevra Kadisha should meet at regular intervals to review the requisite rituals and practices and the problems that are encountered when it officiates. No individual should be permitted to participate without its express consent, lest its discipline be compromised.

Moving the Deceased

1. Before it proceeds, a commitment should be obtained from the next of kin of the deceased that there will be no interference with the Chevra Kadisha and that they will conduct themselves in accordance with its rules and regulations.

2. About half an hour after death has been definitely established, the deceased is completely disrobed and covered with a sheet. The Chevra Kadisha, as a preliminary to its work, addresses the deceased, referring to him by his Hebrew name and that of his father, and asks to be forgiven for any indignity they may unwittingly visit upon him.

3. Some straw or excelsior is placed on the floor and covered with a sheet, and the body is gently lowered to the sheet, feet toward the door. The windows of the room are opened.

4. The eyes are closed, the limbs are straightened out and a handkerchief may be tied about the jaw if it falls. A solid object is placed beneath the head so that it will be slightly elevated. Candles are lit and placed near the head, except on Sabbath and religious holidays.

5. The body remains covered at all times and viewing by anyone, except by the Chevra Kadisha in the course of its duties, or for the purpose of identification, is not permissible.

6. Women perform similar duties for the deceased woman. Where no women are available at the moment, men may lower the body, while it is fully clothed, in the same manner as for men.

7. Each member of the Chevra Kadisha should come provided with a copy of the *maaver yabok* which contains the prayers that should be recited at this time as well as during the entire *taharah*.

The Watching
שמירה

1. The body must be watched at all times even during the day or on the Sabbath. The body is *never* left alone. The individual who serves as a watcher, or *shomer*, is exempt from all prayers and other religious duties at that time— he is engaged in the performance of a *mitzvah* and therefore exempt from performing other *mitzvot*. Where two people watch over the body, one performs his religious duties in another room, while the other remains with the body. Psalms and traditional prayers for the departed are recited near the body.

2. The *shomer* should remain in the room with the body, if possible. Where it is not possible, such as in a morgue, the *shomer* should be able to see into the room and observe the body.

3. Smoking, eating, and unnecessary conversation are forbidden in the room which contains the body.

4. Women may serve in this capacity for a deceased woman. Men may serve as *shomrim* for any deceased person, man or woman. It is preferable, where possible, that sons or other relatives of the deceased serve as *shomrim*.

Preparations for the Taharah

1. The *taharah* should take place as close to the time of the funeral service as possible. Ordinarily, no more than three hours should elapse between the *taharah* and the funeral service.

2. Where this is not possible, as in the case when people will not be available at the proper time to perform the *taharah*, or in the summertime when putrefaction may rapidly set in, the *taharah* may be performed earlier. In that event, the utmost care must be taken that the body and the *tachrichim* shall not become soiled again before the funeral.

3. Before the *taharah*, the casket and the *tachrichim* and all the other necessary items must be prepared and ready. Those who will participate should be assigned their functions in advance. No conversation is permitted except that which is necessary for the washing and cleansing of the deceased.

4. During the washing and the *taharah*, the father-in-law, mother's husband and brother-in-law of the deceased may not be present. At the *taharah* of a woman, the females in similar relation to her may not be present.

5. It is desirable that five, or at least four, members of the Chevra Kadisha should participate in the *taharah*.

The Washing

1. The members of the Chevra Kadisha must wash their hands in the same manner as the ritual washing each morning: each hand, beginning with the right, is alternately washed three times with a container.

2. The body is placed on its back on the *taharah* board, with the feet toward the door. At no time should it be placed face downward—it is inclined first on one side and then on the other side during the washing.

3. In respect for the person and his integrity, care should be exercised to keep the body covered at all times, particularly the private parts, except when they must be exposed in order to be washed.

4. A large container is filled with lukewarm water, into which a smaller vessel is dipped and poured upon the parts of the body to be washed.

5. The order of the washing is as follows: first the entire head, then the neck, the right hand, the right upper half of the body, the right lower half of the body, the right foot, the left hand, the left upper half of the body, the left lower half of the body and the left foot. The body is then inclined on its left side and the right side of the back is

washed in the same order as above. The body is then inclined on its right side and the left side of the back is
washed.

6. The fingernails and toenails are cleansed and the
hair is combed. Care should be taken that the fingers or
other joints of the body do not bend or close. The body is
washed completely. Internal cleansing is not customarily
performed.

7. The blood that flows at the time of *death* may *not* be
washed away. When there is other blood on the body that
flowed during *lifetime*, from wounds or as a result of an
operation, the washing and *taharah* are performed in the
usual manner.

8. Where the deceased died instantaneously through
violence or accident, and his body and garments are completely spattered with blood, *no* washing or *taharah* is performed. The body is placed in the casket without the
clothes being removed. Only a sheet is wrapped around it,
over the clothes. The blood is part of the body and may not
be separated from it in death.

9. Where only part of the body was injured and covered
with blood, and it is possible to perform a *taharah* on the
remainder, rabbinic authority should be consulted.

10. Where blood flows continually after death, the
source of the flow is covered and not washed. The clothes
which contain the blood that flowed after death are placed
in the casket at the feet.

The Taharah
טהרה

1. After the body has been thoroughly washed and
cleansed, the Chevra Kadisha members again wash their
own hands, as described above. A clean sheet and the
tachrichim are made ready.

2. Two or three of the participants raise the body until
it stands vertically on the ground. Some straw or wood is
placed underneath the feet.

3. Twenty-four quarts of water (nine *kavin,* according to Hebrew measurement) are poured over the head, so that the water flows down over the entire body.

4. This is the principal *taharah,* and enough members of the Chevra Kadisha should participate so that it may be performed properly.

5. Where this is not possible, the body is raised onto several pieces of wood and the nine *kavin* of water are poured over the entire body.

6. The nine *kavin* of water do not have to be contained in one vessel or poured at one time. The usual procedure is that two members of the Chevra Kadisha take a pail of water, each containing a minimum of 12 quarts, or three members each take a pail containing a minimum of 8 quarts each. The water is then poured in a continuous stream over the head and body not simultaneously, but in succession. Before the first vessel is emptied, the second starts, and the pouring of the third begins before the second has been emptied. No more than three vessels may be used and at no time may the flow cease until the water from all the vessels has been successively poured over the body.

7. While the *taharah* is being performed, the *taharah* board is thoroughly dried by other members of the Chevra Kadisha. After the *taharah,* the body is placed on the board and covered with a clean white sheet with which it is completely dried.

8. The white of a raw egg, according to some custom, is mixed with a little wine or vinegar, and the head is washed with the mixture.

The Tachrichim
תכריכים

1. The *tachrichim* should be made of white linen, sewn by hand with white linen thread, by pious women (past the age of menopause).

2. Where these shrouds are not obtainable or they are too costly, cotton or other inexpensive material may be used. In any event, the *tachrichim* should not be too costly.

3. They should have no binding, seams, knots, or pockets. In dressing the body, only slip-knots are made where the garments are tied around parts of the body.

4. The *tachrichim* consist of the following seven garments:

a) *mitznephet*, a head dress. b) *michnasayim*, trousers. c) *k'tonet*, a chemise. d) *kittel*, an upper garment. e) *avnet*, a belt. f) *tallit*, a prayer shawl. g) *sovev*, a linen sheet.

5. The *tachrichim* must be clean. If they have become soiled, they must be washed before use. The Chevra Kadisha should have several sets of *tachrichim* on hand for emergencies.

Order of Dressing

1. The *mitznephet* is placed on the head and drawn down to cover the entire head, the neck and the nape of the neck.

2. The *michnasayim* extend from the belly to the ankles. Two participants draw the trousers up to the belly. They are tied at the belly by making three forms that are shaped to resemble a *shin*. Around the ankles, each foot is tied with a band. No knots are made.

3. The *k'tonet* should be large enough to cover the entire body. It has an opening at the top to be slipped over the head, and sleeves for the arms. Two of the participants carefully draw the sleeves over the hands and arms, slip it over the head and down over the body. At the neck, the bands are knotted with bows and shaped to resemble a *shin*.

4. The *kittel* may be open like a shirt or closed like the *k'tonet*. It has sleeves for the arms and is drawn over the

body. If there is a *kittel* which the deceased wore during his life that should be used, but the metal snaps or buttons must be removed. Care should be taken, when the *kittel* is put on the body, that the sleeves of the *k'tonet* not be moved from their position and that they extend to the waist. The *kittel* is tied at the neck in the same manner as the *k'tonet*.

5. The *avnet* is wound around the body three times, over the *kittel*. Both ends are knotted at the belly with three bows in the shape of a *shin*.

6. The *tallit* should be one that the deceased wore during prayer in his lifetime. If that is not available, another may be used. All ornaments of that *tallit* must be removed.

7. In placing the body into the casket, some straw and a handful of earth from the Holy Land are first put into a linen bag and placed inside the casket. The *sovev* is spread on the casket and the *tallit* over the *sovev*.

8. The body is placed in the coffin and the *tallit* is unwrapped around the body. One of the *tzizit* is either torn or tied up and placed in a corner of the *tallit*. The *sovev* is unwrapped first around the head. It is customary to place broken pieces of earthenware called *sherblach* in Yiddish.

9. Women are clothed in the following: A cap, *michnasayim*, *k'tonet*, *kittel*, *avnet*, a face cloth or a *sovev*.

10. The Chevra Kadisha asks forgiveness of the deceased and the coffin is covered. Under no circumstances may it be opened again before burial, except in those communities where it is customary to insert the *sherblach* at the cemetery.

Infant Deaths

An infant who does not live for thirty days is called a *nefel*, and is not considered viable in terms of Jewish tradition. The laws of *aninut* and mourning do not apply to the family at all. However, the infant should be given the last purification rites of *taharah*, in accordance with the specific procedures determined by the Chevra Kadisha burial society. Adult-type shrouds are not necessary; a plain white blanket is appropriate. Burial should not take place on holidays except for unusual circumstances, and this to be determined by the local rabbi. There is also no need for a cortege of family members to accompany the deceased. Three persons should be present at interment, but none of the burial ceremonies such as the recital of Tzidduk Hadin and Kaddish prayers, and the formal consolation service, need be performed.

The infant, male or female, should be given a name that merely need be recited before burial. If this was omitted it may be given even after burial. The rending of the garment need not be done, and the blessing usually recited at the *keriah* may not be said. The custom is to circumcise infants, usually during the *taharah*, who have not undergone circumcision until then. The technical procedural requirements of Jewish law for circumcisions need not apply, but it should be performed by a Jew, if no *mohel* is available preferably by a member of the Chevra Kadisha. This circumcision may not be performed on a major holiday, even on the second day of such a holiday, and no blessings should be recited over it.

One of the greatest contemporary rabbis, Rabbi Ezekiel Bennet, willed that he be buried among the infant dead. May God keep us from such tragedy.

Bibliography

Following is a partial listing of the sources upon which halachic decisions appearing in the text have been based. Specific reference is not made in the text proper.

HEBREW SOURCES

Torat Ha'adam, Nachmanides
Ma'avar Yabok, Aharon Berachia of Modena
S'dei Chemed, Chayim Chizkiah Madini
Aruch Ha'shulchan, Yechiel Michel Epstein
Emek Halachah, Yehoshua Baumol
Kol Bo Al Avelut, Leopold Greenwald
She'arim Ha'metzuyanim Be'Halachah, Shlomo Braun
Gesher Ha'chayim, Y. M. Tukachinsky
Otzar Dinim U'minhaggim, J. D. Eisenstein
Mishmeret Shalom, Vol. II, Shalom Shachna Tcherniak

In addition to the biblical portions cited in the text, the Talmud tractates *Semachot* and *Mo'ed Katan,* Maimonides' *Hilchot Avel* (14 chapters), and Joseph Karo's *Shulchan Arukh, Yoreh De'ha* (chapters 335 through 403) were constantly consulted.

ENGLISH SOURCES

The Kadish, David De Sola Pool
The American Way of Death, Jessica Mitford
Death, Grief and Mourning, Geoffrey Gorer
Man's Search for Himself, Rollo May
The American Funeral, Leroy Bowman
The Meaning of Death, Ed. Herman Feifel
The Loved One, Evelyn Waugh
For the Living, Edgar N. Jackson

In addition, numerous psychological and religious periodicals have been consulted. In many cases direct reference is noted in the text proper.

Glossary

Adar—The twelfth (and last) month of the Hebrew calendar.

Adar sheni—The thirteenth month, added in leap years immediately following Adar. Literal meaning: Adar the Second.

Alav ha'shalom—"May he rest in peace." A phrase used after mentioning the name of the deceased.

Alenu—A prayer which concludes all religious services.

Aliyah—A Torah honor which denotes being called to the reading of the Torah.

Amidah—The silent devotion known as the *Shmone Esrai* which is recited in a standing position. It is of the essence of Jewish prayer, and follows the benediction immediately after the *"Shema Yisroel."*

Aninut—The state of mourning between death and interment.

Av—The fifth month of the Hebrew calendar.

Avel—A mourner.

Avelut—The period of mourning.

Bar Mitzvah—A boy at the age of thirteen years and one day, as he becomes obligated to observe all *mitzvot* (commandments).

Bechi—Bewailing, mournful crying.

251

Bein ha'shemashot—The brief duration of time between sunset and sundown, between day and night, as it were.

Birchat ha'gomel—The benediction which thanks God for recovery from serious illness or escape from mortal danger.

B'rit—The circumcision ceremony at which time the eight-day-old boy enters the Covenant of Abraham.

Chen—Grace, charm.

Chevra Kadisha—Literally, "Holy Society." The group of people which prepares the body for burial and performs the rite of purification.

Cheshvan—The eighth month of the Hebrew calendar, sometimes referred to as *Mar Cheshvan*.

Chilul ha'Shem—The desecration of the name of God.

Chodesh—Month.

Chol ha'moed—The festive weekdays between the first and last days of Passover and Succot.

Dayan ha'emet—The blessing which the mourners recite after death. Literal meaning: True Judge.

El Malei Rachamim—Literally, "God, full of compassion." A memorial prayer, sometimes referred to as the *"Malei."*

Elul—The sixth month of the Hebrew calendar.

Erev—The eve of.

Gan Eden—Garden of Eden. Paradise.

Gehinnom—The valley of Hinnom, outside of Jerusalem, the location of pagan altars for child sacrifice. Later it was the place for burning the refuse of the city. It is the Jewish equivalent of hell.

Gemillat chasadim—Acts of kindness.

Haftorah—A passage from the Prophets read after the Sabbath Torah reading.

Halachah—Literally: the way. The law, which encompasses both the written Torah and the oral tradition.

Hallel—Songs of praise from the Book of Psalms recited on holidays after the *"Amidah."*

Hanukkah—The holiday which celebrates the Maccabean victory over the Syrian Greeks in the second century before the common era. The Festival of Lights. Sometimes spelled *Chanukah.*

Havdalah—Separation. The ceremony which concludes the Sabbath, "separating" it from the weekday that follows.

Hazkarat neshamot—Memorial prayer for the deceased.

Hesped—Eulogy.

Iyyar—The second month of the Hebrew calendar.

Kabbalat Shabbat—The service of welcome to the Sabbath, read on Friday eve, before sunset.

Kaddish—The prayer recited for the deceased parent for eleven months or one year from the date of burial.

Kalut rosh—Lightheadedness, frivolity.

Kav, kavin—A Hebrew liquid measure, approximately 2.6 quarts. (Nine *kavin* equals twenty-four quarts, as used in the *Taharah* procedure.)

Kefiat ha'mitah—The overturning of the bed. A ritual performed in past times to indicate the despair of mourning.

Keriah—The rending of the garment of the mourner after death occurs.

Kevod ha'met—Respect for the deceased.

Kiddush ha'Shem—The sanctification of the name of God.

Kippah—A headcovering. Skullcap or *yarmulke.*

Kislev—The ninth month of the Hebrew calendar.

Kohen—A priest in the Jewish religion. A descendant of Aaron who served in the ancient Temple.

Kol Nidre—The prayer recited at the beginning of the Yom Kippur eve service, asking God for release from the vows made to Him.

Lag ba'Omer—The thirty-third day of the *Omer*, which extends from the second day of Passover to Shavuot. It

celebrates the surcease from the plague which killed
Rabbi Akiba's students. A minor festival which releases
the Jew from period of semi-mourning.

Le'chayim—A toast. Literally: To life.

Levi—In terms of religious status, the Levi is second to
the Kohen. He is called to the Torah for the second *Aliyah*.

Maariv—Daily evening service.

Maftir—The last portion of the weekly Sabbath Torah reading. It is the honor accorded one who will recite the *Haftorah* immediately after the Torah scroll is bound.

Malei Rachamim—See *El Malei Rachamim*.

Matzevah—Monument.

Megillah—A scroll. Although, technically, there are five
scrolls, or *Megillot*, only the Book of Esther is known as
the Megillah. It is read on Purim eve and Purim morning.

Met mitzvah—An unburied corpse which does not have a
sufficient number of Jews in attendance to perform the
burial and the interment.

Midrash—Literally: inquiry or investigation. A genre of
literature which interprets the Bible, usually homileti-
cally, to extract its full and hidden meanings.

Mikveh—A pool of water designed for the rite of purification, primarily used by women after the monthly completion of the menstrual period.

Minchah—The daily afternoon service, usually recited shortly before *Ma'ariv*.

Minyan—A quorum of at least ten Jewish males above the
age of thirteen.

Mishnah—The primary collection of laws and opinions of
the Sages known as *"Tannaim."* Compiled in 200 C.E. by
Rabbi Judah the Prince. It forms the basis of the Talmud.

Mitzvah—Commandment. Sometimes used to connote a good
deed.

Mitzvot—Plural of *mitzvah*.

Mo'ed Katan—The name of a book of the Talmud which records many of the laws of mourning.

Mohel—One who performs the circumcision.

Nechamah—Consolation.

Nissan—The first month of the Hebrew calendar.

Olam ha'ba—The world to come.

Onen—A mourner between the time of death and interment.

Onenim—Plural of *onen*.

Passover—The eight-day holiday which celebrates the exodus from Egypt.

Pidyon ha'ben—The redemption of the first-born son. This ceremony is held on the thirty-first day after birth.

Prozdor—Corridor, vestibule.

Rachamim—Mercy.

Rosh Chodesh—The first day of the Hebrew month, or New Moon. It is celebrated as a minor holiday.

Rosh Hashanah—The religious New Year. It is referred to as a High Holiday.

Sandek—The one who receives the honor of holding the infant during the ceremony of circumcision.

Sefirah—Literally: counting. The forty-nine days of the *Omer*, from the second day of Passover to Shavuot, observed as days of semi-mourning.

Shabbat—The seventh day of the week. A day of rest.

Shabbat shalom—Sabbath peace. The customary Sabbath greeting.

Shalach manot—Gifts sent to the poor and to friends on Purim.

Shalom—Literally: peace. Hello or goodbye.

Shalom aleichem—Literally, peace be unto you. Hello.

Shalom zachar—A celebration held on the first Friday eve after the birth of a son.

Shavuot—Pentecost. Celebrated seven weeks after Passover. A major holiday.

Sheloshim—The thirty-day period following interment.

Shemini Atzeret—Eighth day of assembly. Celebrated as the last days of the Succot holiday.

Sherblach—Pieces of pottery or earthenware.

Sheva berachot—The seven blessings recited at a wedding and on each night for seven nights following the wedding.

Shevat—The month of the Hebrew calendar.

Shin—Next-to-the-last letter of the Hebrew alphabet. It is formed of a base with three "fingers" extending from it.

Shofar—The horn blown at Rosh Hashanah services as a rallying call to Jews to repent of their evil deeds.

Shochet—One who slaughters meat for kosher consumption.

Siddur—A prayerbook.

Simchah—Joy, celebration.

Simchah shel mitzvah—A religious celebration such as held at a Bar Mitzvah, a *B'rit*, a wedding, or upon the conclusion of studying a book of the Talmud, etc.

Simchat Torah—The holiday of the rejoicing of the Torah. It is the second day of Shemini Atzeret, and the last day of the Succot festival period.

Sivan—The third month of the Hebrew calendar.

Siyyum masechet—The celebration held upon the conclusion of study of a book of the Talmud.

Succot—Tabernacles. The holiday which celebrates the Jewish wandering in the desert following the exodus from Egypt.

Tachanun—Prayers of petition, following the *Amidah*.

Tachrichim—Shrouds.

Taharah—Purification or cleansing.

Tallit—Prayer shawl.

Talmud—The literature which contains the *Mishnah* (see above) and the *Gemara*, the discussion on the *Mishnah*. It was compiled and edited by Rav Ashi in the fourth century C.E.

Tammuz—The fourth month of the Hebrew calendar.

Tefillin—Commonly called "phylacteries." They are small black cases which contain passages from the Bible and are affixed, by means of black straps, to the head and arms. These are not amulets, as phylacteries might connote, but rich Jewish symbols. They are worn only during weekday morning services.

Tevet—The tenth month of the Hebrew calendar.

Tisha b'av—The ninth day of Av, which commemorates the destruction of both ancient Temples. It is observed through fasting and semi-mourning.

Tishre—The seventh month of the Hebrew calendar.

Torah—The first five books of the Bible or, more commonly and correctly, the whole body of Jewish teaching.

Tzidduk ha'din—The "Justification of God" prayer recited at the interment or immediately thereafter.

Tzitzit—Fringes on the four corners of the *tallit*.

Yahrzeit—The memorial anniversary of the date of death.

Yekara de'hayye—"For the good of the living."

Yekara d'schichba—"For the honor of the deceased."

Yizkor—The memorial service recited on Yom Kippur and on the final days of Passover, Shavuot, and Succot.

Yom Kippur—The Day of Atonement. The second of the High Holidays.

Index

A

Aaron, High Priest, 86, 126
Abin, Rabbi, 138
Abortion, 11
Abraham, 50, 158
Absalom, 168
Adam, 16, 55
After-life, see Life after death
Agnon, S. Y., 156
Akiba, Rabbi, 29, 160, 164, 165
Albo, Joseph, 225, 234
Aliyah, for Torah reading, 163, 203
Amos, 86
Aninut, see *Onen*
Apostates, mourning for, 83
Autopsy, 8-12, 19
Avelut, see Mourning

B

Bar Mitzvah, 109, 176, 178, 180-
   181, 209, 215
Bathing, for *Onen*, 23
   for mourner, 125
Ben Azzai, 29
Benches, for Shiva, 104
Body
   position after death, 4
   legal custodian, 8-9
   ownership, 10
   mutilation, 14
   rate of decomposition, 16
   defilement by contact, 212-15

resurrection, 228 f.
washing by Chevra Kadisha, 241
Bride, 40
   attend Funeral Services, 54
   who becomes a mourner, 80
   when marry, 184-7
B'rit (circumcision)
   109, 110, 111, 176, 180, 183
Brother, 22, 39, 55, 79, 182, 213
   adopted, 80
Buber, Martin, 34
Burial, see Interment
Burial service, 59-64
Burial Society, see *Chevra Kadisha*

C

Candles
   immediately after death, 4
   in house of mourning, 101-102
   Yizkor, 200
   Yahrzeit, 202
   at *Taharah*, 241
Cantor, 24
Carlyle, Thomas, 130
Casket, 16-18, 19, 60, 64, 71-2
Cemetery
   Funeral Service, 37
   Keriah, 40
   attendance at, 53-4
   carrying of casket, 60
   plot, 67-70
   National, 73
   etiquette, 74-5

condolence begins, 139
Kaddish, 171
Yahrzeit observance, 203-4
Kohen, 214-5
burial of suicides, 219
Chapel (Funeral Home), 18, 20
the Service, 37
Keriah, 40
the night before, 54 (see Wake)
Kohen, 214
Charity, 76, 174-5, 197-8
Chevra Kadisha, 5, 6, 7
appendix, 239-247
Chol Ha'Moed
Onen and Tefillin, 26
Keriah, 41
burial, 89
counting shiva and sheloshim, 96
meal of condolence, 101
shiva candles, 102
work similar to shiva, 113
condolences on, 139
grave visitation, 192
Christian, 15, 18, 232
the wake, 35
"Lord's Prayer," 52
cemetery, 68
Jew buried in cemetery, 72
Clothes, new, 130-132
Concrete Vault, 57-58
Cohen, Hermann, 225
Condolence, consolation, comforting, 28, 35, 36, 98-101, 109, 123, 136-141, 153, 220
Conjugal relations
Onen, 23, 24
during Shiva, 133
Converts,
cemetery plot, 70
mourning observances, 82
Cosmetics, 126
Cremation, 56-57, 84
Crescas, Hasdai, 225
Criminals, 84

D

Dates of Yahrzeit, 204-6
Daughter, 22, 39, 55
Keriah, 44
married, on cemetery plot, 69

of intermarried parents, 70, 85
as mourner, 79
adopted, 80
setting hair, 128
saying Kaddish, 166-7
at wedding, 182
defilement of Kohen, 213
Daughter-in-law, 40
David, King, 38, 61, 159, 168, 227
Death, meaning of, 235-238
Defilement, 212-15
Delayed News, 208-211
Keriah, 41
brief delay, 208
extended delay, 210
Deuteronomy, 19, 56, 194, 197
Dignity of man, 29, 103
Disinterment, 70-71
Divorced mates, 39
attend funeral services of, 54
separated mates, 68-9
mourning observances, 82
Dressing, 7, appendix
Duran, Simon ben Zemah, 225

E

Earth, 17
Eating
near deceased, 5
for Onen, 23
Onen on Holiday, 24
on cemetery, 74, 195
meal of condolence, 100
mourner at joyous occasions, 179
wedding dinner, 182
on Yahrzeit, 201, 203
Ecclesiastes, 6, 44, 61, 138, 178
Embalming, 12-15
Enemies
as pallbearers, 60
in cemetery plot, 69
Engagements, 185
Epstein, B. H., 38
Escorting the dead, 52-55
bride and groom, 81
Etiquette,
at cemetery, 74, 195
in house of Shiva, 122-4, 140-141
Eulogy, 20, 50-52, 195, 219
Ezekiel, 113, 121, 122, 154, 228

F

Fasting, 201
Father, 22, 39, 55, 79, 169, 182, 201, 213
  adopted, 80
Flowers, 18, 75
Funeral Director, 6
Funeral Service, 36-37, 45-49
  timing, 18
  as a finale, 31-32
  location, 37

G

Genesis, 16
Gentile, 55
Gifts, 75, 124-5, during Sheloshim, 145
Gorer, Geoffrey, x, 38, 141
Greetings, 122-124
Grave, 17, 64-65, 67, 71
  visitation, 192-3
Groom, 40
  attend Funeral Service, 54
  who becomes a mourner, 80
  shaving, 129
  when he may marry, 184-7

H

Haircutting, Onen, 23, 126-129
Hanukkah,
  Onen, 25
  eulogy, 51
  Tzidduk Ha'din, 64
  meal of condolence, 101
  services in house of mourning, 108
  condolences, 139
  celebrating holiday meal, 183
Holidays (Festivals, see also specific holidays)
  burial, 20, 89
  Onen, 24
  Keriah, 41
  eulogy on day after, 51
  Tzidduk Ha'din, 64
  bride and groom, 81
  burial prior to, 88
  during shiva and sheloshim, 94-97

  meal of condolence, 101
  services in house of Shiva, 108
  haircutting, 128
  condolences, 139
  toward remarriage, 185-6
  before High Holidays for grave visitation, 192
  Yahrzeit, 202
  delayed news arriving on, 209
Homicide, 11
Hospitals
  autopsy practices, 9-12
  death occurring in, 6
  mourner in, 23
  donation of limbs to, 58
Housewarming, 183

I

Image of God, 3, 10, 19, 29-30, 72, 103, 239 f.
Immortality, 224-226
Intermarriages
  cemetery plot, 69-70
  offspring, 85
Interment, 55-56, 64-65
  delay, 19-21
  of limbs, 58
  at twilight, 87
  out-of-town, 89
  temporary, 90
  in case of labor strike, 90
  of suicides, 219
Isaac, 136, 158
Isaiah, 29, 136
Israel, burial in, 70

J

Jacob, 38, 59, 67, 86, 161, 188
Jeremiah, 127, 134
Job, 38, 111, 134, 138, 150, 154, 173
Joel, 39
Joab, 159
Johanan, 212
Judges, Book of, 196
Joseph, 38, 70, 86
Joshua ben Chanania, Rabbi, 233
Joyous occasions, 175-187
Judah, the Prince, 37, 105

K

Kaddish, 49, 149-175
  Onen, 24
  for the cremated, 57
  Burial Kaddish, 65-66
  by converts, 82
  burial delayed by labor strike, 90
  Mourner's Kaddish, 149
  history, 150
  five forms, 152
  function, 153
  as education, 157
  significance, 158
  observances, 162
  on Sabbaths, 162
  which mourners recite, 164
  is it transferrable, 167
  for whom recited, 169
  when recited, 171
  delayed news, 211
  for suicides, 219
Kalut Rosh, 74
Kennedy, John F., 17
Keriah, 38-44, 187
  for suicides, 219
Kohen, 19, 53, 79, 82, 111, 120, 189,
  211-215

L

Lamentations, 134
Laundering, 130-132
Levi, Rabbi, 16
Leviticus, 79, 212
Liebman, Joshua Loth, 77
Life after death, 221-224
Limbs, Burial, 58, Donation, 58
Lindemann, Dr. Eric, 140, 141-4
Lo'eg Larash, 75

M

Maimonides, 38, 122, 137, 138, 224,
  225, 226
Mana, Rabbi, 138
Marriage, 184-7
Mausoleum, 57-58
Meal of condolence, 98
Memorial Prayer, 45, 48, 193, 194,
  195, 197, 203, 204
Mentally ill, 92, 210

Messiah, 226-228
Met Mitzvah, 53, 213-14
Midrash, 60, 134, 138, 215
Military, 23
Minors, 22, 39
  under 30 days, 54, 83, 101
  as legal mourners, 80
  Bar Mitzvah during Shiva, 91
  Washing during Shiva, 126
  infant's clothes, 131
Minyan, 53
  Onen, 23
  for Kaddish, 66
  in House of Shiva, 105
  if no minyan at home, 110
  shoes when leaving for, 122
  for Kaddish, 136-4
  at wedding, 181
  at unveiling, 195
  for Yizkor, 200
Mirrors, 4, 102-104
Mishnah, 193, 224
Missing persons, 92, 171
Mitford, Jessica, 13, 14
Mitzvah, 20, 24, 109, 136, 175, 242
Mohel, 110, 120
Monument, 188-192
Moses, 61, 86, 87
Mother, 22, 39, 55, 79, 128, 169,
  182, 201, 213
  adopted, 80
Mourning, 66
  pattern, 77-80
  begins, 87
  if neglected, 91
Music, 177, 178, 179, 181, 184

N

Nail trimming, 130

O

Onen, 21-26
  labor strike and delayed inter-
    ment, 90
  for suicides, 218
Orthodox, 17

P

Pallbearers, 59-60
Party, 175-187, Onen, 23

Passover
  Onen, 24
  eulogy, 51
  Tzidduk Ha'din, 64
  in counting Shiva and Sheloshim,
    95
  meal of condolence, 101
  for Yizkor, 197
Physically handicapped, 40, 214
Physicians, 116
Pidyon Ha'ben, 111, 120, 180
Post-Mortem, see Autopsy
Prayers
  Onen, 24
  in house of mourning, 104-108
Pregnant woman
  "sitting" during Shiva, 112
  shoes, 121
  bathing, 125
  consideration for remarriage, 186
Priest, see Kohen
Proverbs, 30, 48
Proxy
  for Kaddish, 167-169
  for Yahrzeit, 206-7
Psalms
  number 23 & 91, 5
  number 23, 45-6
  number 91, 61
  before Kaddish, 66
  number 16, 66
  for converts, 82
  number 49, 108
  number 17, 108
  number 119, 194
  at graveside, 194
  at Unveiling, 195
Psychology
  quick burial, 19
  Onen, 21
  viewing the corpse, 32-3
  Keriah and anger, 38
  burial service, 65
  pattern of mourning, 77
  mourning by children, 91
  meal of condolence, 99
  shiva as withdrawal, 109
  condolence call, 136-8, 140
  symptoms of grief, 141-4

of Kaddish, 153 f., 165
of suicides, 217-18
Public officials, 120, 128
Purim
  Onen on, 25
  eulogy on, 51
  Tzidduk Ha'Din, 64
  meal of condolence, 101
  service at synagogue, 111
  condolence call, 139
  gifts during Sheloshim, 145
  for grave visitation, 192

R
Rabbi, 120, 181-2
Rachel, 188
Reinterment, 71-75
Respect
  immediately following death, 3-6,
    211
  service at synagogue, 37
  in house of mourner, 105
  in death as in life, 201
Resurrection of the Dead, 226, 228-
    233
"Righteous Judge" Blessing, see
  "True Judge"
Roosevelt, Franklin Delano, 17
Rosh chodesh,
  eulogy, 51
  tzidduk Ha'din, 64
  meal of condolence, 101
  services in house of Shiva, 108
  condolence call, 139
  before, for grave visitation, 192
  Yahrzeit dates, 204
Rosh Hashanah,
  Burial, 89
  in counting Shiva and Sheloshim,
    96
  meal of condolence, 101
  as festival for remarriage, 186

S
Sabbath, 5-6, 42
  Onen, 24
  Keriah, 41
  burial prior to, 38
  burial on, 89

during Shiva and Sheloshim, 94
meal of condolence, 101
Shiva candle, 102
greetings, 123
haircut for, 128
laundered clothes, 132-3
conjugal relations, 133
condolences, 139
joyous occasions, 183
Yahrzeit candles, 202
Yahrzeit observance, 206
arrival of delayed news, 209
Taharah, 241
Sarah, 67
Saul, 38
Second marriages, cemetery plot, 69
Sefirah, 24-5
Sephardic tradition, 199
Shalom zachar, at birth of son, 183
Sheloshim, (Thirty days), 44, 144-47
eulogy, 51
stage of mourning, 79
bride and groom, 80-1
duration, 93
haircutting, 126
shaving, 129
laundered clothes, 132
joyous occasions, 178, 179 f.
wedding, 181
marriage, 184 f.
monument erection, 190
grave visitation, 192
brief delay determination, 208 f.
Shaving, 129-30
Onen, 23
Shavuot
eulogy on, 51
Tzidduk Ha'din, 64
burial on first day of, 89
in counting Shiva and Sheloshim, 95
meal of condolence, 101
for Yizkor, 197
Shemini Atzeret
in counting of Shiva and Sheloshim, 96-97
as festival for remarriage, 186
for Yizkor, 197

Sheva Berachot, (post-wedding celebrations) 183
Shiva, 20, 23, 40, 51, 55, 57, 78, 86-144
minors, 80
bride and groom, 80-81
by converts, 82
instructions to ignore, 85-6
origins, 86
when begins, 87-93
labor strike, 90
duration, 93
Sabbath during, 94
where observed, 97
changes in prayer, 106-8
"Sitting" Shiva, 111-12
business during, 112
end of, 144
grave visitation, 192
delayed news, 208 f.
Shoes, 121-2, 210
Shomer (or *Shemirah*), 4, 5, 242
Shrouds, 7-8, 19, 242-3, 245-7
Simchat Torah
in counting of Shiva and Sheloshim, 96
Simeon bar Yohai, Rabbi, 159
Sinners
arrogant, 83
non-intentional, 84
Kaddish for, 170-1
Sister, 22, 39, 55, 79, 213
adopted, 80
setting hair, 128
at wedding, 182
Sitting, 111-12, 210
Social reproach, 127, 129, 148
Solomon, 61
Son, 22, 39, 55
married, on cemetery plot, 69
of intermarried parents, 70, 85
mourner, 79
adopted, 80
prime mourner in saying Kaddish, 164
minor, saying Kaddish, 165
adopted, saying Kaddish, 165
paying for Kaddish, 167

at wedding, 182
defilement by Kohen, 213
Son-in-law, 40
Spouse (husband, wife, mate), 22, 39, 55, 79, 128, 213
Succot, (Tabernacles)
  Onen on, 24
  eulogy on, 51
  Tzidduk Ha'din, 64
  in counting of Shiva and Sheloshim, 95
  meal of condolence, 101
Suicide, 215-220
  reason for autopsy, 11, 22
  cemetery plot, 70
  are they mourned, 84-5
  meal of condolence, 101
  Kaddish for, 170
Synagogue,
  Funeral service, 37
  memorial gifts, 75

T

Tachrichim, see Shrouds
Tacitus, 56
Taharah, 6-8, 219, 239-247
Talmud, Babylonian
  18, 29, 37, 53, 72, 105, 126, 134, 138, 151, 158, 159, 174, 176, 201, 212, 215, 231, 233
  celebration of, 182-3, (*siyyum masechet*)
Talmud, Jerusalem, 39, 98, 134
Tzidduk Ha'din, 62-64, 157
Teacher of Torah, 135
Tefillin
  Onen, 25-6
  delayed news, 26
  on cemetery, 75
  groom, 81
  in case of delayed news, 210
Tisha b'Av, 111, 192
Titus, 230
Torah Scroll, equated with man, 3, 30, 111
  on cemetery, 75
  in house of Shiva, 105
Torah
  study, for Onen, 23
  suspended, 53
  study for mourners, 134-136

Bar Mitzvah lad, 178
  study of, for Yahrzeit, 203
"True Judge" Blessing ("Righteous Judge"), 4, 81, 210, 211
Twelve month period, 147-149

U

Unveiling, 194-6
  Kohen at, 215

V

Viewing the remains, 17, 26-35

W

Wake, 35
Washing
  hands, 67, 98, 210
  the deceased, 243-4
Watching, see *Shomer*
Wedding ceremony, 109, 120, 176, 177, 181-2
"What is man?", 47
Work, during Shiva, 112-120
  retail stores, 115
  partners, 115
  physician, 116
  poor, 117
  severe loss, 117
  sexton, 119
  teacher, 119
  shochet, 120
  rabbi, 120
  mohel, 120
  public officials, 120
  on delayed news, 210

Y

Yahrzeit, 79, 194, 201-206
  Onen reciting Kaddish for, 24
  day for grave visitation, 192
  observances at home, 201
  at synagogue, 203
  on cemetery, 203-4
  determination of date, 204
  for suicides, 220
Yizkor, 79, 164, 194, 196-200, 220
Yom Kippur, 19, 121
  in counting of Shiva and Sheloshim, 96
  as festival for remarriage, 186
  original time for *Yizkor*, 196, 197